50 YEARS

lon

MW00364393

BANFF, JASPER & GLACIER NATIONAL PARKS

Jasper National Park
p122

Alberta

Banff National Park
p55

British
Columbia

Waterton Lakes
National Park
p208

CANADA

USA

Glacier National Park
p167

Washington   Idaho   Montana

Jade Bremner, Brendan Sainsbury

Moraine Lake (p108)

CONTENTS

Canoeing,
Maligne Lake (p144)

Cycling near Whitefish (p182), Glacier National Park

RIGHT: CRAIG MOORE/GETTY IMAGES ©
TOP RIGHT: MUMEMORIES/SHUTTERSTOCK ©

3

OLEKSANDR MOKROHUZ/SHUTTERSTOCK ©

Cory Pass (p99)

BANFF, JASPER & GLACIER NATIONAL PARKS
THE JOURNEY BEGINS HERE

I've traveled all over North America researching guidebooks for Lonely Planet, but what particularly impresses me about the Canadian Rockies (and their jagged cousins in Montana) is the way in which they mix footloose adventure with accessibility and convenience. It's a paradoxical allure. I've lost count of the times I've rolled into Jasper or West Glacier on a train or bus, struck out on a super-steep alpine trail, and been back in time for a craft beer and a Neapolitan-style pizza by nightfall.

I love the parks because they strike a delicate balance between the modern world and a grittier, more primordial one. The trails might be well trafficked and meticulously marked, but the thought that a grizzly bear might be waiting around the next corner serves to keep me guarded and on my toes, rudely reminding me of my inconsequential place in the planet's ancient ecosystems.

Brendan Sainsbury

@sainsburyb

Brendan is a Canada-based Brit and the author of 66 Lonely Planet guidebooks covering everywhere from Angola to Alaska.

My favorite experience is Banff's Cory Pass hike, because it's tough, uncrowded, incredibly varied and located just 8km (5 miles) from the townsite. I love the way it ascends so quickly into taxing and rugged terrain. It's challenging but not overly technical.

WHO GOES WHERE

Our writers and experts choose the places that,
for them, define Banff, Jasper and Glacier national parks.

Glacier National Park's handsomely carved glacial valleys are like a gift from the hiking gods –
with seemingly endless high-mountain plateaus, absurdly sublime views, rushing waterfalls, alpine
lakes, dense forests and copious nature living among it all. But this dense and imposing wilderness
is more fragile than it appears – its glaciers, like Grinnell Glacier (pictured; p202), are rapidly
melting, meaning there's not long to experience the park with its namesake attractions.

Jade Bremner
@jadeob

Jade is a writer, editor and author of more than 40 books. She specializes in travel culture, travel and news.

Banff Sunshine
Hit the slopes at the Rockies' best all-round ski resort (p88)

Banff Town
Bathe with a view at Banff Upper Hot Springs (p60)

Skyline Trail
Hike Jasper's quintessential above-the-tree-line trail (p150)

Valley of the Five Lakes
Ride Jasper's multifarious single-track bike route (p140)

Athabasca Falls
Feel the power of Jasper's most dramatic waterfall (p162)

Lake Louise
See grizzlies from a gondola (p102)

Egypt Lake
Camp in Banff's bountiful backcountry (p93)

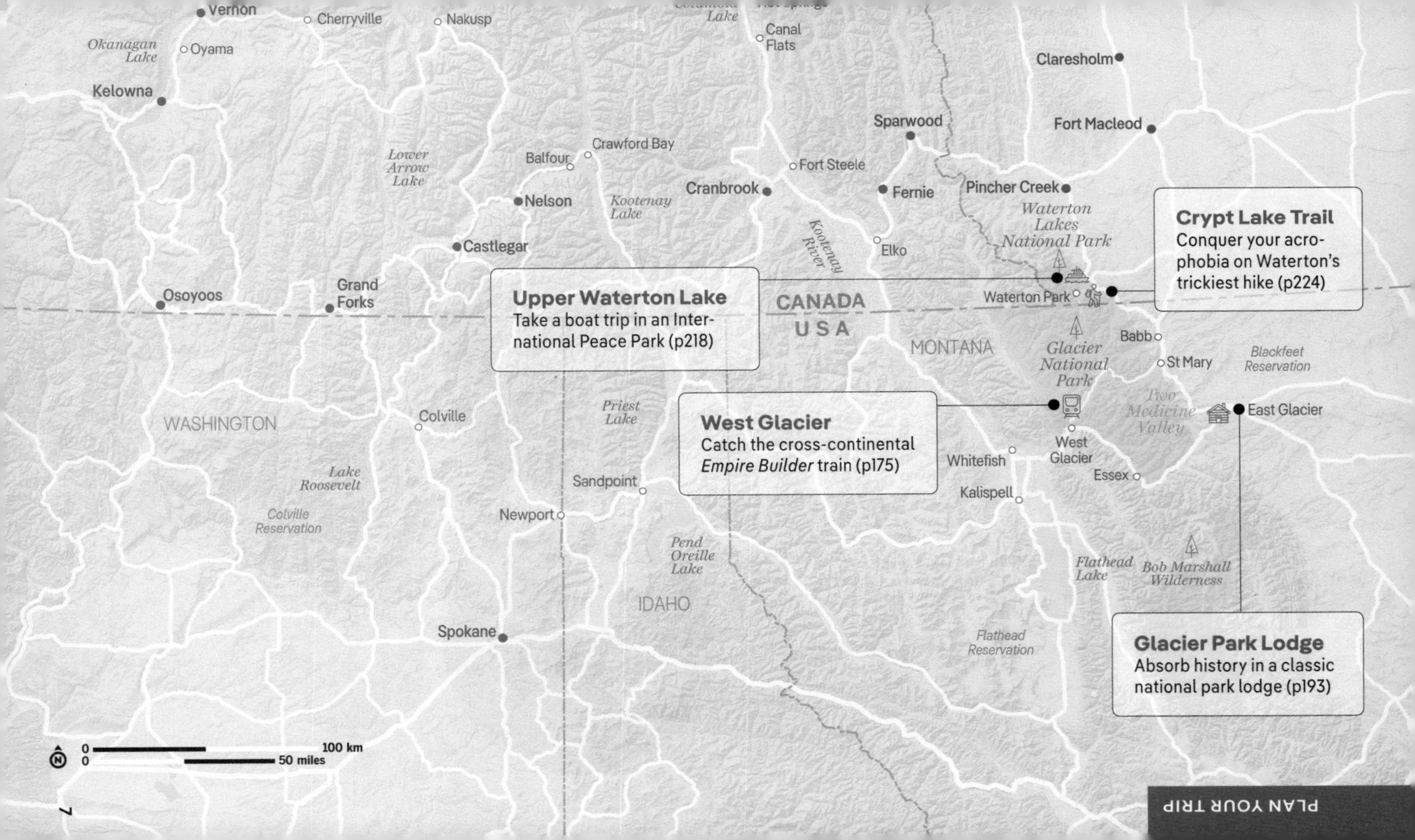

Crypt Lake Trail
Conquer your acrophobia on Waterton's trickiest hike (p224)

Glacier Park Lodge
Absorb history in a classic national park lodge (p193)

Upper Waterton Lake
Take a boat trip in an International Peace Park (p218)

West Glacier
Catch the cross-continental *Empire Builder* train (p175)

Claresholm

Fort Macleod

Pincher Creek

Waterton Lakes National Park

Waterton Park

Sparwood

Fernie

Elko

Fort Steele

Kootenay River

Canal Flats

Lake

Cranbrook

Crawford Bay

Kootenay Lake

Balfour

Nelson

Castlegar

Lower Arrow Lake

Nakusp

Cherryville

Vernon
Oyama

Okanagan Lake

Kelowna

Osoyoos

Grand Forks

Colville

Priest Lake

Sandpoint

Newport

Spokane

Lake Roosevelt

Colville Reservation

WASHINGTON

IDAHO

Pend Oreille Lake

Flathead Reservation

Flathead Lake

Kalispell

Whitefish

West Glacier

Essex

Glacier National Park

Two Medicine Valley

Babb

St Mary

Blackfeet Reservation

East Glacier

Bob Marshall Wilderness

MONTANA

CANADA
U S A

100 km

50 miles

7

FROM LEFT: MITCHELL COYLE PHOTO/SHUTTERSTOCK ©, KARLIE BUTLER/SHUTTERSTOCK ©, DON LAIDLAW/SHUTTERSTOCK ©

ANIMAL MAGIC

A distant glimpse of a grizzly bear, the bugling of rutting elk, the sudden dart of an osprey dive-bobbing a trout – the Rocky Mountain parks are like a *National Geographic* photo spread come to life. Get ready for an adrenaline-stoked safari North American style, except you won't need a jeep and a warden to drive you around. Just a map, some bear spray and a heightened sense of your own surroundings.

Animal Spray

—

They should rename bear spray 'animal spray' – it can be used as a last line of defense against any type of major fauna. Never hike without it.

Meet the Elk

—

Elk might seem like benign ungulates, but females are prone to be aggressive if approached during the spring calving season. Keep a wide berth.

Glacier: Bear Capital

—

Glacier National Park has way more bears – around 900 (300 of them grizzlies) – than the three Canadian parks put together.

BEST WILDLIFE EXPERIENCES

See grizzlies from the safety of an enclosed gondola above a protected wildlife corridor on Whitehorn Mountain in **Lake Louise ❶**. (p102)

Observe moose, bears and marmots in the hills and swamps that rim the shores of Jasper's **Maligne Lake ❷**. (p144)

Light traffic and ample foliage on the **Bow Valley Parkway ❸** mean you're almost guaranteed to see something with four legs on this quiet backroad. (p95)

Logan Pass ❹ is the highest point on the Going-to-the-Sun Road and a fine place to see mountain goats, bighorn sheep and grizzlies despite the crowds. (p179)

Watch for moose on the approach road and spy bears around the passes that overlook the shores of **Two Medicine Lake ❺**. (p190)

Fairmont Banff Springs (p63)

GRAND HOTELS

Built by railway companies for their vacationing passengers in a style that blends seamlessly with their natural surroundings, the early national park lodges invented a new type of architecture, coined 'parkitecture' by enamored guests. While fires destroyed some of the early prototypes, several of the original hotels remain, welcoming modern visitors with their retro ambience.

Afternoon Tea

A British tradition transplanted to Canada, afternoon tea with jam and cream scones can be enjoyed in many of the region's historic railway hotels.

Tee Off

Bring the clubs. Three of the Rocky Mountain heritage hotels – the Banff Springs, Jasper Park Lodge and Glacier Park Lodge – have golf courses.

BEST HOTEL EXPERIENCES

Not just an irresistible hotel, but also one of Canada's greatest architectural marvels, the **Fairmont Banff Springs** ❶ stands tall above the lush forests of Banff. (p63)

Sink your feet into thick carpets at the **Fairmont Chateau Lake Louise** ❷ as you look out over Canada's most famous lake. (p104)

Clustered like a deluxe village around Lac Beauvert, the **Fairmont Jasper Park Lodge** ❸ is embellished with a golf course, boathouse and planetarium. (p136)

A timber-framed lounge and huge windows characterize the beautiful **Prince of Wales Hotel** ❹ overlooking Upper Waterton Lake. (p213)

History weaves its magic through the corridors of the early-20th-century **Glacier Park Lodge** ❺ crafted from 900-year-old logs. (p193)

ROCKY MOUNTAIN RAILWAYS

Cross-continental railways were integral to the early development of the Rocky Mountain parks, bringing in tourists to a backwoods haven still mostly devoid of cars. While the railways' role as a mass transportation option may have diminished with the rise of private vehicles, the romance of the train journey has never gone away.

BEST RAILWAY EXPERIENCES

Book a trip on the **Rocky Mountaineer** ❶, a deluxe private loco that rattles along three different routes between Jasper, Banff and Vancouver. (p78)

Canada's national rail service, **VIA Rail** ❷, offers sleeper cars on its continent-spanning *Canadian* train that calls in twice weekly at Jasper. (p140)

Arguably, the park's most handsome building, **Jasper Train Station** ❸ is a notable architectural monument built in a dashing arts-and-crafts style. (p131)

Cross the Continental Divide at Marias Pass in the **Amtrak Empire Builder** ❹ and stay in a railway hotel in East Glacier. (p175)

Lake Louise Station

The historic train station in Lake Louise Village (p106), dating from 1910, is a grand log building that today serves as a deluxe restaurant and terminus for the *Rocky Mountaineer* train.

Splurge with the Rocky Mountaineer

Pay extra for deluxe carriages, gourmet meals and narrated tours on the privately run *Rocky Mountaineer* (p78) with services between Vancouver and Banff, and Vancouver and Jasper.

Sleep in a renovated train carriage and dine in a restaurant surrounded by railway memorabilia at the **Izaak Walton Inn** ❺ on the cusp of Glacier National Park. (p195)

Book a Sleeper

Reserve your own private overnight train compartment on the *Empire Builder* (Seattle–West Glacier) or the *Canadian* (Vancouver–Jasper), and arrive at the parks refreshed and rejuvenated.

TRAMPING THE TRAILS

If there's one activity that sums up the spirit of the Rockies, it's hiking. To come here and not hit the trails is like going to Disneyland and not utilizing the rides. No matter where you travel in the parks, there's a trail with your name on it, from the wheelchair-accessible path around Lake Annette to the knee-quivering scramble to the top of Mt Rundle overlooking Banff, and hundreds more in between.

Stay on the Trail

Walking off-piste and taking shortcuts causes soil erosion, damages plants, and leads to the formation of ugly braided paths.

Trailcams

Parks Canada maintains a number of motion-activated cameras attached to trees on various national park trails to monitor wildlife movements and log visitor numbers.

Know Before You Go

Fickle weather, forest fires and animal activity can lead to sporadic trail closures. Study the latest reports and wildlife warnings at park visitor centers or online.

BEST HIKING EXPERIENCES

Climb through the forest to the high-mountain lunar landscapes that soar above the Maligne and Athabasca river valleys on Jasper's **Skyline Trail ❶**. (p150)

Immerse yourself in the kaleidoscopic flower carpet of **Sunshine Meadows ❷** on the border of Alberta and British Columbia. (p90)

A profusion of wildlife and dramatic swathes of flaxen trees color **Larch Valley ❸** in Lake Louise in the autumn. (p109)

Accessible from Waterton's diminutive townsite by boat, the **Crypt Lake Trail ❹** is one of the Rockies' great alpine day hikes. (p224)

The strenuous overnight **Dawson–Pitamakan Loop ❺** departs from the wildlife-rich trail hub of Two Medicine and ascends two lofty mountain passes. (p188)

Valley of the Five Lakes (p140)

BEST CYCLING EXPERIENCES

TREK ON TWO WHEELS

The simplest and most environmentally friendly machine yet invented by humans has an enduring and universal appeal that's not lost on national park trails (Glacier excepted). Speed along the fabulous paved trails and quiet backroads of Banff but, for a real mountain-biking experience, decamp to to the stimulating single-track trails of Jasper.

A traffic-calmed spur road with minimal elevation between Banff and Lake Louise, the **Bow Valley Parkway ❶** offers plenty of wildlife-spotting opportunities. (p95)

The **Valley of the Five Lakes ❷** is Jasper's multifarious single-track with jolting roots and tight twisting paths keeping you busy with the gears. (p140)

Classed as off-road mountain biking for beginners, the mostly double-tracked **Goat Creek Trail ❸** links Canmore and Banff via a quiet back route. (p81)

A super-smooth multiuse path that runs parallel to the Trans-Canada Hwy between Canmore and Banff, the **Banff Legacy Trail ❹** offers ample opportunity for wind-assisted sprints. (p79)

The deceptively named **Snowshoe Trail ❺** in Waterton takes summer cyclists along a former fire road with minimal elevation. (p227)

Accessories

Always wear a helmet, take a puncture-repair kit and/or spare inner tubes, and a basic trail tool kit including hex keys, screwdrivers and a chain tool.

Bear Aware

Speedy cyclists are more likely to surprise bears. Carry bear spray, make noise and be alert on blind corners and rises.

MINERAL-RICH SPRINGS

It's the whole point of the park! Banff, the first Rocky Mountain park, was founded on the basis of its hot springs. Visiting the pools (and its cousins in Jasper and Kootenay) isn't just a day out at a spa, it's a historical pilgrimage to the heart and soul of the national park movement.

Smells Like Clean Spirit

Don't like the sulfur smell? Head to Radium (pictured, p101) in Kootenay, the only Rocky Mountain hot springs where the mineral-rich spring water is odorless.

Vintage Costumes

Forgot your costume? No problem. You can rent swimwear at all the hot springs, including retro 1920s-style swimsuits in the Banff Upper Hot Springs (p67).

Water Temperature

While the natural water temperature at the three springs varies (Miette is the hottest), the pool temperatures are all kept at a generic 37°C (99°F) to 40°C (104°F).

BEST HOT SPRINGS EXPERIENCES

A fount of warm, mineral-rich water and superb mountain views, **Banff Upper Hot Springs ❶** also evokes a genuine sense of history. (p67)

You can no longer bathe at **Cave and Basin National Historic Site ❷**, but you can uncover the historical background of Banff, the springs and the whole national park movement. (p69)

Hot, quiet and relatively isolated, **Miette Hot Springs ❸** is only open in summer, but well worth the 60km (37-mile) trek from Jasper Town. (p152)

The main gathering point in BC's Kootenay National Park, **Radium Hot Springs ❹** draws bathers to its relaxing, odorless waters. (p101)

The **Fairmont Banff Springs ❺** doesn't technically use natural spring water, but its spa is first-class and its indoor pool redolent of a European bathhouse. (p63)

15

LAKES & AQUATIC PURSUITS

Rocky Mountain lakes are famed for their blueish hue, the result of the sun reflecting off the fine glacial silt in the water. Every lake seems to have its own shade ranging from teal to sapphire, to turquoise. When you've finished admiring their colors, you can utilize the chilly waters for recreational purposes: cruises on Waterton, paddling around Cameron Lake, fishing in Minnewanka, and braving the icy temperatures for a swim in Lake Annette.

Beaches

The best sandy beach is at Lake Annette, closely followed by Pyramid Lake and Edith Lake (pictured), all in Jasper. Waterton townsite has a broad pebbly beach.

Cruises & Hikes

Glacier National Park offers the most comprehensive schedule of boat cruises with tours on five of its lakes, some of which include guided hikes.

The Big Chill

Almost all the mountain lakes, including expansive Lake Minnewanka, freeze over between December and early May. Aquatic activities don't get fully underway until June.

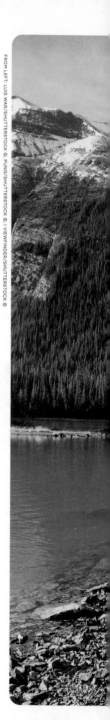

**BEST LAKE
EXPERIENCES**

There's nothing malign about **Maligne Lake ❶**, the go-to place in Jasper for narrated boat cruises and arm-numbing backcountry kayaking excursions. (p144)

Banff's primary aquatic nexus, **Lake Minnewanka ❷** offers the park's largest selection of water activities, from fishing and diving, to kayaking and boat cruises. (p82)

Take a brief passport-less boat trip on **Upper Waterton Lake Valley ❸** to Goat Haunt in the US to celebrate the International Peace Park. (p218)

Enjoy a cruise in a historic 100-year-old boat launch on **Lake McDonald ❹**, courtesy of Glacier Park Boat Company. (p174)

Chill on Jasper's finest beach beside **Lake Annette ❺** with a barbecue, a blow-up raft and perhaps an elk or two for company. (p135)

Canmore Nordic Centre (p77)

BRAVING THE WINTER CHILL

The parks are mostly warm weather havens. But you've only really experienced half the action if you haven't been in the winter. Post-November, the landscape gradually becomes more snow-covered and challenging (even the bears retire). Skiing is the obvious lure. Ice climbing, cross-country skiing and fat biking attract the more adventurous.

Way Less than Zero

Canadian winters can be cold. As recently as January 2020, the mercury dropped as low as -44.8°C (-48.6°F) in Jasper.

Ski Shuttles

All of the parks' four ski areas have free winter shuttles busing skiers between base stations and accommodations in Banff, Jasper and Lake Louise.

BEST WINTER EXPERIENCES

Arguably the Rockies' best all-round ski resort, **Banff Sunshine** ❶ enjoys heaps of fluffy powder, a ski-in hotel and plenty of winter sun rays. (p88)

The frozen waterfalls and guided ice walks around **Maligne Canyon** ❷ form the backbone of Jasper's winter excursion list. (p147)

The cradle of backcountry skiing in Banff, the rustic **Skoki Lodge** ❸ pulls in a steady trickle of ski tourers, and cross-country enthusiasts. (p112)

The cross-country skiing HQ for the 1988 Winter Olympics, the **Canmore Nordic Centre** ❹ has lost none of its world-class polish. (p76)

One of the largest ski areas in Canada, the **Lake Louise Ski Resort** ❺ is known for its varied terrain and fabulous views toward the lake of everyone's dreams. (p102)

NIGHTS UNDER CANVAS

Camping comes in various guises. There's the large front-country campground where you pull up in an RV and cluster around an alfresco amphitheater for evening ranger talks, and the lonesome tent-pad in the wilderness with pit toilets and a cable on which to hang your food. Both invoke happy uncomplicated visions of a simpler life.

Plan Ahead

There are many campgrounds in the parks but demand is high and the summer season is short. Book well in advance, especially for front-country campgrounds.

Camping Giants

The Canadian parks are home to two of the nation's largest campgrounds: Tunnel Mountain in Banff with 1128 sites, and The Whistlers in Jasper with 781 sites.

No Reservations

Six of Glacier National Park's 13 front-country campgrounds operate on a first-come-first-served basis. Of these, only one, Rising Sun, is developed and open to RVs.

BEST CAMPING EXPERIENCES

The superb three- to four-day **Skyline Trail ❶** hike along the rooftops of Jasper offers seven great places to pitch your tent, all of them spectacular. (p150)

Glacier's well-trodden **Gunsight Pass Trail ❷** provides a good intro to camping in the park with sites up for grabs at the basic Gunsight Lake and Sperry Chalet campgrounds. (p181)

Home to Banff's largest backcountry campground, **Egypt Lake ❸** inspires enduring love among park regulars. Book ahead! (p93)

Twenty-five campgrounds and very few takers mean you can enjoy splendid isolation in the wilds of Jasper's **North Boundary Trail ❹**. (p139)

A dramatic contrast to brawny backcountry, Banff's giant **Tunnel Mountain Village ❺** is an ideal place to show off your new RV. (p71)

RIVERS & WATERFALLS

Meandering across glacial valleys, crashing through narrow canyons and spilling over powerful waterfalls, the Rockies are full of clear, fast-flowing rivers radiating from the turreted mountains of the Continental Divide, many with their source in giant glaciers. The Bow, Athabasca, Saskatchewan and Flathead rivers create vast aquatic ecosystems and bubble with recreational possibilities.

Spring Meltwater

Waterfalls are usually at their most impressive in May and June when the rivers are supplemented by glacial meltwater turning them into thunderous forces of nature.

River Safari

Slow-float trips are an excellent way of spotting wildlife, most of which comes down to the river at some point to feed, drink and play.

Three Forks, One River

The Flathead River has three forks – north, south and middle – with the North Fork, which originates in British Columbia, usually considered the main tributary.

BEST RIVER EXPERIENCES

Diminutive but immensely strong, **Athabasca Falls** ❶ is the Mike Tyson of Jasper waterfalls, packing a powerful aquatic punch. (p162)

Go on an overnight rafting-camping trip and partake in fishing and wildlife-watching on the angry North or Middle Forks of the **Flathead River** ❷. (p175)

Banff Town's easily accessible **Bow Falls** ❸ provides a melodious backdrop to the superb views at Surprise Corner. (p64)

A unique waterfall within a waterfall near Two Medicine, **Running Eagle Falls** ❹ is named for a female leader of the Pikuni Blackfeet tribe. (p189)

Look down on the Maligne River at **Maligne Canyon** ❺ as it changes its course and personality multiple times from narrow flume to choppy meandering waterway. (p147)

Ice climber, Maligne Canyon (p147)

EXTREME ADVENTURES

The Rockies hide some starkly beautiful but unforgiving terrain. Winters are brutal and even summer weather can change on a dime. If you like to push yourself and live life in the physical fast lane, you've landed in the right spot. There are plenty of opportunities to turn your knuckles white.

Ask an Expert

Not sure? Book a tour. Learn adventure skills from an established operator. Yamnuska Mountain Adventures in Canmore is the ultimate white-knuckle specialist.

Practice Makes Perfect

Canmore has some great places to fine-tune your outdoor skills: Elevation Place has an indoor climbing wall, while the Nordic Centre has superb mountain biking and cross-country skiing trails.

BEST EXTREME EXPERIENCES

Cory Pass ❶, Banff's best 'black-diamond' hike, is an exhilarating mix of shinnying and scrambling over boulders, rocks and scree slope. (p99)

In winter the ferocious waterfalls of **Maligne Canyon ❷** freeze solid, creating challenging ice walls for aspiring climbers. (p147)

The most lonesome of Jasper's backcountry hikes, the **North Boundary Trail ❸** takes you off the grid for at least a week with sinuous trails and wild campsites. (p139)

Narrow ledges, cable supports, cliff ladders and shadowy tunnels, Waterton's **Crypt Lake Trail ❹** has several unusual technicalities dotted along its course. (p224)

Get up close and personal with the rocks of Mt Norquay in Banff on a safe but spine-tingling **via ferrata ❺** (fixed-protection climbing route). (p74)

21

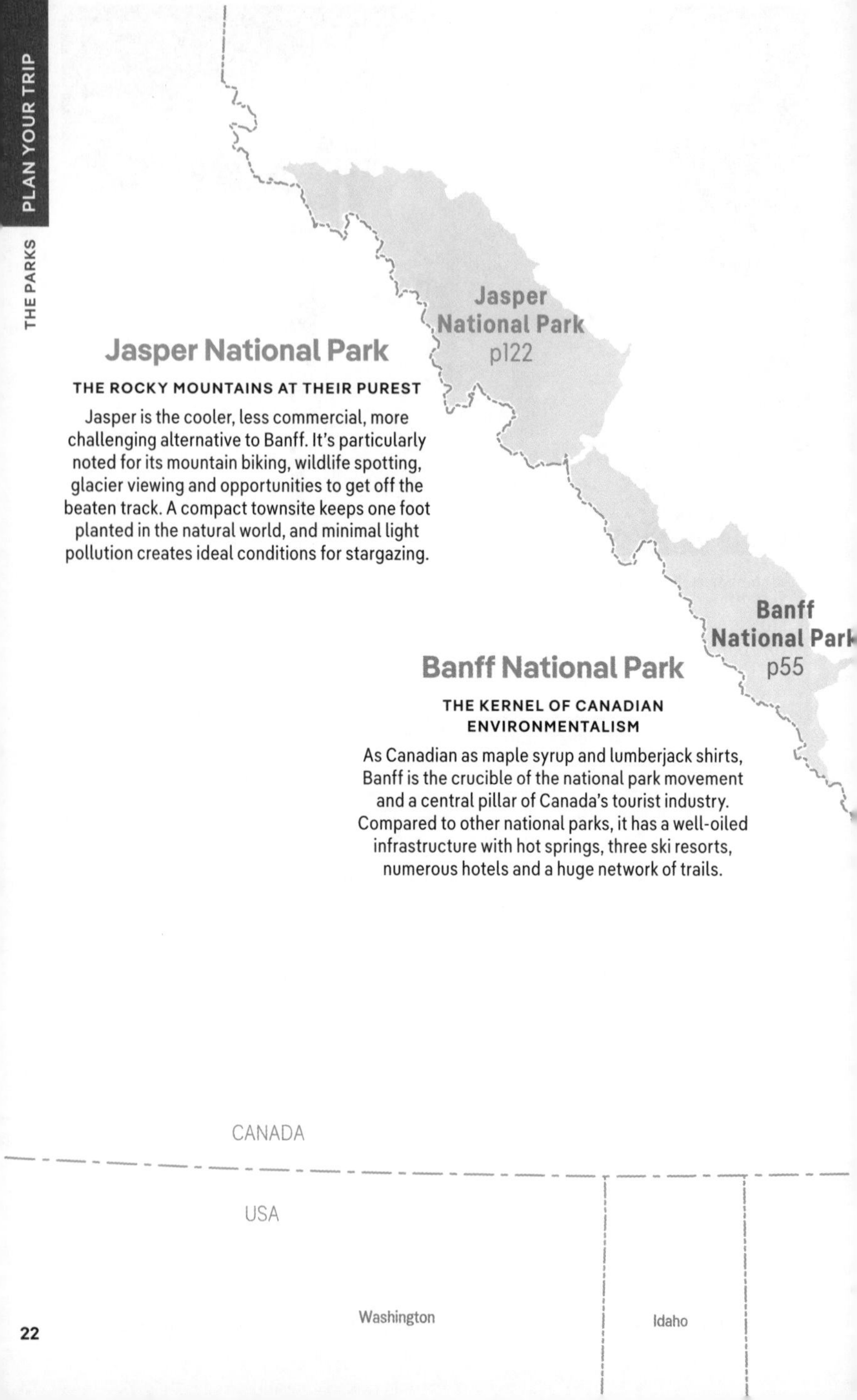

Jasper National Park

THE ROCKY MOUNTAINS AT THEIR PUREST

Jasper is the cooler, less commercial, more challenging alternative to Banff. It's particularly noted for its mountain biking, wildlife spotting, glacier viewing and opportunities to get off the beaten track. A compact townsite keeps one foot planted in the natural world, and minimal light pollution creates ideal conditions for stargazing.

**Jasper
National Park**
p122

**Banff
National Park**
p55

Banff National Park

**THE KERNEL OF CANADIAN
ENVIRONMENTALISM**

As Canadian as maple syrup and lumberjack shirts, Banff is the crucible of the national park movement and a central pillar of Canada's tourist industry. Compared to other national parks, it has a well-oiled infrastructure with hot springs, three ski resorts, numerous hotels and a huge network of trails.

CANADA

USA

Washington

Idaho

THE PARKS

Find the places that tick all your boxes.

Alberta

Saskatchewan

Waterton Lakes National Park

FLAT PRAIRIES MEET ROCKY MOUNTAINS

The park that the rest of the Rockies likes to forget has been quietly attracting in-the-know visitors since 1895. Squeezing many of the region's greatest hits (lakes, alpine hikes, regal hotels) into its diminutive 525 sq km (203 sq miles), it serves as a smaller, under-the-radar version of Banff and Jasper.

Waterton Lakes National Park
p208

Glacier National Park
p167

Glacier National Park

GLACIALLY CARVED NATURAL WONDERLAND

One of the wildest and most pristine US national parks outside Alaska, Glacier takes its 'Crown of the Continent' billing seriously. Strict management policies have protected the park from over-commercialization. Come here for superb hiking, historic lodges and a drive along one of America's most spectacular roads.

Montana

23

JASON PATRICK ROSS/SHUTTERSTOCK ©

Athabasca River (p159)

ITINERARIES

Banff, Jasper & the Parkways

Allow: 7 Days   **Distance**: 288km (180 miles)

Two national parks, two classic mountain towns and the dramatic view-laced road that runs between them – this trip crams as much as possible into a busy 10 days of slow driving and frenetic activity as you take in the Canadian Rockies' greatest hits. Beware: sensory overload is possible!

❶ BANFF TOWN ⏱1 DAY

With its outfitter stores and casual restaurants, **Banff** (p60) is a good place to stock up and enjoy your favorite food fixes before heading north. It's also a prime spot to digest a bit of local history in the Whyte Museum, the Cave and Basin National Historic Site and the iconic Banff Springs Hotel. For exercise, hike up Sulphur Mountain before gondola-ing back down for a dip in the Banff Upper Hot Springs.

🚗 15 minutes

❷ BOW VALLEY PARKWAY ⏱1 DAY

Divert onto Hwy 1A, also known as the **Bow Valley Parkway** (p95), just outside Banff and slowly ply north. There are copious pull-overs with interpretive boards honoring the surrounding ecosystems. An essential stop is Johnston Canyon where you can hike along catwalks through a spectacular gorge.

🚗 50 minutes

❸ LAKE LOUISE ⏱2 DAYS

Head straight for **Lake Louise** (p102), where you can stroll the halls of the famous chateau before heading up into the mountains for refreshments at the Lake Agnes Teahouse. In the afternoon, take the gondola up Whitehorn Mountain for potential grizzly-bear sightings. On day two, book the shuttle to Moraine Lake and spend your time creating photo art and exploring the Larch Valley.

🚗 90 minutes

FROM LEFT: RYBARMAREKK/SHUTTERSTOCK ©, FOKKE BAARSSEN/SHUTTERSTOCK ©, MATT GRIMALDI/SHUTTERSTOCK ©

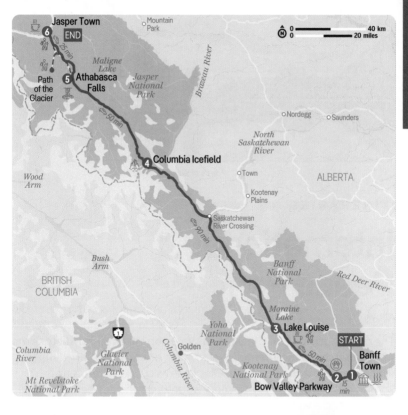

4 COLUMBIA ICEFIELD ⏱ 1 DAY

Take it slow as you head north on the Icefields Parkway stopping off at the many viewpoints. Hector Lake, Bow Lake and Mistaya Canyon are all recommended. For a longer excursion, hike to the 'red chairs' on the Wilcox Pass trail before hitting the Icefield Discovery Centre for a late lunch and an excursion on the **Columbia Icefield** (p160) in an Ice Explorer Snocoach.

🚌 *50 minutes*

5 ATHABASCA FALLS ⏱ 1 DAY

After a night in the Glacier View Lodge, continue your slow passage north along the Icefields Parkway, lingering at Tangle Falls and Sunwapta Falls before descending on the super-powerful **Athabasca Falls** (p162).

🔁 *Detour: Head up the skirts of Mt Edith Cavell to hike the Path of the Glacier Loop (p159) to an iceberg-filled lake. ⏱ 4 hours*

🚌 *25 minutes*

6 JASPER ⏱ 1 DAY

Embrace the salubrious mountain airs of **Jasper Town** (p128), loading up on coffee and cakes at The Other Paw and earthy nosh at Terra. Walk the urban section of the Discovery Trail, admire the handsome train station and, time permitting, rent a bike to take you around the lakes and trails of the Athabasca River Valley, stopping at the Jasper Park Lodge en route.

SHAWN.CCF/SHUTTERSTOCK ©

Prince of Wales Hotel (p213)

ITINERARIES

International Peace Park

Allow: 6 days   **Distance:** 150km (94 miles)

The conjoined parks of Glacier and Waterton Lakes stretch across the 49th parallel and the international frontier, offering two very different visions of the same mountains. Glacier is wild, unadulterated and spread out, while Waterton is more structured and condensed with a townsite and a well-organized commercial core.

❶

LAKE MCDONALD ⏱ 1 DAY

The southwestern shore of the large natural **Lake McDonald** (p174) is about as built-up as Glacier gets. The tiny 'village' of Apgar acts as the main service center for the park west of Logan Pass and is a great place to go for a paddle, talk to a ranger, pick up shuttle schedules and sample the park's essence. Several accommodations hug the lakeshore.

🚗 *60 minutes*

❷

LOGAN PASS ⏱ 1 DAY

Get off the free shuttle bus at **Logan Pass** (p179) and say hello to bighorn sheep, stubborn patches of snow and a plethora of enamored visitors. To escape the bulk of them, hike as far as possible along the Highline Trail, a spellbinding traverse in the shadow of the Crown of the Continent, aiming to reach the backcountry Granite Park Chalet before turning back.

🚗 *40 minutes*

❸

ST MARY ⏱ 1 DAY

On the park's eastern border, you can indulge in some of Glacier's more esoteric activities around **St Mary** (p199), such as stargazing and dance performances at the visitor center, and Native American Speaks at local campgrounds. For refueling try the berry pies at Park Cafe in St Mary village and the around-the-world cuisine at Two Sisters Cafe in Babb.

🚗 *30 minutes*

FROM LEFT: FRANCISCO BLANCO/SHUTTERSTOCK © , KIT LEONG/SHUTTERSTOCK © , ZACK FRANK/SHUTTERSTOCK ©

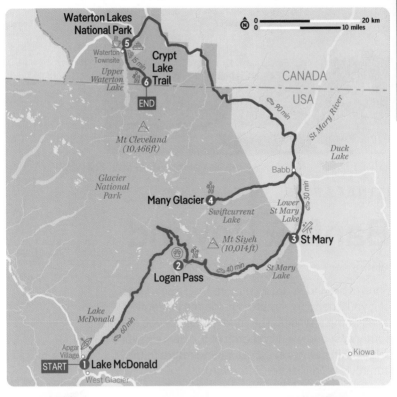

MANY GLACIER ⏱ 1 DAY

Spend the morning in **Many Glacier** (p204) languishing guiltily in the handsome confines of the Many Glacier Hotel clocking assorted taxidermy, chatting to staff in lederhosen and enjoying wonderfully wild views over Swiftcurrent Lake from the Ptarmigan Dining Room. In the afternoon, hit the short Apikuni Falls Trail if you're feeling lethargic or the 17km (10.6-mile) Grinnell Lake Trail if you're not.

🚗 90 minutes

WATERTON LAKES NATIONAL PARK ⏱ 1 DAY

Spend a day enjoying the creature comforts of **Waterton Park** (p212), where you can procure the relative luxuries of multiflavored ice cream, a round of golf, afternoon tea in the Prince of Wales Hotel (pictured) and songs around the campfire at the town's expansive campground. Save time for a cruise on the lake to the international border.

⛴ 15 minutes

CRYPT LAKE TRAIL ⏱ 1 DAY

A fitting end to a spectacular trip, the **Crypt Lake Trail** (p224) involves a challenging but exhilarating day hike to a hidden lake that includes a short boat transfer, a traverse along a narrow ledge (with cables for support), a short ladder climb and a scramble through a dark tunnel. Good fitness and a head for heights are essential. Celebrate your bravery at a Waterton watering hole afterwards.

DAVID P. LEWIS/SHUTTERSTOCK ©

Hiking, Yoho National Park (p111)

ITINERARIES

Banff & Beyond

Allow: 6 days **Distance:** 305km (190 miles)

Banff is big and to uncover more than a smidgeon of it you'll need to venture outside the protective shell of the townsite. This itinerary sends you north, south, east and west in search of the park's rawer edges with plenty of opportunity to return to the comforts of 'civilization' afterwards.

1 BANFF TOWN ⏱ 1 DAY

Orientation day in **Banff Town** (p60). Stroll Banff Ave (pictured) to check out dining possibilities, following the whiff of coffee to Whitebark Cafe and the aroma of beer to Bear Street Tavern. Peruse a museum or two, double-take views of the Fairmont Banff Springs Hotel at 'Surprise Corner' and get the Google Earth view of town from Tunnel Mountain.
🚲 75 minutes

2 CANMORE ⏱ 1 DAY

Venture briefly outside the park gates for a day to the mountain town of **Canmore** (p76). No car required. Spend the morning cycling along the fast, flat, paved Legacy Trail from Banff before chilling in a Canmore cafe and eyeing its art galleries. After lunch in Rocky Mountain Flatbread Co, take the off-road Goat Creek Trail back to Banff, or stick your bike on a bus.
🚌 15 minutes

3 LAKE MINNEWANKA ⏱ 1 DAY

Spend a day exploring **Lake Minnewanka** (p82) by car or bike. Start with a morning boat cruise, followed by a short stroll to Stewart Canyon. Grab a picnic lakeside and head back around the road loop, stopping at Lower Bankhead for an insight into Banff's erstwhile mining history. Detour: Just beyond Bankhead, hiking fanatics can tackle the steep but rewarding clamber to C-Level Cirque.
🚌 20 minutes

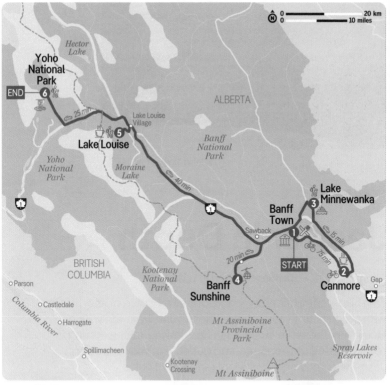

4 BANFF SUNSHINE ⏱1 DAY

Summer and Sunshine Meadows go together like maple syrup and bacon. Take the gondola up to **Banff Sunshine** (p88), grab some poutine in the Mad Trappers Saloon, and ride the Standish chairlift (pictured) up to the Continental Divide. Spend the rest of the day wandering around the lakes and meadows of Alberta and British Columbia. The super-athletic can hike over to Healy Meadows and descend on foot from there.

🚌 *40 minutes*

5 LAKE LOUISE ⏱1 DAY

Re-pack your bags and head for **Lake Louise** (p000) by car or bus. Get acquainted with the 'village' over a coffee in Trailhead Cafe before hiking up to the lake, where you can spend the day admiring the hotel, tramping the trails and popping into a teahouse or two. Book an atmospheric dinner by the tracks in the heritage Station Restaurant.

🚌 *25 minutes*

6 YOHO NATIONAL PARK ⏱1 DAY

Smaller than its surrounding national park brethren, **Yoho National Park** (p111) packs a lot into its diminutive 1313 sq km (507 sq miles). Make a base in Field and endeavor to explore the natural wonders clustered on the north side of the Trans-Canada Hwy including forest-ringed Emerald Lake, lofty Takakkaw Falls (pictured) and the ancient Burgess Shale fossil beds.

Sulphur Skyline Trail (p153)

ITINERARIES

Jasper in Depth

Allow: 7 Days   **Distance:** 328km (205 miles)

This hike-centric itinerary incorporates a couple of short trails with a significantly longer one (the Skyline Trail). On your non-hiking days, reserve time for glacier viewing, lolling around in revitalizing mineral springs, and quenching your appetite in Jasper's surprisingly abundant (and good) cafes.

1
JASPER TOWN ⏲ 1 DAY
Spend a day hanging around **Jasper Town** (p128), getting orientated on the Discovery Trail, visiting the historic train station, and perusing the shops and heritage buildings of Patricia and Connaught Sts. Carb-load in the Wicked Cup Cafe, excite your taste buds in the Raven Bistro, and indulge in alcoholic drinks at Jasper Brewing Co. Finish off with a visit to the planetarium at the Jasper Park Lodge.
🚶 *45 minutes*

2
PYRAMID BENCH ⏲ 1 DAY
Follow your lazy intro with a more energetic excursion to the **Pyramid Bench** (p134), the well-trammeled network of forest and lakes directly above the town. Visit Pyramid Lake (pictured) for its beach, canoeing and diminutive island, and look out for waterfowl on the Mina and Riley Lakes Loop. Pop into the Jasper-Yellowhead Museum & Archives on your way back into town.
🚗 *60 minutes*

3
MIETTE HOT SPRINGS ⏲ 1 DAY
Jasper's hot springs, **Miette Hot Springs** (p152), are more isolated than Banff's but the drive over is worth it, especially if your legs are still knackered after a day on the 'Bench.' If they're not, you can give them another run around on the Sulphur Skyline hike, a steep climb to a stormy ridge.
🚗 *50 minutes*

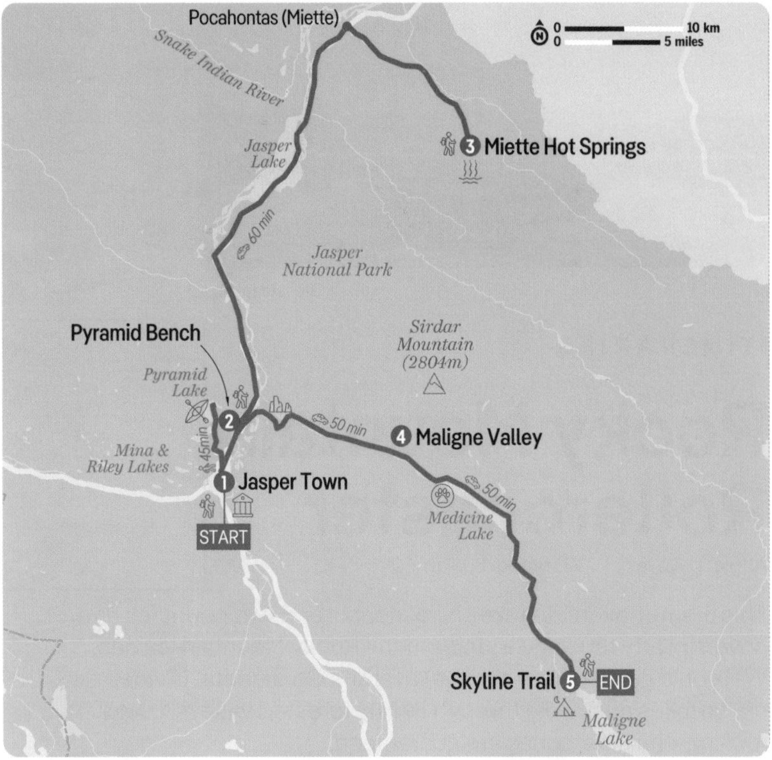

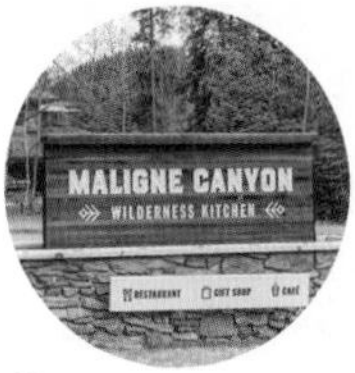

4

MALIGNE VALLEY ⏱ 1 DAY

Pitch south toward the **Maligne Valley** (p149), stopping off at Maligne Canyon on the way for a loop around its five main bridges and a snack at the exquisite Wilderness Kitchen. Stop two is Medicine Lake where wildlife is usually abundant and, finally, the shores of Maligne Lake where you can take an elongated boat cruise before hiking the short Moose Lake Loop.

50 minutes

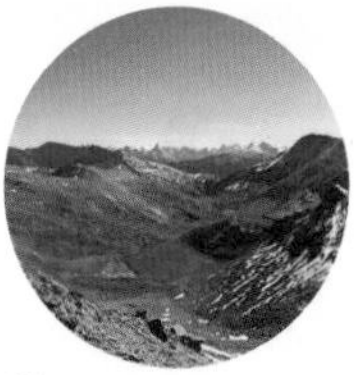

5

SKYLINE TRAIL ⏱ 3 DAYS

Release your energy on one of North America's finest alpine trails with an early start at Maligne Lake. Spread over three days, the 45km (28-mile) **Skyline Trail** (p150) has various camping options (arrange in advance). Nights at the Little Shovel and Tekarra campgrounds will enable you to take your time and absorb the landscapes on the rooftop of the Rockies.

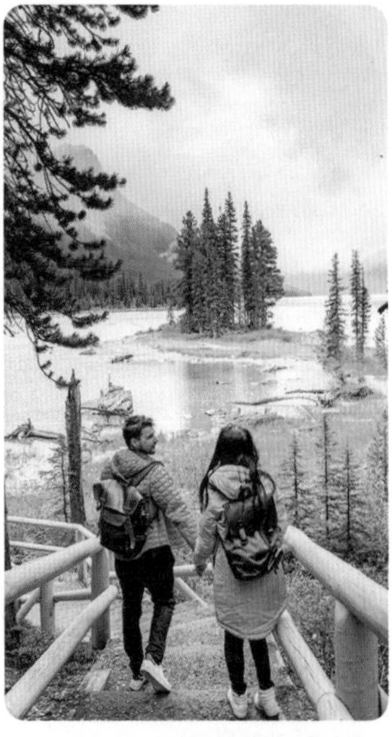

Maligne Lake (p144)

Lake McDonald (p174)

ITINERARIES

Rocky Mountain Rollercoaster

Allow: 14 Days   **Distance:** 805km (504 miles)

This cram-it-all-in trip takes in four parks and two countries and covers pretty much everything in the Rocky Mountain lexicon. Walk on a glacier, hike (or drive) over the Continental Divide, cruise lakes and cycle through thickly forested valleys. Lucid rocking-chair memories are guaranteed.

❶ GLACIER NATIONAL PARK
⏱ 3 DAYS

Start out with three days exploring **Glacier National Park** (p167) using the Going-to-the-Sun Rd (pictured) as your vestibule. Warm up with some short hikes around Many Glacier and gravitate, if you have the time, to a spine-tingling tramp up toward the Grinnell Glacier. Quench your appetite in Apgar Village and dip an oar in Lake McDonald before pitching north to Canada.

🚗 2 hours

❷ WATERTON LAKES NATIONAL PARK ⏱ 2 DAYS

Undertake more hiking in **Waterton Lakes National Park** (p208), incorporating what is for many the best alpine day hike in the Rockies: the resplendent Carthew-Alderson Trail (pictured) that'll deliver you back to the townsite in time for dinner. Spend part of day two enjoying that most British of traditional repasts, afternoon tea, accompanied by spectacular vistas at the Prince of Wales Hotel.

🚗 4 hours

❸ BANFF NATIONAL PARK
⏱ 5 DAYS

Spend the next day driving north to **Banff National Park** (p55), your base for the next four days. There are many ways to divide your time, but make sure you factor in the gondola ride up Sulphur Mountain (pictured), wildlife spotting around Vermilion Lakes and a boat trip across Lake Minnewanka. Day 10 is set aside for more mind-blowing scenery around Lake Louise and Moraine Lake.

🚗 40 minutes

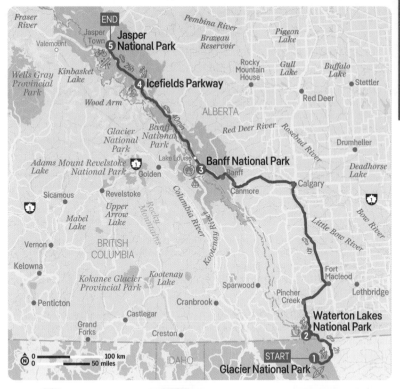

❹
ICEFIELDS PARKWAY
⏱ **1 DAY**

On day 11, gear up for a drive north on the **Icefields Parkway** (p156) – it won't take long for you to realize why it's often dubbed the world's most spectacular road. Of the multitude of potential stops, the unmissables include Bow Lake, Parker Ridge (for the best short hike) and the Columbia Icefield where you can walk on a glacier.

🚗 *2½ hours*

❺
JASPER NATIONAL PARK
⏱ **3 DAYS**

Round the trip off with three days in **Jasper National Park** (p122), where you can puff out your adventurous resume with some of the park's specialty activities: rafting on the Sunwapta River, mountain biking in the Valley of the Five Lakes (pictured), and stargazing in and around the planetarium at Jasper Park Lodge. If you missed the mineral waters in Banff, Miette Hot Springs offers a quieter alternative.

Icefields Parkway (p156)

WHEN **TO GO**

To enjoy the full gamut of trails, facilities and activities in
the parks, come between late May and late September.

High season in the Rocky Mountain parks is late May to
Labor Day weekend (early September). July and August
are the busiest months with mostly warm weather
and sunny skies, although thunderstorms can descend
quickly.

Hiking restrictions are often implemented on certain
trails during buffaloberry season from mid-July to early
September, when bears are more active.

Spring comes late, with snow lingering until May or
June, especially in alpine areas where trails can remain
closed due to avalanche danger. June is invariably the
wettest month.

Late March to May and October to November is the
quiet shoulder season when many facilities remain closed
and some public transportation doesn't run.

Weather permitting, ski areas usually open from early
December to early May.

Accommodations Lowdown

Prices are lowest in the shoulder season but bear in mind
that many campgrounds are closed outside of high season.
Demand for accommodations is high in the summer
and the parks can often fill up completely. Book ahead.

⊗ I LIVE HERE

**BANFF
NATIONAL PARK**

**Amar Athwal is a Visitor
Experience Team Leader
at Cave and Basin National
Historic Site.**

One of my favorite hikes
in Banff National Park is
the Healy Pass Trail. Early
summer to see the variety of
beautiful wildflowers and in
the fall to see the amazing
golden-colored larch trees.
There's a small chance
you might see a bear in the
meadow, but mostly I've been
able to sit back and watch
the birds with my binoculars.
It's always good to bring
extra layers so you can be
comfortable at the top.

SPRING THAW

Conditions vary year to
year but park lakes generally
start thawing in early May with
Lake Minnewanka leading the way
followed by Maligne Lake in late
May, and Lake Louise in early
June. Moraine Lake is usually
the last to shake off its
ice pack.

LEFT: ALBERTOGONZALEZ/SHUTTERSTOCK ©
RIGHT: MACK MALE/FLICKR/CC BY-SA 2.0 ©

Moraine Lake (p108)

Weather Through the Year

❄ JANUARY	☔ FEBRUARY	☁ MARCH	☁ APRIL	☀ MAY	☀ JUNE
Average daytime max: -6°C (21°F)	Average daytime max: -2°C (28°F)	Average daytime max: 3°C (37°F)	Average daytime max: 11°C (52°F)	Average daytime max: 16°C (61°F)	Average daytime max: 21°C (70°F)
Days of rainfall: 4	Days of rainfall: 4	Days of rainfall: 5	Days of rainfall: 6	Days of rainfall: 7	Days of rainfall: 9

SNOWED-IN ROADS

The summer opening of Glacier's Going-to-the-Sun Road can vary depending on the winter snowpack. The earliest opening was May 16 in 1987 when the road remained accessible for six full months. Other years, it hasn't opened until the beginning of July.

Jasper in January

Outdoor Chill

Jasper in January is the town's atmospheric winter festival hosting plenty of family-friendly events, including cross-country skiing, sleigh rides, skating and a chili cook-off.
❄ **January**

Snow sculptures, block parties, snow-sliding events, big-name bands and a huge game of street hockey characterize Banff's **Snow Days** that celebrates the frigidity of winter with comforting warmth.
❄ **January**

The **Canmore Highland Games** sees the town celebrating its Scottish roots with a day of caber tossing, piping, sheepdog trials and a traditional ceilidh to round things off.
🍂 **September**

Jasper's annual **Dark Sky Festival** (p132) celebrates the national park's status as one of the world's leading Dark Sky Preserves with classical concerts and outdoor trips to incredible stargazing sites.
🍂 **October**

☑ I LIVE HERE

JASPER NATIONAL PARK

Deryl Kelly is a Visitor Safety Specialist at Parks Canada.

This vibrant, small mountain town throbs with contagious energy! Perpetually fueling my passion for a rider's life on my mountain bike. I am absolutely enamored with exploring the vast network of trails. The best part, Jasper National Park offers year-round biking opportunities, whether it's the flat-packed winter trails on a fat bike, sustained climbing into the clouds on my road bike or hurtling down the infamous single track, 'WaterTower' descent in the summer.

Cultural Happenings

The largest of several celebrations held on the Blackfeet Indian Reservation throughout the year, the **North American Indian Days** event in Browning has displays of traditional drumming and dancing.
☀ **July**

Culture takes center stage for the month-long **Banff Summer Arts Festival**, a showcase of artistic activity at the Banff Centre, hosting everything from opera, theater and street performance to art exhibitions. ☀ **July to August**

Top folk acts descend on Canmore for the **Canmore Folk Festival**, a lively musical gathering held every year since 1978 over the Heritage Weekend. The main stage is in Centennial Park, but there are extra gigs at many cafes and bars around town, too. ☀ **August**

Since the mid-1970s, the seven-day **Banff Mountain Film & Book Festival** has celebrated the spirit of mountain adventure through films, videos, readings and lectures. 🍂 **October to November**

CAN'T STAND THE HEAT

In recent years Banff has seen a warming trend, breaking longstanding summer temperature records. In 2018 it logged an August record of 34°C (93°F), and in 2021 it busted the records for June at 38°C (100°F) and for July at 37°C (99°F).

JULY	AUGUST	SEPTEMBER	OCTOBER	NOVEMBER	DECEMBER
Average daytime max: 24°C (75°F)	Average daytime max: 24°C (75°F)	Average daytime max: 18°C (64°F)	Average daytime max: 12°C (54°F)	Average daytime max: 3°C (37°F)	Average daytime max: -4°C (25°F)
Days of rainfall: 7	Days of rainfall: 8	Days of rainfall: 7	Days of rainfall: 5	Days of rainfall: 5	Days of rainfall: 4

LEFT: SONGQUAN DENG/SHUTTERSTOCK ©. FAR RIGHT: PICTORIAL PRESS LTD/ALAMY STOCK PHOTO ©

Hiking, Moraine Lake (p108)

GET PREPARED FOR BANFF, JASPER & GLACIER NATIONAL PARKS

Useful things to load in your bag, your ears and your brain.

Clothes

Forget the dandy outfits. How you dress in the Rockies is more about practicality than impressing the fashion police. No restaurant in Banff is going to eject you for not wearing a three-piece suit. Here are the outdoor essentials.

Dependable footwear Broken-in hiking boots or your favorite running shoes – whichever you feel more comfortable in. Slides or flip-flops for the evenings.

Rain gear and windproof jacket Add rain pants and gaiters if you're heading for the backcountry.

Cold-weather protection Even in summer, you'll need long underwear, wool or fleece base layers, a down or synthetic jacket, and a hat and gloves.

Manners

Canadians are fastidiously polite and famous for saying 'sorry' at almost any opportunity.

It's customary to thank the driver on Canadian buses when you disembark, even if it means shouting the words down the aisle.

Don't be shy. Like many Midwesterners, Montanans are open and friendly and will often strike up random conversations with strangers in restaurants and on buses.

Sunwear Shorts or convertible trousers, a hat, sunglasses, skin cream, and a swimsuit for spontaneous lake swims.

Animal protection You shouldn't hike anywhere in the parks without bear spray and preferably a bear horn too.

📖 READ

Night of the Grizzlies
(Jack Olsen; 1969)
Shocking account of a
night in Glacier National
Park in 1967 when two
young women were
killed by grizzly bears in
two separate incidents.

Ridgerunner (Gil
Adamson; 2020) Mixing
the genres of Gothic
and Western fiction,
this novel is set in Banff
during WWI in a place
at the crossroads of
change.

**Old Indian Trails of
the Canadian Rockies**
(Mary Schäffer; 1911)
Early-20th-century
account of Schäffer's
wilderness adventures
in and around Jasper.

**Handbook of the
Canadian Rockies**
(Ben Gadd; 1995)
Comprehensive guide to
everything from geology
and history to birds,
plants and animals
spread over 800 pages.

Words

First Nations A
term used to identify
Indigenous Peoples in
Canada who are *not*
Inuit (from the Arctic
or subarctic) or Métis
(of mixed Indigenous-
European roots). In the
Rocky Mountains it
includes the Stoney-
Nakoda, Assiniboine and
many more.

Indigenous An umbrella
term for pre-contact
people in Canada,
including Inuit and Métis.

Native Americans
Indigenous Peoples in
the US.

Park ranger A national
park employee in the US.

Park warden A national
park employee in
Canada.

Parks Canada A
government agency
running Canada's 48
national parks. Founded
in 1911.

**National Park
Service** A US federal
agency running all
the country's national
parks, monuments and
properties. Founded
in 1916.

Minnewanka Means
'lake of the spirits' in the
Stoney language.

Sunwapta Means
'turbulent water' in the
Stoney language.

Athabasca A word of
Cree origin meaning
'where there are reeds.'

Yoho A Cree expression
of amazement.

🎬 WATCH

Brokeback Mountain (Ang Lee;
2005, pictured) An unorthodox
cowboy tale partly filmed in
Kananaskis Country near Banff.

River of No Return (Otto Preminger;
1954) The peroxide glamor of
Marilyn Monroe is pitted against
Banff and Jasper's natural beauty.

Days of Heaven (Terence
Malick; 1978) Terrence Malick's
magnum opus utilized Banff for
its stunning cinematography.

The Revenant (Alejandro Iñárritu;
2015) A trapper's harrowing wilderness
journey after a grizzly attack, partially
filmed in Canmore and the Kananaskis.

🎧 LISTEN

All the Right Reasons
(Nickelback; 2005)
The bestselling album
of Alberta's most
famous international
rock band mixes post-
grunge with alt-rock
and heavy metal.

Unbreakable (The
Bearhead Sisters; 2023)
Three-piece band from
the Cree-Nakoda Paul
First Nation whose
album won a Juno
prize for Traditional
Indigenous Artist of
the Year in 2023.

**Banff International
String Quartet
Competition**
(banffcentre.ca/bisqc/
watch-and-listen)
Watch and listen to
footage from Banff's
prestigious annual
classical music festival.

Headwaters Podcast
(nps.gov/glac/learn/
photosmultimedia/
headwaters-podcast.
htm) Tune into podcasts
from the Glacier
National Park media
team about the region's
history and nature.

LEFT: DIRKVD/SHUTTERSTOCK ©; RIGHT: KISSCAT/SHUTTERSTOCK ©

Sunshine Meadow Hike (p90)

THE OUTDOORS

The Rocky Mountain parks epitomise the great North American outdoor experience. Come here to embrace nature, push personal boundaries, and insert yourself back into a simpler, more primordial world.

The role of the Rocky Mountain national parks is to preserve the region's delicate ecosystems while, at the same time, delivering memorable experiences for visitors.

Beyond Banff's ice-cream shops and Jasper's railway paraphernalia, the real thrill for most arrivals lies in the opportunity to indulge in a raft of self-propelled outdoor pursuits of which hiking, biking and canoeing sit center stage. Reminding us of a time when homo sapiens were infinitely closer to nature, the parks offer us a chance to reconnect.

Hiking

Welcome to hiking heaven! The comprehensive national park trail networks are exceptionally well marked, both with downloadable maps, available on the Parks Canada and National Park Services websites, and extensive on-the-ground signage. Large informative map boards are usually posted at trailheads, and distance and directional signage is available at almost every major trail junction. It's practically impossible to get lost.

To help choose for your ability, hiking trails are color-graded on maps, in green (easy), blue (moderate) and black (difficult). Green trails are flat, relatively smooth, and appropriate for beginners. Black paths are steep, uneven and only suitable for experienced hikers.

Park authorities are meticulous about clearing trails of dead trees and other obstacles, and special signs will warn of wildlife activity in the area. Sometimes trails are closed completely (eg during the elk calving season) or enforce seasonal restrictions (eg hikers must travel in groups of four around Lake Louise in the buffaloberry season).

Other Activities in the Parks

VIA FERRATA
Guided fixed-protection climbing routes on Mt Norquay (p74) turn novices into mountaineers in one short session.

WHITE-WATER RAFTING
Enjoy a placid float trip or take a tempestuous journey through wild water on the Flathead River (p175).

SKIING
The Rocky Mountains have four downhill ski resorts, including Banff Sunshine (p88), and ample options to ply tracked trails in the backcountry.

FAMILY ADVENTURES

Take a gondola ride above **Lake Louise** (p102) with the chance of seeing grizzly bears grazing on the slopes below.

See Glacier's dramatic landscapes from the a vintage open-topped **Red Bus** (p177).

Go canoeing on **Vermilion Lakes** (p70) and watch beavers sliding under your boat.

Discover off-road cycling on the moderate **Goat Creek Trail** (p81) and reward the family with tea and cakes in the Fairmont Banff Springs hotel afterwards.

Visit the **Jasper Planetarium** (p132) at the Jasper Park Lodge for a peep through the Rocky Mountains' largest telescope.

Ease into hiking on the 8km (5-mile) **Rowe Lakes Trail** (p221) in Waterton Lakes, for quick access to a gorgeous alpine lake.

Take a boat cruise on **Lake Minnewanka** (p82) and enjoy a picnic on the lakeshore afterwards.

Mountain Biking

Mountain biking in the Rockies ranges from the superb – Jasper – to the non-existent – Glacier (where dedicated trails are all but banned). Jasper's liberal policies on mountain biking draw a dedicated contingent of downhill warriors.

Multiuse trails depart directly from the townsite with many crisscrossing the partly forested Pyramid Bench. Two of the best longer trails are the rootsy Saturday Night Loop and the highly technical Valley of the Five Lakes.

There are plenty of bike-rental companies in all three Canadian parks. Some offer shuttle services to trailheads or guided trips along the more classic routes.

Kayaking & Canoeing

Canoeing was the modus operandi of Indigenous Peoples in the Rockies for thousands of years before the arrival of Europeans. Early fur traders and settlers followed their example, and modern-day visitors have carried on the tradition.

Non-motorized boats (canoes, dinghies and kayaks) are allowed on nearly all waterways in the national parks. There's a plethora of options if you bring your own boat. If not, canoes and kayaks are readily available for hire at many of the larger lakes.

Banff's best places for canoeing are Lake Louise and Moraine Lake (both have mega-expensive rental outlets). Nearer to town you can slip through the waters of the Bow River and Vermilion Lakes by renting a boat from Banff Canoe Club. In Jasper, Maligne Lake and Pyramid Lake are the two best places for paddling. In Glacier, hire boats and cruises are offered on Lake McDonald, St Mary, Swiftcurrent Lake and Josephine Lake. In Waterton, Cameron Lake is the most comprehensive lake for sailing, with rowboats, kayaks and canoes for rent.

BEST SPOTS

For the best outdoor spots and routes, see map on pp40–41.

Kayaking, Moraine Lake (p108)

HORSEBACK RIDING	CLIMBING	STARGAZING	FISHING
Follow in the hoof-marks of the park's early pioneers with guided trail rides on Jasper's Pyramid Bench (p134).	Decamp to Canmore (p76) near Banff, ground zero for Canada's rock-climbing and mountaineering culture.	Jasper's lack of light pollution ensures psychedelic views of the planets, stars and northern lights in its Dark Sky Preserve (p132).	Numerous rivers and lakes teem with native and introduced fish species, especially around aptly named Whitefish (p183).

ACTION AREAS

Where to find the best outdoor activities in Banff, Jasper and Glacier national parks.

Extreme Adventures
1. Hiking the Cory Pass Loop (p99)
2. Flathead river rafting (p175)
3. Mt Norquay's via ferrata (p74)
4. Ice-climbing Maligne Canyon (p147)
5. Hiking the North Boundary Trail (p139)

Cycling
1. Valley of the Five Lakes (p140)
2. Bow Valley Parkway (p95)
3. Goat Creek Trail (p81)
4. Banff Legacy Trail (p79)
5. Snowshoe Trail (p227)

Skiing/Snowboarding
1. Mt Norquay (p75)
2. Canmore Nordic Centre (p76)
3. Banff Sunshine (p88)
4. Marmot Basin (p163)
5. Lake Louise Ski Resort (p102)

Blackfeet
Reservation

East Glacier

Claresholm

Fort Macleod

Babb

St Mary

Glacier
National
Park

Bob Marshall
Wilderness

Waterton
Lakes
National Park

West
Glacier

Essex

Flathead
Lake

Pincher Creek

Waterton Park

Sparwood

Fernie

Elko

Whitefish

Kalispell

Fort Steele

Flathead
Reservation

Columbia
Lake

Radium
Hot Springs

Kootenay
River

CANADA

U S A

MONTANA

Crawford Bay

Cranbrook

Kootenay
Lake

Pend
Oreille
Lake

IDAHO

Nelson

Priest
Lake

Nakusp

Castlegar

Sandpoint

Rossland

Newport

Spokane

Upper
Arrow
Lake

Lower
Arrow
Lake

Grand
Forks

Colville

Vernon

Okanagan
Lake

Kelowna

WASHINGTON

Hiking

1. Highline Trail (p181)
2. Grinnell Glacier Trail (p202)
3. Egypt Lake (p93)
4. Skyline Trail (p150)
5. Parker Ridge Trail (p120)
6. Lake Agnes (p105)
7. Crypt Lake Trail (p224)

Kayaking/Canoeing

1. Moraine Lake (p108)
2. Lake Minnewanka (p82)
3. Vermilion Lakes (p70)
4. Pyramid Lake (p134)
5. Maligne Lake (p144)
6. Lake McDonald (p174)
7. Cameron Lake (p220)

100 km

50 miles

N

PATRICIA THOMAS/SHUTTERSTOCK ©

Bowman Lake (p198)

Plan a Multiday Hike

For a true hiking experience you need to spend a few nights in the wilderness. There are hundreds of off-the-grid routes scattered around the parks. Some alternate day hikes with nights spent at a backcountry base, others venture out on multiday loops or point-to-points that penetrate distant and little-visited corners of the national parks.

Planning Your Route

The key questions to ask when route planning are: how fit are you? What do you want to see? And, how much time do you have to spare? You'll also want to carefully measure distances between campgrounds and check what sites are available. There are a number of backcountry hikes in the parks that follow well-established routes designed to maximize scenic impact. Most last from between two and four days.

Passes & Permits

Overnight hikers require a wilderness pass and backcountry campground reservations. This information helps park authorities manage trail usage and ensure that they know where you are should you get into difficulties.

Campgrounds, Huts & Lodges

Backcountry accommodations is mostly in rudimentary campsites (with privy toilets and food lockers) of which there are many: Jasper alone has over 80. On top of this there is a scattering of basic huts and cabins, and a handful of more upscale backcountry lodges, including the Shadow Lake and Skoki lodges in Banff, Shovel Pass in Jasper, and the Granite Park and Sperry chalets in Glacier.

What to Take

You'll need to pack food, a tent and sleeping bag, first-aid supplies, a mobile phone, water filter/purification tablets, bear spray and all other equipment, and pack out all your rubbish.

TRAIL TIPS

- The more-popular trails are well marked and well trodden, although snow can make route-finding tricky. Always carry a decent map.
- Use the national park websites and information centers to check trail status before setting out.
- Beware of avalanche danger between early winter and early summer.
- Pay attention to seasonal restrictions and take heed of any posted wildlife warnings.
- Preferably hike in a group or with a friend. If hiking alone, leave your route and itinerary with a trusted contact.
- Make noise so as not to surprise bears and other wildlife.

Grizzly bear, Jasper National Park (p122)

TRIP PLANNER

WILDLIFE

Sometimes elusive but always impressive, the iconic big fauna in the Rocky Mountain parks is one of the primary reasons why people continue to flock here. Roadside sightings are almost guaranteed to stop the traffic. After years of hunting, trapping and habitat loss, wildlife preservation is now a central tenet of national park culture.

Black Bears

Found all over North America, black bears roam montane and subalpine forests throughout the Canadian Rockies in search of their favorite foods: grasses, roots, berries and the occasional meal of carrion. They can frequently be seen along roadsides feeding on their favorite treat – dandelions. While most black bears are black in color, they can also be light reddish brown (cinnamon). Although sometimes confused with grizzlies, black bears are somewhat smaller with more-tapered muzzles, larger ears and less-fearsome claws. These claws help them climb trees to avoid their main predator, grizzly bears, which are known to drag black bears out of their dens to kill them. Although they are generally more tolerant of humans and less aggressive than grizzlies, black bears should always be treated as dangerous.

Most black bears run away from human presence, although they can be aggravated when surprised on trails or when they feel their cubs are threatened. If a black bear attacks you, the general rule is to fight back.

Grizzly Bears

Rarer and with a narrower geographical range than black bears, grizzlies once roamed widely in North America, but most were killed by European settlers who feared their intimidating ursine presence. Thanks to conservation efforts, their numbers have increased since they were listed as endangered in 1975. Even with rebounding populations, they aren't particularly easy to spot as they roam widely on high mountain slopes and generally avoid human contact. Male grizzlies reach up to 2.4m (8ft) in length and 1.05m (3.5ft) high at the shoulder, and can weigh more than 315kg (700lb) at maturity. Although some grizzlies are almost black, their coats are typically pale brown to cinnamon, with 'grizzled,' white-tipped guard hairs (the

43

HIBERNATING BEARS

Sometime in October, black and grizzly bears wander upslope to where snows will be deep and provide a thick insulating layer over their winter dens. There, the bears scrape out a simple shelter among shrubs, against a bank or under a log and sink into deep sleep (not true hibernation, as their body temperatures remain high and they are easily roused).

To get them through the winter, bears become voracious before hibernating. Black bears will eat for 20 hours straight and gain an incredible 1.8kg (4lb) each day before retiring to their dens; grizzly bears are known to eat 200,000 buffaloberries a day.

Winters are particularly hard as bears live entirely off their fat and lose up to 40% of their body weight. A female who has been able to gain enough weight will give birth to several cubs during the depths of winter, rearing the cubs on milk while she sleeps.

EMILAGRACEH/SHUTTERSTOCK ©

Gray wolf

long, coarse hairs that protect the shorter, fine underfur). They can be distinguished from black bears by their concave (dish-shaped) facial profile, smaller and more rounded ears, prominent shoulder hump and long, non-retractable claws.

Grizzlies generally segregate themselves from black bears, roaming in more open areas higher up mountain slopes. They are particularly abundant in Alaska and British Columbia. Glacier National Park, with a healthy population of around 300, is one of their last refuges in the contiguous US. Banff and Jasper have about 180 grizzlies between them.

Wolves

The gray wolf, once the Rocky Mountains' main predator, was nearly exterminated in the 1930s, then again in the 1950s. It took until the mid-1980s for them to reestablish themselves in Banff and Jasper in Canada, and Glacier in the US where they can be found in North Fork Valley. Wolves look rather like large German shepherds. Colors

range from white to black, with gray-brown being the most common hue. They roam in close-knit packs of around eight animals ruled by a dominant (alpha) pair. The alpha pair are the only members of a pack to breed, though the entire pack cares for the pups. Four to six pups are born in April or May, and they remain around the den until August. Packs of wolves are a formidable presence, and they aren't afraid of using their group strength to harass grizzly bears or kill coyotes, but more often they keep themselves busy chasing down deer, elk or moose. Jasper has five known wolf packs, Banff around four and Glacier a more healthy weight.

Elk

Weighing up to 450kg (1000lb) and bearing gigantic racks of antlers, male elk are the largest mammals that most visitors will encounter in these parks. And they're easy to see, especially in Jasper where they often roam around the railway yard and graze on the tracks.

Best Places to See Wildlife	BIGHORN SHEEP **November to April** Lake Minnewanka (Banff), Highline Trail (Glacier).	BLACK BEAR **May to October** Bow Valley Pkwy (Banff), Maligne Lake Rd (Jasper).	ELK **March to May** Vermilion Lakes (Banff), Maligne Lake Rd (Jasper).

OTHER IMPORTANT SPECIES

Mountain goat
Keeping mainly to ultra-steep cliffs and hillsides, pure-white mountain goats are nimble-footed and live mostly above the tree line. Your best chance of seeing one is when they descend to salt licks near roads.

Deer
Both white-tailed deer and mule deer roam the Rockies – the former in forests; the latter in more open areas.

Beaver
Beavers create vibrant wetlands and forge whole ecosystems by cutting down as many as 200 trees a year.

Marmot
Common to mountain meadows and the rocky alpine, these plump rodents make a distinctive whistling sound to warn of approaching predators.

Woodland caribou (reindeer)
Recently extirpated in Banff, caribou remain highly en-dangered in Jasper where there are only three herds left.

Wolverine
Territorial animals that stick to the deep wilderness, wolverines are strong and ferocious relative to their size. They are of little danger to humans and are highly threatened due to habitat loss.

Bighorn sheep
Shy creatures who can detect human presence from 300m (1000ft) away but have a penchant for roadside salts. Males face off during the fall rut, ramming into each other at speeds of 96km/h (60mph).

Cougar
Mountain lions are solitary, nocturnal big cats that stalk and ambush their prey, usually deer and elk for which they compete with wolves. They generally keep away from humans but should be avoided if encountered.

Come September, valleys resound with the hoarse bugling of battle-ready elk; a sound that is both exciting and terrifying, as hormone-crazed elk are one of the area's most dangerous animals. Battles between males, harem gathering and mating are best observed from a safe distance or from your car. Equally tricky are potentially aggressive female elk during calving season in May. Elk populations in the Rockies have fluctuated with the presence of the wolf, their main predator.

Moose
The ungainly moose is the largest North American deer; its 495kg (1100lb) is easily big enough to total a powerful car. Visitors love to spot this solitary animal with its lanky legs and periscope ears, but they are uncommon, despite their size, and not easy to find.

Moose spend their summers foraging on aquatic vegetation in marshy meadows and shallow lakes, where they readily swim and dive. The best chance of seeing one is in Jasper's Miette Valley and Maligne Lake corridor, around Banff's Upper Waterfowl Lake, and in the McDonald Valley of Glacier. The male's broadly tined antlers and flappy throat dewlap are unique, but like their close relative the elk, moose can be extremely dangerous when provoked.

Moose are no longer as common as they were in the days when they freely wandered the streets of Banff; numbers have been reduced due to vehicle traffic (roadkills) and a liver parasite.

Raptors
Avowed ornithologists aside, most visitors to the Rocky Mountains prefer to ignore birds in favor of bears, moose and other big beasts. Notwithstanding, more than 300 species have been found in the region spearheaded by two splendid raptors: eagles and ospreys. Working their way along rivers and lakes, white and brown ospreys specialize in diving into water to catch fish, then flying off to eat their scaly meal on a high perch.

Golden eagles, meanwhile, migrate both north and south along a narrow corridor on the east side of the main mountain divide. Spring migration peaks at the end of March, and fall migration in October.

GRIZZLY BEAR	MOOSE	MOUNTAIN GOAT	WOLF
May to October	**May to August**	**Year-round**	**November to April**
Many Glacier (Glacier), Carthew-Alderson Trail (Waterton).	Moose Lake (Jasper), Kootenai Lake (Glacier).	Logan Pass (Glacier), Icefields Parkway (Jasper).	North Fork Valley (Glacier), Lake Minnewanka (Banff).

MARINA POLISHKINA/SHUTTERSTOCK ©

Showshoeing, Banff National Park (p55)

TRIP PLANNER

WINTER IN THE PARKS

Half of national park infrastructure shuts down in winter, while the other half metamorphoses into an adventurous cold-weather alternative. Lakes become skating rinks, hiking and biking routes become cross-country skiing trails, waterfalls become ice climbs, wildlife migrates to lower climes, and – last but by no means least – prices become far more reasonable.

Skiing & Snowboarding

Building a ski resort inside a national park, with all its associated roads, runs and infrastructure, wouldn't happen today. The four resorts that embellish Banff and Jasper are a legacy of a different era when 'visitor experience' took precedence over the park's ecological integrity.

From the early 20th century onward, the ski areas in Banff – starting with Mt Norquay in the 1920s – began to refashion the park as a year-round attraction.

Initially an extreme sport accessible only to a handful of rich adventurers, skiing morphed into a mass-participation affair by the 1960s. Towropes, chairlifts and,

ultimately, gondolas provided easy access to the higher slopes and, by the 1980s, most of the park's hotels had been winterized to accommodate a growing influx of skiers. Today, Banff pulls in around one million winter visitors.

Banff's trio of modern ski resorts is known collectively as the Big Three (skibig3.com) and you can buy a single lift pass to cover all of them (individual passes are also available).

The parks' all-round alpine facilities are some of the finest in Canada, with ski and snowboarding schools, childcare facilities, terrain parks and half-pipes for snowboarders, as well as public

Hot springs Banff Upper Hot Springs and Radium Hot Springs stay open year-round. Jasper's Miette Hot Springs is closed from October to May.

Gondolas Banff's three gondolas run in the winter. The Lake Louise and Banff Sunshine gondolas take skiers and sightseers up to the tops of snowy runs. The Sulphur Mountain gondola delivers visitors to restaurants and an interpretive center. The Jasper SkyTram is closed between October and May.

Wildlife-watching Not everything hibernates. Look out for mountain goats, cougars, elk, moose and deer.

Stargazing Visit Jasper's planetarium and take advantage of the longer nights to study stars and the northern lights.

Historic hotels The Canadian parks' old railway hotels were winterized in the 1960s and 1970s. Walk the carpeted halls and stop by for a meal or a cup of tea around a crackling fire.

Winter camping A small percentage of campgrounds stay open in winter, including Tunnel Mountain II in Banff, Wapiti in Jasper, Pass Creek in Waterton, and the Apgar and St Mary campgrounds in Glacier.

Join a tour Numerous outfitters continue to run tours in winter. Enroll in a Maligne Canyon ice walk, a Jasper train tour, plus dogsledding, sleigh-riding and snowshoeing.

Museums Stay warm digesting regional history in local museums in Jasper and Banff.

WINTER FESTIVALS

Canmore Winter Carnival
This boisterous January festival attempts to raise the winter spirits with log-sawing, ice-carving and beard-growing contests, but the Trapper's Ball is the highlight.

Snow Days
Snow sculptures, block parties, snow-sliding events, big-name bands and a huge game of street hockey characterize Banff's celebration of all things snowy in January.

Banff Craft Beer Festival
Forsaking the chilly claws of early winter, Alberta's best microbreweries join forces with Banff's finest pubs and restaurants at this annual food and drink festival at Cave and Basin National Historic Site in late November.

transportation to the slopes, groomed runs and extensive snow-making equipment.

Lake Louise is the largest area (and one of the largest in Canada), Banff Sunshine is renowned for its heavy snow dumps, while Mt Norquay is where locals go to dodge the lines. All have good day lodges replete with food outlets and après-ski bars. Sunshine is the sole resort with ski-in accommodations.

Jasper is the only other Canadian national park with a ski resort. Action is centered at Marmot Basin just off the Icefields Parkway. While Marmot has no mountain-ascending gondola, it does operate the longest high-speed quad-chair in the Rockies. Due to its relative isolation vis-à-vis Banff, it's known for its lack of crowds and minimal lift lines.

Cross-Country Skiing

For every 50 downhill skiers, you'll probably only encounter one die-hard cross-country skier. But Nordic skiing, with its cheaper equipment and light environmental impact (no lifts, roads or heavily logged mountainsides), is far more congruous with delicate park ecology than downhill. Plus, no chairlifts and fewer people mean you'll get an up-close and rewarding glimpse of the Rockies in their tranquil wintry glory.

Banff and Jasper have a well-mapped network of groomed and tracked trails, color-coded for difficulty, along with several outfitters that rent the necessary equipment (skis, poles, gloves and boots).

Backcountry skiing is a tougher, more self-sufficient variation of cross-country skiing that involves travel through unpatrolled, ungroomed wilderness with potential avalanche danger. In Banff, the most popular and benign routes lead out to a couple of ski-in backcountry lodges – the Skoki and Shadow Lake – the latter of which logs a relatively easy approach along the track-set 13km (8.1-mile) Redearth Creek trail.

Trails aren't always signposted and can be difficult to make out under heavy snow cover. Check conditions before you set out and hire a guide if you're unsure.

Backcountry skiers should carry emergency supplies: an avalanche beacon, a full repair kit, a compass and a detailed topographical map.

Snowshoeing

Snowshoeing has been practiced by Indigenous Peoples in the Rockies for thousands of years, and it remains one of the easiest ways to explore the winter wilderness.

Many of the trails kept open for cross-country skiers also have parallel tracks for snowshoers, and there are other routes to explore around the townsites in Jasper, Banff and Glacier. As always, parks staff can help with route maps and condition reports for current trails.

Snowshoes can be hired from outdoor-equipment stores and activity providers in Banff, Lake Louise, Jasper and Glacier. Some heavily used walking trails where the snow is well trodden and tightly packed can be hiked (or even run) with crampons or portable cleats that slide onto the soles of your shoes. Popular winter trails include the path to the top of Sulphur Mountain, the Johnston Canyon-Inkpots trail, the Lake Louise shoreline in Banff, and the paths around the Pyramid Bench and Athabasca River in Jasper.

Ice Climbing

With a road called the Icefields Parkway, copious glaciers, and a surfeit of surreal waterfalls frozen mid-flow, it's no surprise the Rocky Mountains harbor an ice-climbing bonanza.

Ice climbing is a specialist sport that requires sturdy equipment and relevant expertise. You can arm yourself with both by taking a course or going on a trip with Yamnuska Mountain Adventures.

For a low-hazard highlight, try Johnston Canyon in Banff and Tangle Falls and Maligne Canyon in Jasper. Remember, ice climbing is particularly prone to avalanche danger – do your homework first.

FAT BIKES

A recent surge in fat biking has turned cycling in the frozen north into a year-round sport.

Fat bikes are bicycles with comically large tires and extra-wide forks that lend them a high degree of traction and the ability to move swiftly across soft, uneven surfaces like snow.

Their usage worldwide has been increasing rapidly since the early 2010s and, in 2014, an American cyclist rode one across Antarctica to the South Pole.

Popular fat-biking routes in Banff and Jasper shouldn't be as taxing, but they do allow bike access to areas once only reachable on skis or snowshoes.

Camping, Tunnel Mountain (p71)

HOW TO... Camp in the Backcountry

Backcountry or wilderness camping is radically different to a night in an RV at The Whistlers. Wave goodbye to electrical hookups, communal shower blocks, gravel access roads, and bins into which you nonchalantly toss your garbage; and say hello to a world of leave-no-trace travel ethics and off-the-grid self-sufficiency.

Choosing a Campground
You don't have to hike far in any of the parks to find a tent pad. Jasper has 83 campgrounds, Glacier 67, Banff 51 and Waterton 10. The facilities vary in size from 15 sites (Egypt Lake in Banff) to one (Camas Lake in Glacier), with five on average. One tent and four people are allowed per tent pad.

Visitor numbers for backcountry trails are limited, so you'll usually need to specify which campgrounds you intend to stay at when you purchase your wilderness pass. In some very remote areas, wild camping is allowed – choose a site at least 50m (164ft) from the trail, 70m (230ft) from water sources and 5km (3 miles) or more from the trailhead.

Camping Essentials
You'll need a tent, sleeping bag (with optional sleeping pad), portable stove, some form of water purification, bear-resistant food container, sealable garbage bags, cooking utensils, pocket knife, food, water bottle and toiletries.

Most campgrounds are sited near a water source and offer a selection of campsites (tent pads), food storage (either lockers or poles/cables), and some kind of toilet (usually pit toilets in an outhouse). Extras may include picnic tables and fire rings.

Booking
- Backcountry camping requires a permit, known in Canadian parks as a wilderness pass and in US parks as a backcountry permit.
- Popular spots fill up quickly in peak months so advance reservations are highly recommended. For Parks Canada see *reservation. pc.gc.ca*; for Glacier visit *nps.gov/glac/planyourvisit/ backcountry-reservations.htm*.
- You can make reservations for summer on the park's 'launch-day' (usually in mid-March).
- The maximum stay at any campground is generally three nights.
- In Glacier 30% of all campground spots are kept for walk-ins, although you'll still need a permit.

LEAVE NO TRACE
- Pitch on previously used sites to avoid unnecessary damage to the landscape.
- Keep your campsite clean to avoid attracting animals.
- Store food, toiletries and cooking equipment in bear-proof lockers if available, or suspend them between two trees at least 4m (13ft) above the ground and 1.3m (4ft) from each trunk.
- Use biodegradable soap and wash dishes well away from rivers and streams.
- A portable stove is more ecofriendly than a campfire, as it prevents unnecessary scorching of the ground.
- Check current fire restrictions before setting out and adhere to them on the trail; If you do have a fire, don't cut down anything to burn as fuel – dead wood is OK, green wood isn't.

49

White-water rafting, Kicking Horse River, Yoho National Park (p111)

TRIP PLANNER

EXTREME PURSUITS

Hiking through bear country not scary enough for you? No problem!
The mountain parks have plenty of other ways to spike your adrenaline,
from battling the waves on the Sunwapta River to skiing down the off-
piste Delirium Dive on Banff Sunshine's Lookout Mountain.

White-Water Rafting

The Rockies is home to some turbulent
white water. Navigable rapids in the region
range from sedate class I (fast-moving
water with small waves) to stormy class
IV (intense, choppy rapids) on the six-grade
international classification system. For the
strongest rapids in the parks, head to the
Middle Fork of the Flathead River on the
southern cusp of Glacier, which tosses up
powerful class IV rapids during its spring
peak. Just outside Banff National Park,
Kicking Horse River (in Yoho National Park)
and Horseshoe Canyon on the Bow River
near Canmore have similarly tempestuous
waves (class IV), while Jasper's Sunwapta

River reaches a bumpy class III in its
rougher sections. For a calmer family float,
sample the easier class I and II rapids of
the Athabasca River in Jasper and the
Kananaskis River near Banff.

To tackle these watery crapshoots, you'll
need to enlist in an organized tour with
one of several well-established companies
in Jasper, Banff and West Glacier. Half-
and full-day trips include equipment, safety
gear, trained guides and transportation to
and from the put-in points.

The rafting season runs May through
September, with the highest river levels
(and therefore the most rapids) usually in
June.

Scrambling occupies the gray area between hiking and rock climbing. While you won't require any specialist equipment aside from sturdy shoes, you *will* need strong nerves, sure-footedness, route-finding skills and a head for heights.

The sport was partly inspired by the book *Scrambles in the Canadian Rockies* by Alan Kane, first published in 1991 (most recent edition 2016), which lists over 150 routes between Waterton and Jasper.

Parks Canada has since got in on the act, producing three separate guides to scrambles on Mt Rundle, Cascade Mountain and Mt Temple. Stuffed with copious safety information, they're essential reading for all aspiring scramblers.

Via Ferrata

Via ferratas are fixed-protection climbing routes equipped with cables, ladders and bridges that, through the use of special climbing harnesses, allow relative novices to climb crags normally only accessible to experienced mountaineers. Imported from Europe, the idea has proliferated in Canada in the last decade, and you can now climb five different via ferrata routes on Mt Norquay in Banff. Unlike Europe, where climbers are free to go it alone, the Norquay via ferrata is guided only. Equipment and instruction are included.

Rock Climbing

The Rocky Mountain parks are well-known destinations for rock climbers, but the variable sedimentary rock formations can be technically challenging and more suited to experienced alpinists, rather than novices.

The Alpine Club of Canada (alpineclubof canada.ca) and Yamnuska Mountain Adventures (yamnuska.com), both in Canmore, are the go-to specialists for advice, training and organized trips.

Rock climbing, Canmore (p76)

OTHER EDGY ACTIVITIES

White-water rafting and scrambling are mere gateway drugs to a whole world of outdoor extremism. Below are a few highlights:

- Tackle the adventurous side of caving, including crawling, climbing and rappelling around the depths of the Rat's Nest cave system beneath Grotto Mountain east of Canmore.
- Fit skins onto your backcountry skis, check the avalanche forecast and sally forth to the backcountry Skoki Lodge in February.
- Upgrade your climbing credentials and sign up for a guided summit attempt on Mt Edith Cavell in Jasper under the expert tutelage of Yamnuska Mountain Adventures.
- Get a helicopter to fly you into Assini-boine Provincial Park for several days of subalpine hiking bookended by comfortable nights in the backcountry Mt Assiniboine Lodge.
- Fine-tune your stamina and attempt to complete the iconic Skyline Trail in an epic day of trail-running.
- Head up to Banff Sunshine to tackle the advanced black diamond ski runs off the summit of Goat's Eye Mountain.
- Forsake the Brewster Snocoaches and go for a guided ice walk on the crevasse-riddled Athabasca Glacier.
- Load up the panniers and test your mettle on the 233km (145-mile) Icefield Parkway with only a bicycle for company.
- Hammer your ice axe into the frozen waterfalls of Maligne Canyon or navigate slippery ascents at the Weeping Wall on the Icefields Parkway.

THE GUIDE

Chapters in this section are organized by hubs and their surrounding areas. We see the hub as your base in the destination, where you'll find unique experiences, local insights, insider tips and expert recommendations. It's also your gateway to the surrounding area, where you'll see what and how much you can do from there.

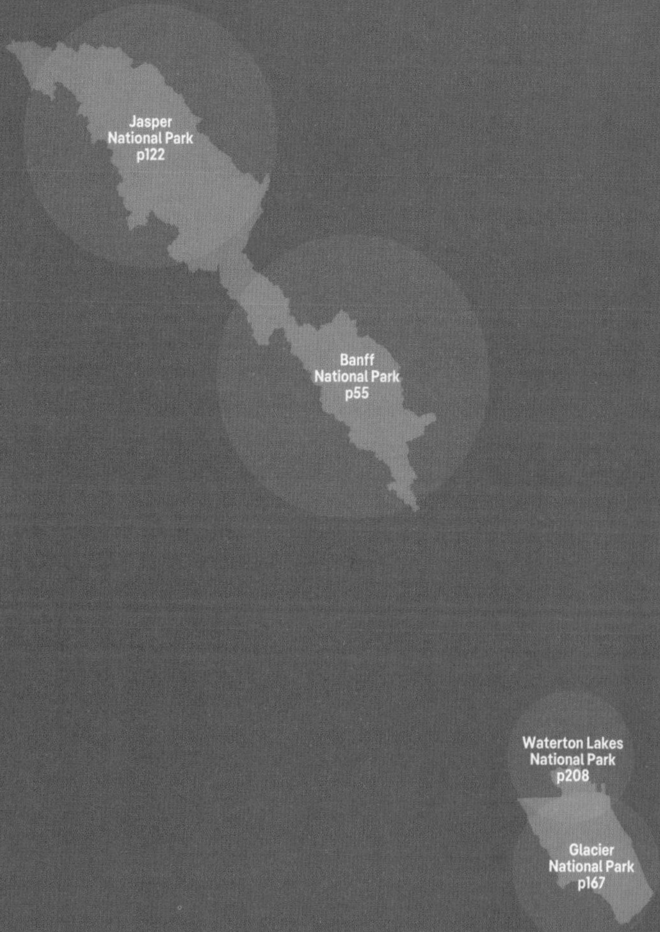

Jasper
National Park
p122

Banff
National Park
p55

Waterton Lakes
National Park
p208

Glacier
National Park
p167

Valley of the Five Lakes (p140)

Bow Lake (p119)

THE MAIN AREAS

BANFF TOWN
Park hub packed with dining
and accommodations.
p60

LAKE MINNEWANKA
Recreation area with ample
water activities.
p82

SUNSHINE VILLAGE
Winter skiing and summer
flower meadows.
p87

BANFF NATIONAL PARK

THE KERNEL OF CANADIAN ENVIRONMENTALISM

In Canada's oldest national park, the words 'accessible wilderness' are no oxymoron. Nowhere is the raw power of nature within such easy reach.

Banff is a Canadian icon. Created as the world's third national park in 1885, this finely sculpted corner of the Rocky Mountains helped shape Canadian history and pave the way for the growth of modern tourism in North America in the late 19th century. As an early exponent of environmental protection, Banff was a blueprint for national parks that came later and, in more recent times, has emerged as a litmus test for how they should act today, balancing ecological integrity with all-round visitor experience.

Geographically, the park is split into two opposing parts. There's the cozy comfort of Banff Town anchored by its busy main avenue versus the raw energy of the expansive wilderness that lies beyond. It's the close juxtaposition of these two very different worlds that makes Banff so intriguing. One minute you're sinking a beer in crowded Banff Avenue; the next you're scrambling up a precipitous scree slope with only mountain goats for company. The distance between the two experiences might only be a few kilometers, but it often feels more like a thousand.

Due to its early development in the days before tight environmental restrictions, Banff is one of a handful of Canadian national parks with a townsite within its borders. Supporting the local infrastructure are three ski resorts, commercial hot springs, and a major highway – the Trans-Canada – providing access to the rest of the country.

BOW VALLEY PARKWAY	LAKE LOUISE	ICEFIELDS PARKWAY
Roaming wildlife alongside historic backroad.	Teahouses and astounding natural beauty.	One of the world's most spectacular highways.
p95	p102	p114

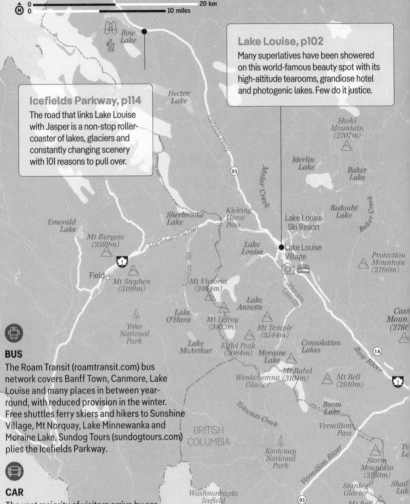

Lake Louise, p102

Many superlatives have been showered on this world-famous beauty spot with its high-altitude tearooms, grandiose hotel and photogenic lakes. Few do it justice.

Icefields Parkway, p114

The road that links Lake Louise with Jasper is a non-stop roller-coaster of lakes, glaciers and constantly changing scenery with 101 reasons to pull over.

BUS

The Roam Transit (roamtransit.com) bus network covers Banff Town, Canmore, Lake Louise and many places in between year-round, with reduced provision in the winter. Free shuttles ferry skiers and hikers to Sunshine Village, Mt Norquay, Lake Minnewanka and Moraine Lake. Sundog Tours (sundogtours.com) plies the Icefields Parkway.

CAR

The vast majority of visitors arrive by car. Trans-Canada Hwy (Hwy 1) cuts through the center of the park via Canmore, Banff Town and Lake Louise Village. The single-lane Bow Valley Parkway (Hwy 1A) runs parallel to Hwy 1, but is closed periodically in spring to protect wildlife.

BIKE

Banff is well geared for cyclists, with a wide network of trails and plenty of bike shops and rental companies dotted around the town. Very few trailheads have cycle racks, but some rental companies offer shuttle services to main trails.

Sunshine Village, p87

Year-round activity center that shifts from ultra-snowy winter ski resort to subalpine summer hiking hub. It's the best place in Banff to see wildflowers.

Find Your Way

The Trans-Canada highway (Hwy 1) runs right through Banff and, in recent years, authorities have increased the provision of public transportation to help cut pollution and ease congestion in the park during the summer.

Bow Valley Parkway, p95

The park's original highway is today a sleepy backroad with seasonal limits on cars, allowing ample opportunities to view the park's signature fauna.

Lake Minnewanka, p82

The park's biggest lake is a summer nexus for boat trips, diving and kayaking. Hiking paths fan out from the shoreline to hidden canyons and lofty cirques.

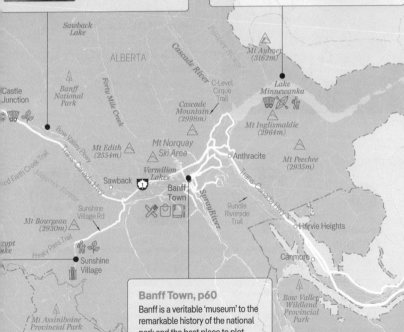

Panther Mountain (2943m)

Sawback Lake

ALBERTA

Cascade River

Palliser Range

Mt Aylmer (3162m)

Castle Junction

Banff National Park

Forty Mile Creek

C-Level Cirque Trail

Lake Minnewanka

Cascade Mountain (2998m)

Mt Inglismaldie (2964m)

Bow Valley Pkwy

Mt Edith (2554m)

Mt Norquay Ski Area

Anthracite

Mt Peechee (2935m)

Trans-Canada Hwy

Redearth Creek Trail

Massive Range

Sawback

Vermilion Lakes

Banff Town

Spray River

Rundle Riverside Trail

Mt Bourgeau (2930m)

Sunshine Village Rd

Healy Pass Trail

Harvie Heights

Egypt Lake

Sunshine Village

Canmore

Banff Town, p60

Banff is a veritable 'museum' to the remarkable history of the national park and the best place to plot, plan, eat and replenish before and after a wilderness excursion.

Mt Assiniboine Provincial Park

Bow Valley Wildland Provincial Park

Spray Lakes Reservoir

57

Plan Your Time

Banff is, arguably, Canada's best-organized national park, blessed with easy access and a good infrastructure. You can see a great deal in a few days and really get under the skin of it in a week.

Tunnel Mountain (p71)

Just Passing Through

Start (where else?) in Banff Town by getting orientated on 'the Avenue'. The classic Banff day out involves hiking to the top of **Sulphur Mountain** (p65), having lunch at the summit and descending on the gondola for a soak in the **Banff Upper Hot Springs** (p67). If you've still got time, hit the **Fairmont Banff Springs hotel** (p63) for afternoon tea, stop to see the spray at **Bow Falls** (p64) and finish off with a pizza and pint in the **Bear Street Tavern** (p68).

If you have another day to spare, uncover park history at the **Whyte Museum of the Canadian Rockies** (p65) and the **Cave and Basin National Historic Site** (p69) before hiking over to **Sundance Canyon** (p65).

Seasonal Highlights

Summer, between Victoria Day (May) and Labor Day (September), is by far the best time to visit, with trails open and services running. Winter attracts a sizable skiing and winter sports contingent.

JANUARY
Annual **ice-magic competition** at the Fairmont Lake Louise where teams of ice carvers battle it out to create epic sculptures.

FEBRUARY
Canmore's **Winter Carnival** attempts to raise the cold-weather spirits with log-sawing, ice-carving and beard-growing contests.

MAY
After Victoria Day in late May, most of the park's summer facilities are open and trails become more accessible.

FROM LEFT: GELU POPA/SHUTTERSTOCK ©, RIEKEPHOTOS/SHUTTERSTOCK ©, JORDAN FEEG/SHUTTERSTOCK ©

TRAVELLIFE18/SHUTTERSTOCK ©

An Active Week

After your two-day intro to Banff, break out of town and head over to **Lake Minnewanka** (p82) for a boat cruise and an eyeful of mining memorabilia at **C-Level Cirque** (p85).

On day four, rent a bike and pedal around **Vermilion Lakes** (p68) and along the Bow Valley Parkway to **Johnston Canyon** (p98) for a spectacular gorge walk. You'll require two days to scrape the surface of Lake Louise. Hike up to the **Lake Agnes Teahouse** (p105), view bears safely from the gondola and rent a bike to get you over to **Moraine Lake** (p108) where you can escape the crowds on the **Consolation Lakes Trail** (p107).

Total Immersion

If time isn't your enemy, you'll be able to explore some of Banff's quieter corners, stretches of brawny backcountry where grizzlies and cougars roam. Get the gondola up to **Sunshine Meadows** (p90) and view the wildflowers in all their finery. Those with extra days to spare can penetrate further into backcountry by overnighting at campgrounds at **Egypt Lake** (p93) or **Lake Magog** (p94).

Back in Banff prick your adventurous spirit on Mt Norquay's **via ferrata** (p74) before testing your nerve on the **Cory Pass hike** (p99). For a grand finale, drive or organize a bus tour along the Icefields Parkway, stopping at **Peyto Lake** (p115) and **Parker Ridge** (p120) en route.

JULY	SEPTEMBER	NOVEMBER	DECEMBER
Alpine areas are mostly snow-free from mid-July and exhibit vivid displays of wildflowers. It's time to hit the high-country trails.	Fall brings a blaze of color to the park, making it one of the most spectacular seasons for hiking.	The **Banff Mountain Film Festival** runs concurrently with the annual **book festival** and marks the highlight of the town's cultural calendar.	The ski season gets underway, with snow descending from the mountaintops to the slopes of Banff's Big Three resorts.

BANFF TOWN

Banff Town

Banff is and always has been a tourist town. Established around the hot springs that were brought to national attention by a trio of opportunistic 19th-century railway workers, the first bathhouses and hotels were built in the 1880s to attract visitors to the area on the nascent Canadian Pacific Railway.

These days, most people arrive by car, and Banff has grown into a community of 8000 people. But this is no ordinary town. In order to protect the park's delicate ecology, urban boundaries are fixed, all residents must meet a 'need to reside' requirement, and business activity is tightly controlled. Some complain about the commercialization of Banff (few other national parks have townsites) but, despite the expensive souvenir shops and perennial summer queues for selfies and ice cream, the town still has one foot firmly implanted in the outdoors and raw adventure lies only a few pedal turns away.

TOP TIP

Most of Banff's hotels and inns line the north side of Banff Avenue. Rendered in local stone and wood, they offer good facilities but are pricey and hard to procure in summer. Book well ahead. For old-school luxury, head south of the river to the Fairmont Banff Springs hotel or the Rimrock Resort.

NICK FOX/SHUTTERSTOCK ©

Banff Avenue (p62)

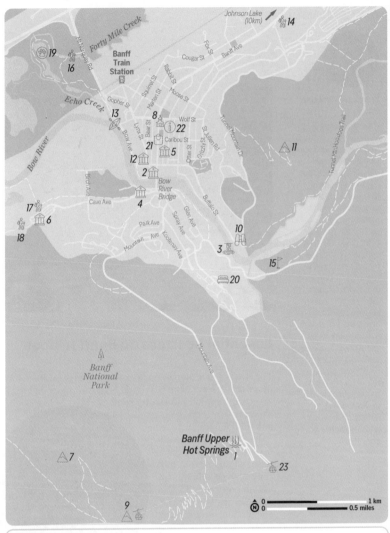

HIGHLIGHTS
1 Banff Upper Hot Springs

SIGHTS
2 Banff Park Museum
3 Bow Falls
4 Buffalo Nations Luxton Museum
5 Cascade Dance Hall
6 Cave and Basin National Historic Site
7 Sanson Peak
8 St Paul's Presbyterian Church
9 Sulphur Mountain

10 Surprise Corner
11 Tunnel Mountain
12 Whyte Museum of the Canadian Rockies

ACTIVITIES
13 Banff Canoe Club
14 Banff Legacy Trail
15 Banff Springs Golf Course
16 Fenland Trail
17 Marsh Loop
18 Sundance Canyon Trail
19 Vermilion Lakes

SLEEPING
20 Fairmont Banff Springs hotel

SHOPPING
21 Banff Avenue

INFORMATION
22 Banff School Auditorium/ Banff Visitor Centre

TRANSPORT
23 Banff Gondola

WHY I LOVE BANFF

Brendan Sainsbury, writer

I like roughing it in the wilderness as much as the next Canadian, but sometimes it's nice to round off a strenuous day of trail-running, bear sightings and privy toilets with a plate of al dente pasta and a glass of chilled pinot grigio. Banff can satisfy all these requirements and a few more besides (hot springs, hipster-roasted coffee, home-brewed beer!). Sure, I love Canada's oldest national park for its white-knuckle hiking trails and bumpy backcountry cycling routes, but I'm also partial to recharging my batteries in its old-school Irish pubs and posh hotels plying afternoon tea.

CHILL CHILLZ/SHUTTERSTOCK ©

Fairmont Banff Springs hotel

Essential Business on Banff Avenue

BANFF'S MAIN DRAG

The street that 99% of national park tourists visit, and many never really leave, **Banff Avenue** is the town's commercial artery, a 5km-long (3.1-mile) conglomeration of shops, restaurants, pubs and lodges.

On a busy day in summer, up to 30,000 people descend here to stroll, shop, eat or relax after an energetic day in the mountains. To ease the congestion, in 2023 the town elected to close several blocks of the street to car traffic.

OTHER TOWNSITES

Townsites were only developed in Canada's very early national parks. You'll find other urban hubs at **Jasper Town** (p128), **Waterton Park** (p202) and Yoho National Park – around the small park nexus of **Field** (p111).

 WHERE TO STAY IN BANFF TOWN

Moose Hotel & Suites
Like a mountain lodge pumped up on steroids with rooftop pools, hot tubs and sauna looking out at the peaks. **$$$**

Samesun Banff
Central location, a full lineup of daily activities and 112 beds spread across modern, compact dorm rooms. **$**

Banff Aspen Lodge
Rare Banff hotel that's not part of a corporate chain, the Aspen offers friendly service and tasteful modern rooms. **$$$**

It wasn't always so busy. A little over a century ago, Banff Avenue *was* Banff; home to a handful of hotels, homesteads and trail outfitters vying to accommodate the park's tiny trickle of tentative tourists. Development of the town took off following the arrival of the Canadian Pacific Railway in 1885 (p78) and the opening of the Banff Springs Hotel three years later.

Much of the current architecture is modern, yet sympathetic to the natural environment and punctuated with local wood and stone. Several pioneer buildings still stand. The most notable is the timber-framed **Banff Park Museum**, with its clerestory (high-level) windows and cantilevered truss supports, which has changed little since its 1903 construction. Further north, look out for the curvaceous **Cascade Dance Hall** dating from 1921, the timber-framed **Banff School Auditorium** (built in 1939 and now occupied by the Banff Visitor Centre), and **St Paul's Presbyterian Church**, a small Gothic structure built using local stone in 1930.

The Ave is where visitors get most of their essential business done, from organizing a rafting trip to reloading on beer and ice cream (join the queue outside Cows).

A Landmark Hotel

SYMBOL OF BANFF

Looking like a cross between Harry Potter's Hogwarts and a Loire Valley castle, the **Fairmont Banff Springs hotel** (fairmont.com/banff-springs) competes with the surrounding Rocky Mountains for size and grandeur. Constructed as one of the nation's 'grand railway hotels' in 1928, it replaced an earlier wooden structure that was built to serve the park's first tourists in the 1880s but was destroyed by a fire in 1926. The remodel was designed in the prevailing Canadian Châteauesque style that sought to imitate the Renaissance castles of the Loire in France. It quickly became a leading contender for Canada's most iconic building.

Looking around the hotel's palatial interior it's easy to forget that people actually stay here. You'll bump into as many day-trippers as guests. The steeply gabled roof and sharp turrets conceal an extravagant collection of ballrooms, tearooms, lounges, staircases, wood-paneled bars and the monastic Mount Stephen Hall that looks like it might have sprung from a set from *Game of Thrones*.

Sleepy? Bed down in one of 757 rooms. Hungry? Choose from one of a dozen restaurants. Afternoon tea is the hotel's quintessential if expensive Banff indulgence. There's a golf course, of course, and a terrace hosting opulent weddings.

THE HOODOOS

The Hoodoos are a cluster of jagged rock stacks beside the Bow River just outside Banff.

The result of natural erosion, they are made predominantly of limestone, with a hard cap of magnesium-rich rock at the top. Millennia of wind and rain have carved them into a complex topography of con-torted towers and strange spires.

You can hike to the Hoodoos from the parking lot at Surprise Corner overlooking Bow Falls. Descend on a trail through larch and pine woodland to the river, passing several inlets and small beaches to a wide, open meadow.

After climbing gently, you'll join the Hoodoos Interpretive Trail from where you can look down on the pointy spires from above. Retrace your steps back to Banff or catch a bus.

Fairmont Banff Springs	Peaks Hotel & Suites	Brewster Mountain Lodge
Sleep with ghosts of royalty, Hollywood and Banff pioneers in one of Canada's most iconic accommodations. **$$$**	A handsome slice of Scandinavian-inspired design with log-shaped desks and fancy coffee machines. **$$**	Comfy lodge owned by the sixth generation of Banff's original outfitters and travel operators. **$$**

One of the real joys, however, is just wandering around the halls trying to work out who's staying over and who ain't.

Naturally, the hotel reels off a long list of celebrated former guests, many of them movie stars (the Rockies is a favorite location for filmmakers). Marilyn Monroe, Leonardo DiCaprio and Clint Eastwood have graced the carpeted corridors at some point. For a tasty fee (C$500 and up), you can too.

Bow Falls Viewpoints

WATERFALL ON CUSP OF TOWN

Small but spectacular and invitingly walkable from Banff Town (1km away), **Bow Falls** is at its finest during the spring snow melt when it turns the eponymous Bow River into a churning whirlpool of white water.

Well-marked paved trails run along either side of the river and bring in a steady stream of foot traffic during peak season. In the summer months, visit early or late in the day for more elbow room. The west-bank viewpoint is the best place to see the waterfall, which is 9m (30ft) at its highest point, thundering over treacherous rocks. The east-bank trail leads to the deliciously named **Surprise Corner**, with a view across the falls toward the Fairmont Banff Springs hotel. It also marks the start of the Hoodoos Trail, which leads along the Bow River to a cluster of bizarre rock pillars eroded into spiky shapes by the Rocky Mountain weather.

The river and falls were used as a filming location in the 1954 movie *River of No Return* starring Marilyn Monroe and Robert Mitchum, who were bivouacked at the nearby Banff Springs Hotel for the duration of their stay. Monroe allegedly nearly drowned during filming after she slipped on a rock in the river and sprained her ankle.

The river itself begins 100km (63 miles) upstream as meltwater from the Bow Glacier on the cusp of Banff National Park, just northwest of Lake Louise. After flowing through Banff Town it heads to Canmore before meandering gracefully through the city of Calgary. Merging with the South Saskatchewan River, it ultimately empties into Hudson Bay.

WALKABLE WATERFALLS

For another attractive waterfall close to a Rocky Mountain townsite, gravitate to **Takakkaw Falls** (p111) not far from Field in Yoho National Park.

WHERE TO GO FOR COFFEE & CAKE IN BANFF TOWN

Good Earth Coffeehouse
Where hot, smooth, earthy coffee pairs beautifully with unique coconut and beetroot muffins.

Whitebark Cafe
Trendy but mega-popular cafe in Aspen Lodge with a modish interior and an abundance of non-stodgy snacks.

Evelyn's Coffee World
Old Banff stalwart that sells assorted coffee paraphernalia and giant cookies shaped like scones.

Sulphur Mountain

Two Ways up Sulphur Mountain

HIKING TRAIL AND GONDOLA

For drone-like views of Banff Town and the Bow Valley, it's necessary to ascend **Sulphur Mountain**, Banff's sentinel 2451m (8041ft) peak named for the famous hot springs that bubble beneath its wooded slopes. There are two ways up: a physically taxing hike that zigzags skyward for 5.6km (3.5 miles), incorporating a series of increasingly steep switchbacks, or a seductive gondola ride.

A weather station has existed on the peak since 1903 and pioneering meteorologists forged the original trail up the mountain in the early 20th century to make their observations. A teahouse was built near the summit in the 1940s (horses were used to take up supplies) and, in 1959, Sulphur Mountain acquired its first gondola. It's been through numerous updates and owners since and **Banff Gondola** now operates year-round with enclosed four-person cabins gliding to the top in eight minutes. There are several restaurants at the upper terminal plus an interpretive center with large explanatory panels and a cinema.

BOUNDARY CHANGES

Since its foundation as the world's third-oldest national park in 1885, Banff's boundaries were redrawn several times before it arrived at the 6641 sq km (2564 sq miles) it is today.

The original park encompassed a diminutive 26 sq km (10 sq miles) set up to protect the Cave and Basin springs but was enlarged substantially in 1887 when it changed its name to Rocky Mountains Park.

In 1902, the park morphed again to cover an area twice the size of its current scope but, after an outcry from farmers and logging companies, it was scaled back to a more manageable 4663 sq km (1800 sq miles).

It reached its current size and was named 'Banff' with the passing of the National Parks Act in 1930.

⚔ WHERE TO EAT IN BANFF TOWN'S HOTELS

Rundle Bar
Five-star high tea, five-star views and five-star service in the stately Fairmont Banff Springs. **$$$**

Juniper Bistro
Artistically presented locally sourced food in the Juniper Lodge at the foot of Mt Norquay. **$$$**

Eden
Eight-course tasting menus worthy of a big city including vegetarian variations in the Rimrock Resort. **$$$**

COSMIC RAY STATION

Inaugurated in 1957, the year of the Sputnik, the world's first unmanned space flight, the Sulphur Mountain Cosmic Ray Station was built to monitor high-energy particles that collide with the Earth's atmosphere from outer space.

One of several such facilities constructed in Canada, Sulphur Mountain's station was of premier importance due to its high elevation and was subsequently fitted with a novel neutron monitor to obtain more accurate readings.

To lug the equipment necessary to the summit, a road was built from the Cave and Basin springs, contouring steeply up the peak's northwestern slopes on a route still used by hikers.

The station closed in 1978 with the advent of more sophisticated space satellites and was dismantled three years later. A plaque marks the spot where it once stood.

Cosmic Ray Station, Sanson Peak

SUSAN MONTGOMERY/SHUTTERSTOCK ©

If you didn't hike up, you can make use of your stored energy on a short walk via boardwalks and stairways to adjacent **Sanson Peak**, the site of the old weather station and an erstwhile Cosmic Ray research facility. The former – a small stone structure – is still intact; the latter was dismantled in 1981.

For a quintessential Banff day out, consider hiking up Sulphur Mountain, having lunch at one of the summit restaurants and getting the gondola back down. Finish off with a soak in the Banff Upper Hot Springs next to the base terminal.

The gondola is 4km (2.5 miles) south of central Banff and easily accessible on Roam bus 1.

History, Art & Heritage

THREE HISTORIC MUSEUMS

Banff National Park doesn't just host a town, it possesses a prestigious museum worthy of a bigger city.

Inaugurated in 1968, the **Whyte Museum of the Canadian Rockies** draws from a rich collection of art, history and cultural heritage bequeathed by local painters and philanthropists Catharine and Peter Whyte a decade earlier. Ever-changing art displays include multifarious paintings dating from 1800 to

 WHERE TO GO FOR DINNER IN BANFF TOWN

Zyka Elevated Indian Restaurant
High-class Indian food and congenial service at very reasonable prices. **$$**

Tooloulou's
Cajun food with an Acadian twist. Bank on catfish, po'boys and jambalaya prepared with Canadian panache. **$$$**

Lupo Ristorante
Enjoy superbly authentic Italian food and a casual ambience in a large, attractive, informal dining room. **$$$**

the present, executed by regional, Canadian and international artists, with a strong focus on the Rockies. It includes a good cross section of the Whytes' own work heavily influenced by Canada's legendary 'Group of Seven' (a loose group of Canadian landscape painters active in the 1920s).

In the historical realm, there's a permanent collection of artifacts telling the story of Banff and the hardy men and women who forged a home among the mountains, along with an archive of thousands of photographs spanning the history of the town and park.

Born in Banff in 1905, Peter Whyte was one of the town's early pioneers who, aside from painting, was an enthusiastic outdoorsman, and world traveler. With his wife he created the Whyte Foundation in 1958 with the aim of leaving their carefully amassed art collection to Banff in the form of a museum.

In the grounds of the museum there are six original heritage homes from the first half of the 20th century, including the Whytes' former house dating from the 1930s. A block from the Whyte, the **Banff Park Museum** inhabits one of Banff's oldest buildings dating from 1903. Inside, you'll find a taxidermic collection of local animals, including grizzly and black bears.On the other side of the river, the **Buffalo Nations Luxton Museum** tells the story of Alberta's Indigenous Peoples.

Soaking in Banff Upper Hot Springs

PUBLIC SPRING-WATER POOL

Banff's raison d'être is hot water. Not any old hot water but the soothing spring water that gushes out of the depths of Sulphur Mountain at temperatures that oscillate between 32°C (90°F) and 46°C (116°F). This geothermal gift of nature contains numerous revitalizing minerals including sulfate, calcium, sodium and magnesium, and is kept at temperatures of between 37°C (99°F) and 40°C (104°F) in the public pools.

The current **Banff Upper Hot Springs** pool complex (hotsprings.ca/banff) has its antecedents in the 1880s but has been extended many times in the years since to keep up with increasing tourist demand. It's located 5km (3.1 miles) from the original Cave and Basin site ('discovered' by the three railway workers in 1883) and was developed, more or less, in tandem. Its mineral-rich water was considered more desirable than the lower springs largely because it was several degrees hotter.

SHORT HIKES NEAR BANFF TOWN

Johnson Lake
A pond-sized lake ringed by fir forest and encircled by an easy 3km (1.9-mile) trail with views of Cascade Mountain.

Marsh Loop
Easy, sometimes muddy, 3.4km (2.1-mile) loop alongside the Bow River that combines well with a visit to the Cave and Basin National Historic Site. Waterfowl and beavers abound.

Fenland Trail
Popular with Banff dog walkers and joggers, this 2.1km (1.3-mile) circular trail travels through a variety of natural habitats – woodland, marsh, fen, riverbed and wetland – around placid Forty Mile Creek.

HOTTER SPRINGS

Jasper has its own quieter and less commercialized therapeutic waters at **Miette Hot Springs** (p152), which bubble up a good 8-10°C (46-50°F) hotter than those at Banff.

 WHERE TO GO TO THE PUB IN BANFF TOWN

Banff Ave Brewing Co
Positioning itself as Banff's 'living room,' this brewpub occupies an upstairs space in a Swiss-style mall.

Rose & Crown
Banff's oldest boozer mixes a roster of locally brewed beers with a comprehensive schedule of live music.

St James' Gate Olde Irish Pub
Atmospheric beer haven plying draught Guinness and British pub grub classics.

BANFF CENTRE FOR ARTS & CREATIVITY

The Rocky Mountain landscapes of Banff have long acted as a vivid muse for painters and artists. Capturing the creative mood, a cultural center was established here in 1933. Initially a drama school, it quickly expanded to include a full spectrum of fine arts under the tutelage of British-Canadian painter and printmaker Walter J Phillips, who became artist in residence in 1940.

Perched on the side of Tunnel Mountain, the contemporary arts center continues to host a varied program of concerts, lectures, exhibitions and events throughout the year, including the Mountain Film Festival in October/November and the Banff International String Quartet Competition in September. There's also an art gallery named in honor of Phillips.

Initially the Upper Springs was operated as a private facility. Its first structure was a deluxe hotel, the Grand View Villa, built in 1886 by railway company doctor Robert Brett, with a view to luring health-treatment-seeking visitors to the area. It was joined by a second establishment, the Hydro Hotel, in 1890. Both buildings burnt down and were replaced in the 1930s by a new bathhouse open to the general public and fashioned in the prevailing art-deco style.

Renovations have since eradicated some of the bathhouse's original charm. Although the gabled gray-stone building isn't unattractive, the interior at busy times can feel like a public swimming pool complex. Suffice to say, the hot springs still rank as one of Banff's quintessential experiences – a giant communal hot bath with an electrifying view of Mt Rundle opposite.

The pools get busy in season, so aim for an early or late dip if you prefer smaller crowds. Towels and swimsuits – including 1930s retro garments – are available for hire, and there's a rudimentary cafe selling coffee and sandwiches on the 2nd floor. Unlike Radium and Miette hot springs, Banff only has one alfresco pool that's kept deliciously warm. In the chillier months, you can enjoy hot-and-cold shock treatment by exposing your torso to the frigid air for five minutes between immersions. It's particularly invigorating during rain or snow.

Navigating Around Vermilion Lakes

WATER, WILDFOWL AND PHOTOGRAPHY

As the nearest navigable lakes to Banff Town, tranquil **Vermilion Lakes** are an attractive nexus for water activities, hiking, and communing with nature. You can spot a diverse stash of wildlife here: elk, beavers, owls, bald eagles and ospreys are all common around the lakeshore, especially at dawn and dusk. A paved path – part of the **Banff Legacy Trail** bike trail – parallels the lakes' northern edge for nearly 6km (3.8 miles), but the proximity of the Trans-Canada Hwy means an almost constant buzz of traffic noise.

Noise or not, the calm, glassy water is an excellent spot for painters and photographers, with the surrounding mountains clearly mirrored on the surface.

Three lakes lie between the wide meanders of the Bow River, their reedy edges ideal for seeing wildfowl. Channels and waterways interconnect them and it's easy to canoe out from Banff along Echo and Forty Mile Creeks through low marsh. Boats can be rented from **Banff Canoe Club**.

WHERE TO GO FOR PIZZA IN BANFF TOWN

Bear Street Tavern
Huge cheesy pizzas with a signature sauce made of honey, rosemary and chili-pepper olive oil. **$$**

Farm & Fire
Crusty pizzas loaded with local ingredients to form slightly off-the-wall combos like fig, Brie and truffle honey. **$$**

Una Pizza + Wine Banff
Perfectly blistered pies backed up by a strong contingent of pastas, salads and veggie starters. **$$**

Vermilion Lakes

The best way to reach the lakes on foot from Banff is via the 2.1km (1.3-mile) **Fenland Trail** that starts at the Forty Mile Creek Picnic Area, just north of the 'Welcome to Banff' sign on Lynx St.

The trail loops through spruce trees close to Forty Mile Creek incorporating wet- and fenlands with various interpretive boards explaining the local ecology. There are several wooden bridges and plenty of bird-watching potential, although you're just as likely to see canoers as wildfowl in the nearby creek. You can extend the walk by crossing the large bridge about halfway around the loop and heading left down the road to Vermilion Lakes.

Cave and Basin & the Birth of Banff

THE SITE THAT LAUNCHED THE PARK

When three Canadian Pacific Railway employees accidentally fell upon the hot springs half-hidden in a cave on one of their days off in 1883, they probably didn't realize the deluge their discovery would unleash. Not only did they come up with an epiphanic business idea, but they inadvertently helped ignite a national park movement and make Banff into the international phenomenon it is today.

The **Cave and Basin National Historic Site**, 1.6km (1 mile) west of the town center, is where it all started. While you can't bathe here anymore, the place has been preserved

SUNDANCE CANYON TRAIL

The partly paved Sundance Canyon Trail begins just beyond the Cave and Basin National Historic Site and follows a forested route around a river canyon with close-ups of a tumbling waterfall.

Graded as easy, the first section is flat with views of Bow River to your right and Sulphur Mountain to your left, passing through tracts of marsh and wetlands replete with waterfowl and dragonflies.

The unpaved second section incorporates a short loop around the canyon proper, with wooden bridges crossing a bubbling creek and leading to a lookout point with tree-framed views of the Bow Valley and the distant Trans-Canada Hwy.

Offering instant access to a shaded forest filled with birds and butterflies, it provides a great coda to a visit to the hot springs.

 WHERE TO ORGANIZE TRIPS & ACTIVITIES IN BANFF TOWN ───────

Pursuit	**Discover Banff**	**Banff Adventures**
Formerly operating under the name 'Brewster,' this company has been leading the way for tourists in Banff since 1892.	Organizes rafting trips, wildlife tours, Columbia Icefield day trips and even a 10-hour grizzly-bear tour in BC.	Banff's main activity-booking company can organize a huge range of activities and creates its own combo packages.

CANOEING IN BANFF

Canoes and kayaks have a long history in the Rockies, particularly among Indigenous Peoples. With numerous rivers and lakes scattered around the park, oar-power remains popular with modern tourists. You can hire canoes from boathouses at Lake Louise, Moraine Lake and Lake Minnewanka, although they're rather expensive and only available when the water fully defrosts between May and October.

For a cheaper deal, head to Banff Canoe Club (banffcanoeclub.com) in town, ideal for paddles on the Bow River or Vermilion Lakes.

Alternatively, you can bring your own canoe, kayak or stand-up board and paddle on a number of lakes. Be sure to download a self-certification permit from the park website first.

Lake Minnewanka is the only lake that permits motorboats.

Elk, Banff Springs Golf Course

as a museum and National Historic Site allowing access to the shadowy cave, the original outdoor bathing pool, and a terrace that covers the once-popular lower mineral springs pool that welcomed spa-seeking visitors for 78 years. An adjacent boardwalk with interpretive signage leads uphill to additional springs and the cave's upper vent.

The railway workers, of course, didn't really 'discover' the springs – the waters had held special spiritual significance to Indigenous Peoples for thousands of years – but their actions quickly spurred a flurry of private-business activity in the area offering facilities for bathers to enjoy the then-fashionable thermal remedies. To avert a gold-rush-style invasion, the government stepped in, declaring Banff Canada's first national park in order to preserve the springs.

The initial protected area, the so-called 'Hot Springs Reserve,' designated in 1885, was a mere 26 sq km (10 sq miles). It was expanded and became the Rocky Mountains National Park in 1887 and, finally, the current 6641-sq-km (2564-sq-mile) Banff National Park in 1930.

The museum is beautifully laid out in the changing rooms of the rather grand bathhouse, which dates from 1914 and saw its last paying customer in 1992. The Cave and Basin springs went into decline in the 1970s due to poor water quality, structural problems and competition from an increasing number of local pools, notably the posher and hotter Banff Upper Hot Springs. In 1985, the place was declared a National Historic Site and by 1992 only 7% of paying visitors were

 WHERE TO GET STEAK IN BANFF TOWN

Bluebird
Restaurant in one of Banff's oldest buildings that specializes in steak but also does a fine line in brunch. **$$**

Bison Restaurant & Terrace
The rustically elegant Bison is full of trendy Calgarians drawn by its regionally sourced, meat-heavy menu. **$$$**

Maple Leaf
Long-established surf-and-turf specialists in the town center offering sirloin, tenderloin and filet mignon. **$$$**

coming for the pools themselves. Service was discontinued and the site was redeveloped in 2011 as a super-modern museum that ushers you around a succinct history of the cave, the town and the whole national park movement with film, photos and juicy stories.

Easy to miss in a separate building behind the bathhouse is a compelling exhibit about Canadian internment camps in WWI where enemy aliens from Germany and Austro-Hungary were incarcerated. Banff had its own camp at Castle Junction.

A Trail up Tunnel Mountain
DIMINUITVE MOUNTAIN WITHOUT A TUNNEL

Small by the standards of the Rockies, **Tunnel Mountain**, known as *tatanga* or 'Sleeping Buffalo' by the Stoney people, is still one of the town's most recognizable natural citadels. The name is a misnomer. You won't find any tunnel here, although there were once plans to build one. In 1882, Canadian Pacific Railway surveyor Major AB Rogers, while laying proposals for the route of the cross-continental railway through Banff, devised a madcap scheme to blast a 275m (902ft) tunnel through the base of the mountain to avoid a more circuitous route paralleling the Bow River. Incensed at the projected cost, Canadian Pacific Railway manager William Van Horne vetoed the plan and ordered Rogers to find an alternative. The railway was subsequently rerouted north of the mountain at a fraction of the original cost, but the name stuck.

The 1692m-high (5551ft) mountain is almost entirely surrounded by modern Banff, meaning it's easy to pick out the town's landmarks from the summit. The sight of the **Banff Springs Golf Course** stretching verdantly alongside the Bow River is particularly beguiling.

A short 2.3km (1.4-mile) trail ascends from the north side of St Julien Rd, switching back up the mountain's eastern flank to the summit. It mostly traverses forest but there are plenty of open sections offering good views. Due to its low altitude, the trail is usually accessible in the winter months.

The mountain is also home to Banff's largest campground, Tunnel Mountain Village, with 1128 sites (over 300 with hookups) scattered around three different areas. It's one of only two campgrounds in the national park that's partially open year-round.

BANFF SPRINGS GOLF COURSE

One of Canada's most famous golf courses, and the most expensive in the world when it opened in 1928, the Banff Springs Golf Course is a 71-par 18-holer that curls around the Bow River between the skirts of Rundle and Sulphur Mountains.

It's notable for its notoriously difficult fourth hole, the so-called Devil's Cauldron, that involves a chip over a glacial lake onto a heavily bunkered sloping green that's unplayable until May due to dark mountain shadows.

Designed by the legendary Stanley Thompson, the course replaced an original nine-holer first laid out in 1911. The hotel added a further nine-hole course in 1989, the 'Tunnel Mountain 9,' making for a grand total of 27 spectacular greens on which to test your putting skills.

GETTING AROUND

Roam (roamtransit.com) runs Banff's excellent network of public buses. Five local routes serve Banff Town and its immediate surroundings, including route 1 to Banff Upper Hot Springs, 2 to Tunnel Mountain, and 4 to the Cave and Basin National Historic Site. All routes pass through Roam's main downtown transit hub at Banff High School;

many also stop across the street at the Elk West Transit Hub. Schedules and route maps are available online and at all bus stops. You can purchase tickets on the bus or in the Banff Information Center.

Taxis (which are metered) can easily be hailed on the street, especially on Banff Ave. Otherwise call Banff Taxi on 403-762-0000.

Cascade Amphitheatre
Mt Norquay
Banff Town
Mt Rundle
Canmore
Kananaskis Country

Beyond Banff Town

The majority of park visitors pull off the Trans-Canada Hwy and never leave the sheltered confines of Banff Town. Time to find out what they're missing.

Once you've tired of Banff Ave, you don't have to stray far to find yourself in a wilder domain with only the eerie rustling of pines for company. This is where the fun really begins as you get your first taste of unguarded wilderness. The most obvious lure is Mt Norquay, one of three ski areas in the park and a summer stomping ground for hikers and climbers.

Just outside the national park gates in the direction of Calgary is the slightly larger town of Canmore where visitors on a tighter budget sometimes prefer to stay. A road and dedicated 26km (16.2-mile) bike path link Canmore with Banff.

TOP TIP

Prices tend to be cheaper in Canmore than inside the park and, in high summer, the town often still has rooms to offer when Banff is full.

TREVOR CLARK/SHUTTERSTOCK ©

Mountain biking, Canmore (p76)

SEAN O'NEILL/ALAMY STOCK PHOTO ©

Skiing, Mt Norquay

Skiing Norquay

WHERE LOCALS GO TO SKI

Although it's the smallest of Banff's trio of ski areas and the closest to town, **Mt Norquay** (banffnorquay.com), 7km (4.4 miles) north of the center of Banff, is no weakling. Contained within its succinct 77 hectares (190 acres) of skiable terrain are some of the trickiest runs in Canada (44% are deemed difficult or challenging). It's also the only place in the national park that offers night skiing.

Norquay is Banff's original ski resort – the first runs were cut in 1926 – and thanks to its proximity to town, it remains the preferred 'local' place to go. Ski snobs are often leery about the quality of the powder and it's true the snowfall here isn't mega, thanks primarily to altitude: Norquay's highest runs are lower than Banff Sunshine's *base* village. To compensate, there are snow machines on 85% of the runs, some of which are notoriously fast. Ski racing has a long history at Norquay dating back to the late 1920s and the area is still used by aspiring Olympic athletes.

Thanks to the absence of the international jet set, who head to Banff Sunshine and Lake Louise, Norquay doesn't get long lift lines and, wedged below the tree line, it's rarely bitterly cold. In 1948, it was the recipient of what was then only Canada's second chairlift, the North American 'Big Chair' that continues to operate year-round.

THE STONEY-NAKODA

Numerous Indigenous groups visited and traded in the Banff area pre-European contact. One of the most notable was the Stoney-Nakoda who speak a dialect of the Dakota language common to the Sioux Nation.

It is thought that the Stoney people separated from the Dakota in present-day Minnesota in the 1640s and migrated west. They ultimately settled in the Rocky Mountain foothills where they traded fur, hunted bison and, later, became indispensable guides to early European explorers and railway surveyors.

Although Banff sits on traditional Stoney-Nakoda land and is punctuated with important spiritual sites, the group were largely excluded from the national park in its early years. It is only recently that they have been able to reconnect with their roots through partnerships with Parks Canada.

 WHERE TO SKI ON MT NORQUAY

Lone Pine
The most notorious of the black diamonds that emanate from the top of the North American chairlift.

Zoomer
Nice trail for beginners in the night skiing area, accessed from the diminutive Cascade quad-chair.

Sun Chutes
Popular narrow chute lined with trees and graded black that's accessed from the top of the Mystic chairlift.

Due to its lower altitude, Norquay logs a shorter season than its national park rivals, usually closing in mid- to late April, a good month before Banff Sunshine and Lake Louise.

Head for Heights on the Via Ferrata

FIXED-PROTECTION CLIMBING ROUTES

Once the sole domain of accomplished sport-climbers, the craggy cliffs of Mt Norquay can now be scaled by mere mortals without fear of falling.

Via ferratas (iron ways) were popularized in the mountains of northern Italy during WWI when they were used purely for military purposes. Their rock-spanning ladders, metal bridges and fixed-line cables helped move armies across rugged alpine terrain during the high-altitude war being played out on the Italian Front.

The routes were improved and adapted for tourism in the Italian Dolomites in the 1930s, enabling non-technical climbers to access otherwise dangerous rocky terrain without advanced mountaineering skills. A harness with two leashes and carabiner clips ensured high levels of safety.

The idea migrated to Canada in the early 2000s and Mt Norquay's via ferrata (banffnorquay.com/summer/via-ferrata), which opened in 2014, is the only one in the national park, with five thrilling route choices ranging from 2½ to six hours. The heart-in-your-mouth Summiteer route includes a three-wire suspension bridge to the top of Mt Norquay. Prices include full safety kit, accompanying guide and passage up the Norquay chairlift to the start point.

Mt Rundle

MT RUNDLE: BANFF'S RUGGED SENTINEL

There are few mountains in Banff as recognizable as 2948m (9672ft) Mt Rundle, or Waskahigan Watchi as Indigenous Peoples call it. The classic and much photographed image of the peak is from Vermilion Lakes, where its distinctive sedimentary rocks slant diagonally skyward like a giant wave about to break.

For a different perspective, and a fuller appreciation of the mountain's true size, it's necessary to view it from the Trans-Canada Hwy. Motoring northwest out of Canmore, Rundle appears like a mini-mountain range stretching for 12km (7.5 miles) with a dozen craggy buttresses rising ominously above the surrounding forest like Hadrian's Wall on steroids.

Rundle is notoriously difficult to climb, and most hikes to the summit are designated 'scrambles' involving loose scree and 50-degree-plus gradients.

 WHERE TO GET A SNACK IN CANMORE

Communitea
Juices, coffee, tea and numerous vegetarian-biased snacks in a cafe that exudes a relaxed modern aesthetic. $

Blondies Cafe
Cabin-sized cafe with Three Sisters views that rustles up wraps, baguettes and revitalizing acai bowls. $

Rocky Mountain Bagel Company
Bagelwiches, pizza bagels or classic maple bagels, this place has it covered. $

Norquay's Summer Chairlift

LOFTY LUNCH SPOT

There is no gondola on Mt Norquay, but the **North American Chairlift** remains open in the summer, offering a short sensory ride to a viewing platform at 2085m (6840ft) – still well below the summit. Here, you'll find a walkway and the **Cliffhouse Bistro**, a former teahouse turned casual restaurant dating from the 1950s. The views of Banff and the Bow Valley from the dining room rival nearby Sulphur Mountain, but without the crowds. The sloping summit of Mt Rundle looks particularly dramatic from this angle.

Higher up, the 2522m (8274ft) summit of Norquay is inaccessible to all but expert scramblers.

A Walk in the Cascade Amphitheatre

MT NORQUAY'S MOST HEAVENLY HIKE

Kicking off at Mt Norquay's winter ski area, this 15.4km (9.6-mile) out-and-back hike bisects grassy ski runs and long stretches of pine forest before switchbacking to its apex: a vast hanging valley anchored by alpine meadows and ringed by dramatic rock faces. You'll hear pikas and marmots scurrying and whistling among the crags as you emerge into the high country while the colossal views up toward 2998m (9836ft) Cascade Mountain will help tug you heavenward.

The trail starts as a service road at the far end of the ski-lodge parking lot and passes the Mystic chairlift before descending into lodgepole pine forest. Continue straight ahead at the Mystic Pass–Forty Mile Summit junction and, after 3km (1.9 miles), you'll reach the banks of gin-clear Forty Mile Creek. Keep to the right and cross over the bridge. From here, the real climb begins as the trail continues through forest to a junction with the Elk Lake Summit Trail at the 4.3km (2.7-mile) mark. Keep right and catch your breath ahead of a series of brutal switchbacks that carry you 2.3km (1.4 miles) up the pine-forested western slope of the mountain.

NATURAL AMPHITHEATERS

Similar to the Cascade Amphitheatre, the **C-Level Cirque hike** (p85) is an uphill grunt through forest to a steep-sided glacial hollow or 'cirque.'

THE PALLISER EXPEDITION

It's hard to escape the legacy of the Palliser expedition in Banff.

Assembled by Irish explorer and geographer John Palliser in 1857, the expedition's aim was to survey and scientifically study the poorly documented fur-trading lands of western Canada and assess their potential for future settlement and transportation. In this sense it closely mimicked Lewis and Clark's pioneering Discovery Corps that had crossed the US half a century earlier.

During three extraordinary years, Palliser and his cohorts roamed the Rockies naming many of the region's natural features after themselves and others, and in 1863 they presented their findings to the British Parliament.

The report quickly became the touchstone for the opening up of the Canadian West by settlers and railway companies in the ensuing decades.

 WHERE TO STAY IN CANMORE

Canmore Downtown Hostel	**Georgetown Inn**	**Falcon Crest Lodge**
Bright, tasteful 2019-vintage hostel with wood-clad dorms and reams of community-led info to enjoy the area. **$**	Slice of old-school pub ambience, the Georgetown's retro rooms are filled with English charm. **$$$**	Modern lodge with tasteful rooms plus kitchenette, fireplace, and a balcony with mountain views. **$$$**

CLIMBING IN CANMORE

Canmore is the epicenter of rock-climbing in the Rockies and the spiritual home of the sport in Canada. It's no coincidence that the Alpine Club of Canada has its national HQ here.

Numerous crags, all within a short distance of each other, surround the town, including Cougar Creek, Grassi Lakes and Grotto Canyon. The holy grail for multipitch routes is Mt Yamnuska (aka Mt John Laurie) with over 100 routes of all grades. In the colder months, Canmore shifts its focus to frozen-waterfall climbing.

The one-stop shop for climbing courses, guided tours and gear is Yamnuska Mountain Adventures (yamnuska.com) in Canmore, with nearly 50 years of experience. For one of Canada's best indoor climbing walls, head to Elevation Place, Canmore's hi-tech sports center.

Just before arriving at the **Cascade Amphitheatre**, the trail levels off and a number of faint paths head to the right. Stick to the main path until you emerge at a lovely alpine meadow, which is dotted with white anemones and yellow lilies in summer.

The trail becomes indistinct but continues for about 1km (0.6 miles) to the upper end of the amphitheater, where the vegetation thins out and boulders litter the ground. Catch a rest before heading back.

Escape to Canmore

BANFF ON A BUDGET

Canmore is Banff without the rules and regulations. Situated just outside the national park boundary, 25km (15.6 miles) from Banff Town, the former coal-mining settlement reinvented itself as an outdoor hub in 1988 after the Calgary Winter Olympics (Canmore hosted the cross-country skiing events). Most of the people who live here today are spiritual descendants of the pioneers who first embraced the Rockies in the 1800s. Linger in a downtown coffee bar and you'll hear their stories: nonchalant locals bantering about pre-breakfast climbing sorties and bear encounters in the backcountry. People live here because they love it. The hiking, the cycling, the skiing and wildlife viewing are some of the finest in Canada. And Canmore acts as the national headquarters for the Alpine Club of Canada, the nation's premier rock-climbing body.

The local **Canmore Museum & Geoscience Centre** divulges the details of the town's coal-mining past and its subsequent reinvention in the 1980s. Nevertheless, most people come here to partake in one of the activities in which Canmore excels. Skiing and mountain biking can be mostly satisfied at the world-class Nordic Centre. Climbers can get to grips with the impressive climbing wall at the Elevation Place sports center before heading outside. The area's showcase hike is the 5.6km (3.5-mile) ascent of Ha Ling Peak, which looms over town like an upturned beaver's tail. Of a less strenuous nature is the Grassi Lakes Loop incorporating waterfalls and two sapphire lakes.

With a population of just under 14,000, the town is well served with restaurants, accommodations and outfitters ready to set you up with everything from bike rental to cave tours.

 WHERE TO HIKE AROUND CANMORE

Ha Ling Peak
Canmore's proverbial fitness test: a steep, busy, well-maintained trail to get hikers quickly above the tree line.

Grassi Lakes
Deservedly popular 90-minute loop incorporating lakes, waterfalls and a well-known rock-climbing crag.

Rundle Riverside Trail
Rootsy trail alongside the Bow River between Canmore Nordic Centre and Banff Town with sporadic river views.

Canmore Nordic Centre

Reigniting the Olympic Spirit

MOUNTAIN BIKING AND NORDIC SKIING

The 1988 Winter Olympics rescued Canmore from potential catastrophe as it struggled to redefine itself after the closure of its coal mines in the 1970s. The saving grace was its **Nordic Centre**, an activity hub that has since morphed into a comprehensive year-round venue, offering cross-country skiing in the winter and mountain biking in the summer.

Wedged at the foot of Mt Rundle en route to the Spray Lakes Reservoir, the huge purpose-built center has one of western Canada's best networks for mountain biking with over 100km (63 miles) of trails mapped out by some of the nation's top trail designers. Routes are graded in the standard green, blue and black, and include easy rides on wide dirt roads to technical single tracks and steep downhills. You can bring your own bike, or hire one from Trail Sports, opposite the center's day lodge. The same goes for skis.

The winter ski trail network measures a slightly more modest 65km (41 miles) – both machine-groomed and natural (ungroomed) – with 6.5km (4 miles) lit for night skiing. The center is a 4km (2.5-mile) drive from Canmore, just off Spray Lakes Rd. Cross the Bow River at the west edge of downtown, take Rundle Dr, continue south along Three Sisters Dr and follow signs to the Canmore Nordic Centre.

ART IN CARNMORE

For what is, essentially, an activity-focused mountain town, Carnmore has a decent art scene.

A good half a dozen art galleries are scattered around the tight, downtown core, displaying canvases and sculptures by talented local artists that document the dramatic landscapes and fearsome fauna for which the area is famous.

Art Country Canada has recreations of Canada's legendary Group of Seven painters and originals from the likes of Robert Bateman. The Ken Hoehn Gallery specializes in wildlife photography, while the Carter-Ryan Gallery exhibits the paintings and soapstone sculpture of contemporary Indigenous artist, Jason Carter.

Look out for jewelry and art pieces fashioned from ammolite, an iridescent gemstone made from the fossilized remains of marine mollusks.

 WHERE TO EAT IN CANMORE

Gaucho Brazilian Barbecue
Authentic southern Brazilian *churrascaria* (steakhouse) with meat served at your table, plus a buffet salad bar. **$$$**

Rocky Mountain Flatbread Co
Flatbread-style pizzas backed up with homemade pasta and daily blackboard specials. **$$**

Crazyweed Kitchen
Flashy bistro on the edge of town with funky artwork and a globetrotting menu of fusion-style dishes. **$$$**

WILDLIFE CROSSINGS

As you drive north from Banff Town toward Lake Louise along the Trans-Canada Hwy, look out for the six arched, tree-covered overpasses spanning the road. These are wildlife crossings specially designed to allow Banff's animals to cross the road without fear of getting mowed down by a passing truck or RV.

The Trans-Canada Hwy sits slap bang in the middle of several key 'wildlife corridors' that crisscross the Bow Valley. Thousands of animals have been killed while trying to cross the highway over the years.

To reduce the risk of accidents and protect the park's increasingly fragile animal population, the wildlife crossings were built at a cost of around C$1 million each, starting in 1988, alongside 38 other underpasses that tunnel beneath the road.

I VIEWFINDER/SHUTTERSTOCK ©

Canadian Pacific Railway, Bow Valley

Beware of wildlife encounters, particularly in the summer, as many of the routes cross through areas of backcountry that form part of the **Bow Valley Wildlife Corridor**. You might find yourself sharing the trails with black bears, moose and occasionally grizzles.

Memories of the Canadian Pacific Railway

THE ORIGINAL TOURIST EXPERIENCE

Banff owes its existence to the railway, more specifically the **Canadian Pacific Railway** (CPR). The cross-continental line reached the Rocky Mountains in late 1883, weaving its way through what is now Banff Town and Lake Louise before climbing over Kicking Horse Pass into British Columbia.

When hot springs were 'discovered' beside the line, the prospect of a tourist bonanza presented itself like a dangling carrot. 'If we can't export the scenery, we'll import the tourists,' proclaimed CPR chairman, William Van Horne. And he meant it!

The railway brought millions of tourists to Banff

THE EMPIRE BUILDER

The Great Northern Railway started the **Empire Builder train** (p195) between Chicago and the Pacific Northwest in 1929. Its trains still run, tracking the southern boundary of Glacier National Park.

WHERE TO GO SCRAMBLING AROUND BANFF

Mt Rundle
Wedge-shaped mountain overlooking Banff that's a relatively easy scramble with its own national park guide.

Cascade Mountain
Banff's sentinel mountain mixes tough, steep hiking with trickier scrambling over loose scree with hand-holds.

Mt Norquay
Norquay can be scrambled as described in Alan Kane's book, *Scrambles in the Canadian Rockies*.

in the first half of the 20th century. Today most arrive by car, but one special train – the elegantly attired **Rocky Mountaineer** (rockymountaineer.com) – still runs. This deluxe tourist train harks back to the adventurous days of Banff's beginnings, when profit-seeking businesspeople attempted to lure affluent tourists to the park by building posh hotels, luxuriant spas and expansive golf courses to soften the wilderness experience.

Since its launch in 1990, the *Rocky Mountaineer* has come to epitomize the vintage appeal of Banff. Its most popular package is the 'First Passage to the West,' a service running between Vancouver and Banff with a night in Kamloops en route (there are no sleeper cars). It's the only passenger train to still utilize the historic CPR line with its famous spiral tunnels completed in 1885, a colossus of 19th-century engineering that took four years to build. The main embarkation/disembarkation is Banff's railway station, a heritage building dating from 1910.

Rocky Mountaineer packages aren't cheap but lay on the luxury with panoramic dome cars, gourmet food and onboard guides.

Cycling the Legacy Trail

PAVED INTER-TOWN BIKE PATH

Of all the initiatives introduced to Banff in the last 15 years, this hugely popular multipurpose trail that parallels the Trans-Canada Hwy for 26.8km (16.7 miles) is arguably the most memorable – and sustainable.

Opened to celebrate the national park's 125th anniversary in 2010, the **Banff Legacy Trail** has logged well over one million users since its inception, sometimes amassing over 3000 cyclists in a single day in summer.

The trail is mostly flat, wholly paved and armed with a number of user-friendly contraptions, including solar-paneled electrified rubber mats designed as invisible 'gates' to protect wildlife. You can cycle over them safely with rubber tires.

Split into two lanes, the route can be done in either direction, although favorable tailwinds usually make starting in Canmore easier.

The official starting point is Canmore's **Bow Valley Trail** opposite the Alberta Visitor Information Centre on the northwest side of town. It's marked by a multicolored guidepost fitted with a count-o-meter that logs daily trail usage.

HORSES FOR COURSES

Banff's earliest European explorers – fur traders and railway surveyors – penetrated the region primarily on horseback.

Kicking Horse Pass between Banff and Yoho, testifies to a story that James Hector of the map-charting Palliser expedition was unceremoniously kicked by his mount there in 1858.

Between the 1880s and the building of the first main road in 1921, almost all tourists explored Banff on horseback.

Today, hiking and biking are the main modus operandi, but you can still follow in the hoofprints of pioneers past on guided rides with Banff Trail Riders (horseback.com), who lead one- to three-hour day trips or longer journeys into the backcountry with overnight stays at its Sundance Lodge. Instruction, guiding and a sore backside are included at no extra cost.

 WHERE TO FIND THE BEST VIEWS AROUND BANFF

Ha Ling Peak
A steep climb of Canmore's guardian mountain reduces the Trans-Canada to a thin ribbon cutting through the Bow Valley.

Valleyview Picnic Area
Rest up on the Legacy multi-use trail halfway between Canmore and Banff with an eyeful of Mt Rundle.

Cliffhouse Bistro
Lunch with an appetizing view at the top of the North American Chairlift on the upper slopes of Mt Norquay.

KANANASKIS COUNTRY

The vast area abutting Banff to the south and east, known collectively as Kananaskis Country (or K-Country), acts as a buffer zone to the national park and is covered by a protective patchwork of provincial parks and wilderness areas.

While tourists descend en masse to Banff for their adventure fixes, many locals prefer to head to K-Country, where the hiking and biking routes are quieter, and the mountain vistas are just as impressive.

Kananaskis has its own ski area, Nakiska, copious opportunities for white-water rafting, and a robust, typically Albertan, horseback-riding culture.

Less rule-bound than Banff, it's long been utilized by film directors for its Wild West–style scenery. Furthermore, with less traffic and no fencing, you're almost guaranteed to see free-roaming Rocky Mountain fauna.

SHAWN.CCF/SHUTTERSTOCK ©

Cycling, Banff Legacy Trail

For most of the journey, the path cuts through low foliage and scattered trees sandwiched between the Trans-Canada Hwy and the railway line. There's one major stop-off point 8km (5 miles) northwest of Canmore called the Valleyview picnic area, where you can slump down in a red Adirondack chair and contemplate the giant buttresses of Mt Rundle opposite.

Refreshingly, there are no major road crossings to negotiate. Instead, as you near Banff town, the trail splits in two with the right fork heading underneath the highway to the **Cascade Ponds** picnic area and Lake Minnewanka, and the left quickly veering away from the highway to merge with the top end of Banff Ave.

Most people call it a day once they get to Banff Town but, technically, the trail continues through the urban district and out the other side, following a paved road that hugs the north shore of Vermilion Lakes. For the final 2km (1.2 miles), the route reestablishes itself as a two-lane multiuse path before reaching its official terminus at the junction of the Trans-Canada Hwy and the Bow Valley Parkway. From here, you can turn around or link up with one of Banff's other great cycling routes (the bike-friendly parkway runs 51km to Lake Louise).

While mainly used by cyclists, the Banff Legacy Trail is also open to walkers, runners, horseback riders, rollerbladers and e-bikes.

 WHERE TO GO FOR A SHORT WALK AROUND BANFF

Policeman's Creek Trail
Flat 4km (2.5-mile) stroll around a river in central Canmore amid birdlife and wonderful mountain vistas.

Spray River Trail
Easy riverside walk that starts south of the Banff Springs Golf Course with an option to loop back along the opposite bank.

Upper Stoney Trail
Short, moderately challenging, mostly forested 4.3km (2.7-mile) loop from the Mt Norquay ski area.

Mountain Biking the Goat Creek Trail

THE BACK ROUTE TO BANFF

In most people's books, Jasper is far superior to Banff in the quantity and quality of its mountain-biking trails. But **Goat Creek Trail** stands as an honorable exception. This easy-to-manage unpaved double-track allows two-wheeled travelers to pedal between Canmore and Banff along an attractive back route that follows an old fire road on the western side of Mt Rundle, well away from the incessant car noise of the Trans-Canada Hwy.

All things being equal, the trail is best done starting at Whiteman's Gap, located 5km (3.1 miles) up the dirt Smith-Dorrien/Spray Trail Rd from Canmore, from where it drops 280 vertical meters (919ft) into Banff. It's good to arrange a shuttle or taxi to get to the start. The car park for Goat Creek sits directly opposite the Ha Ling Peak trailhead and was substantially upgraded in 2022.

The ride begins in pine and spruce forest roughly following the course of meandering Goat Creek, with the Goat Range in Kananaskis Country rising to the south and Mt Rundle to the north. If you've already completed the Banff Legacy Trail, the rugged terrain here will feel wild, unhurried and refreshingly remote. Even better, despite the loose stones and occasional inclines, there are no real technical sections and plenty of opportunities to let rip.

About halfway to Banff, the trail kinks briefly to the west and crosses the Spray River on a handsome bridge. This is a major path junction with the Spray Lakes Reservoir trail, which peels off to the left. Keep right and follow the fire road alongside the Spray River to another bridge where the Goat Creek Trail officially amalgamates with the Spray River Loop (marked as trail No 5 on national park maps). Keeping the river on your right, maintain the brisk pedal revs until you see the Fairmont Banff Springs hotel rising like a French chateau above the golf course. It's a very regal reintroduction to civilization.

All in, the trail measures 18.8km (11.8 miles) one way. To get back to Canmore, there are three options: retrace your steps, stick your bike on the rack of Roam bus 3, or cycle back along the busier, noisier but eminently faster Legacy Trail.

In winter the Goat Creek is tracked for cross-country skiing, a whole different adventure.

FISHING

Although Banff has long promoted itself as a fishing sanctum and many of its early tourists arrived with the express intention of casting a rod and line, 95% of the park's lakes don't naturally support native fish.

The fish that live in them today – and there are plenty – were introduced to the park in the early 20th century in a bid by wildlife and park agencies to 'improve' the visitor experience and lure more sports-minded tourists.

Such meddling with nature has meant that some native fish populations and aquatic ecosystems have suffered, while others have thrived.

If you're keen to fish in Banff, you'll first need to procure a fishing permit and digest a long list of rules and regulations.

GETTING AROUND

Norquay is 7km (4.4 miles) north of Banff Town up the switchbacking Mt Norquay Scenic Dr. A free shuttle bus runs three times a day to and from the town.

Canmore is easily accessible from Banff Town (20 minutes) via the Trans-Canada Hwy (Hwy 1). Bus 3, operated by Roam, makes the 25-minute run between Canmore and Banff every 30 to 60 minutes. Buses stop downtown on 9th St near 7th Ave.

LAKE MINNEWANKA

Lake Minnewanka

Lake Minnewanka (the name means 'lake of the spirits' in the native Stoney language) is located barely 10km (6.2 miles) east of Banff Town, making it a default escape for locals and visitors with their own wheels (be they two or four). Over the years, the lake has been developed as a recreational area for bracing outdoor activities, many of them water-based. Swimming, sailing, boating and fishing are all enthusiastically practiced, plus there are hikes to entertain landlubbers, starting with an easy ramble along the lake's shoreline and culminating with a steep grunt to a nearby glacial cirque.

In days of yore, a full-blown settlement stood on the western shore of Minnewanka, but the town has been long since abandoned and submerged beneath the lake, which was dammed three times between 1895 and 1941. Once much smaller, the lake today is 28km (17.4 miles) long and 142m (465ft) deep, making it the largest body of water in the national park.

TOP TIP

During the buffaloberry season (mid-July to mid-September), hiking restrictions are in place along the Minnewanka shoreline trails (including the Aylmer Pass and Lookout trails) beyond Stewart Canyon. Hikers must travel in groups of four and carry bear spray to minimize disturbance to grizzlies.

Lake Minnewanka

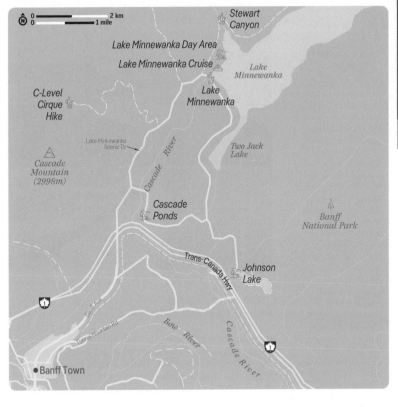

Venturing Out on the Water

THE ROCKIES' LARGEST LAKE

Possibly the most multifarious of the region's lakes, **Lake Minnewanka** (pictured) is a Rocky Mountain classic, surrounded by mountains, frequented by wildlife, and kissed by thick clumps of handsome firs, cedars and aspen groves. Ruins and Indigenous remnants add to the appeal. Evidence of Indigenous settlement (arrowheads and hearth rocks) going back 9000 years has been uncovered at several underwater and shoreline sites, while a whole submerged resort village lurks at the lake's west end.

 WHERE TO CAMP AROUND LAKE MINNEWANKA

Two Jack Lakeside
The prettiest of the Banff area drive-in campgrounds, with 74 reservable sites and 10 'oTENTiks.' **$**

Mount Inglismaldie
Walk-in campground 11km along the lakeshore trail; popular with overnight out-and-back hikers. **$**

Ghost Lakes
A five-site backcountry beauty, 31km (19.2 miles) on foot from civilization. Tranquility guaranteed! **$**

THE TOWN BENEATH THE LAKE

One of Alberta's more interesting diving sites, Minnewanka Landing is a former resort town that got submerged beneath the lake.

The first log hotel was built in 1886 and the area quickly became a popular summer resort village for recreation-seeking Calgary-ites. Within a couple of decades there were several hotels, a handful of restaurants and numerous cottages spread along four parallel avenues.

However, the businesses were ultimately forced to yield to the growing hydroelectric demands of Calgary as the lake was dammed three times, in 1895, 1912 and 1941, causing it to rise by 30m (98ft).

Thanks to Minnewanka's cold, clear glacial water, many of the town's submerged ruins have been well preserved. Divers today can view ghostly foundations, sidewalks, pilings of erstwhile wharves, and even an old bridge.

ACHINTHAMB/SHUTTERSTOCK ©

Boathouse, Lake Minnewanka

Minnewanka is a popular recreational lake that develops a more wilderness feel the further you penetrate its 28km (17.5-mile) course. The western shore, only 10km (6.3 miles) from Banff Town, is a busy hub with a boat dock, picnic area, various trailheads and a seasonal cafe (the **Black Anchor**). The narrated one-hour **Lake Minnewanka Cruise**, bookable through Pursuit (banffjaspercollection.com), is worth it for the succinct history and jovial commentaries, but for a longer, quieter contemplation of what Indigenous Peoples called the 'lake of spirits,' you'll need to hike its northern shoreline. The lakeside path extends from Stewart Canyon (easy stroll) to the Aylmer Pass junction (day hike) and, ultimately, Ghost Lakes (two days out and back).

Kayaks and canoes are another transportation option and rentable from the boat dock. Bear in mind that you'll be competing with motorboats and cruisers: Minnewanka is the only lake in Banff that permits motor-powered watercraft. The lake is also revered for its fishing and allows fishers to keep a small quantity of their catch. Lake trout are native to its waters, although they were substantially topped up in the early 20th century.

The lake freezes in winter.

 WHERE TO PENETRATE THE BACKCOUNTRY AROUND LAKE MINNEWANKA

Cascade Valley
An easy but little trafficked path to a campground and bridge over the Cascade River with opportunities to continue upstream.

Aylmer Lookout
Peel away from the Minnewanka shoreline on this challenging uphill trail to a lookout above the trees with broad lake views.

Lake Minnewanka Shoreline Trail
A long but moderately graded trail that follows the north shoreline of Lake Minnewanka through bear country.

Stewart Canyon Stroll

CINEMATIC RIVER

Stewart Canyon is more modest than deep-cut Johnston Canyon on the Bow Valley Parkway and vertiginous Maligne Canyon in Jasper, but it still offers good hiking opportunities on the wooded shores of Lake Minnewanka. The easy 5.6km (3.5-mile) out-and-back route starts at the lake's main recreational area by the boat dock, which doubles up as a decent spot for a picnic either before or after your hike (there are tables and benches). Alternatively, you can save your sandwiches for a more secluded lunch in the canyon itself.

The trail begins on a forested dirt track with lake views that gradually becomes more uneven and rootsy as you forge north. Within 1.6km (1 mile), you'll come to an attractive wooden bridge above the Cascade River, close to where it drains into Lake Minnewanka. This is where Robert Mitchum and Marilyn Monroe stole a kiss in the 1954 film *River of No Return*. On the far side of the river, there's a fork in the trail: the right-hand branch leads to Aylmer Pass; the left heads up the canyon for 1.2km (0.7 miles), eventually bringing you to the edge of a river gully. From here, you can clamber down across boulders, fallen trees and rocks to the riverside. The canyon itself is named after George Stewart, first superintendent of Banff National Park in the 1880s. It was once visibly deeper, but the water level has risen by about 25m (80ft) since Lake Minnewanka was last dammed in 1941. Local flora and fauna include deer and elk, and purple calypso orchids.

C-Level Cirque Hike

MINE RUINS AND GLACIAL VALLEYS

The cream of Lake Minnewanka's hikes is a steep grunt through forest up the shoulder of **Cascade Mountain** to a glorious opening at the foot of a boulder field and enormous cirque: a concave amphitheater-shaped valley carved out by glacial erosion.

Along the way, it's possible to pick out the remains of several buildings and mine shafts from the long-abandoned Lower Bankhead anthracite coal mine. Indeed, the **C-Level Cirque Hike** takes its name from the level where the miners once worked. More of the ghost town ruins lie nearby on the road to Lake Minnewanka.

A DEEPER CANYON

For the ultimate canyon experience (and plenty of people to share it with) head northwest along the Bow Valley to **Johnston Canyon** (p98), where steep cliffs taper into a narrow fissure.

ACTIVITIES ON LAKE MINNEWANKA

Boat Cruises
Minnewanka is the only lake in the park that allows motorized boats. Daily cruises are offered in the summer.

Diving
Scuba-diving is permitted in the lake, with the best dive sites clustered at the western end around the submerged ruins of Minnewanka Landing. The park has no licensed dive operators, so you'll have to arrange guided trips in either Calgary or Edmonton.

Fishing
Fishing is permitted in many park lakes, but Minnewanka is the only place where you can keep some of your catch (up to two lake trout).

WHERE TO ENJOY A PICNIC AROUND LAKE MINNEWANKA

Lake Minnewanka Day Area	**Johnson Lake**	**Cascade Ponds**
Close to the heart of the action with toilets, shelters, boat rental and a cafe nearby.	The nearest Banff has to a seaside getaway; people motor in with loungers, paddleboards and food hampers.	Series of ponds connected by wooden bridges, with picnic tables and fire pits in the shadow of Cascade Mountain.

BANKHEAD GHOST TOWN

Bankhead was a coal mine that operated between 1903 and 1922 close to the shores of Lake Minnewanka in the days when mineral extraction was still permissible in Canadian national parks (it was finally banned in 1931).

The mine's energy-dense anthracite coal was considered highly profitable and a town of around 900 people quickly sprang up to support the budding industry replete with nascent luxuries of the era, including electricity and plumbing.

When the mine ceased to be profit-able after WWI, the town lost its raison d'etre and promptly died. Many of the buildings were sal-vaged and moved to the growing tourist hub of Banff nearby.

Other artifacts, including a lamp-house, powerhouse and rusty train, have been left *in situ* and can be seen on a 1km (0.6-mile) interpretive loop.

GREENS AND BLUES/SHUTTERSTOCK ©

C-Level Cirque Hike

The route starts from the west side of the Upper Bankhead parking lot and climbs through rootsy forest, often sprinkled with violets, calypso orchids and clematis in summer. After around 45 minutes of climbing, the forest starts to thin out, allowing glimpses of Banff Town, Mt Rundle and the nearby lakes through the trees. Eventually the foliage disappears completely as you emerge exhausted and/or energized into the cirque itself.

Pikas, golden-mantled ground squirrels and whistling marmots can often be seen keeping watch over the path as you continue skirting the rough edge of the cirque, dwarf forest on one side and a vast slope of scree and fallen rocks on the other. Ultimately, you'll join up with a last steep, rubbly section and climb to a high lookout knoll. Rest here and admire the expansive views dominated by the striking blue hue of Lake Minnewanka. The cirque guards the eastern face of Cascade Mountain, which at 2998m (9836ft) is the tallest of Banff Town's sentinel peaks.

 GETTING AROUND

Roam transit's bus 6 runs between Banff and Lake Minnewanka from May to October.
It takes around 15 minutes to drive to the lake by car along the Lake Minnewanka Scenic Drive, or it's a 10km (6.3-mile) cycle ride.

SUNSHINE VILLAGE

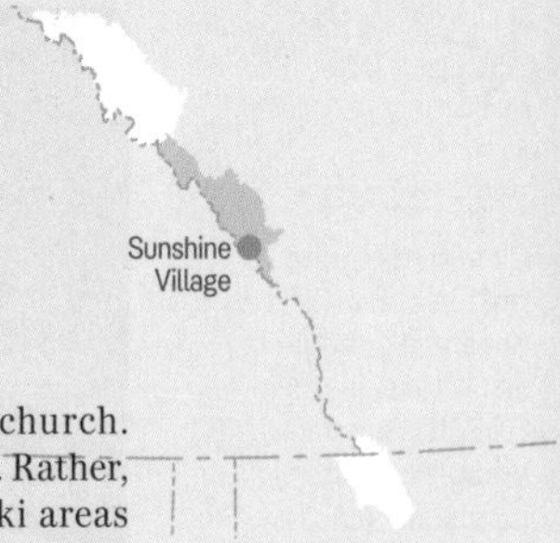

Sunshine
Village

Don't expect thatched cottages and a steepled church. Sunshine Village isn't a village in the traditional sense. Rather, it's home to one of the national park's three main ski areas nestled amid a high-alpine nirvana of meadows, ridges and lakes that straddles the Continental Divide between Alberta and British Columbia.

In winter, skiers congregate in the small purpose-built village to experience some of the best snow in the Rockies. In the spring thaw, the snow melts to reveal the majestic beauty of Sunshine Meadows, a sweeping expanse of ponds and flower meadows backed by crenelated peaks that stretches for 15km (9.3 miles) between Citadel Pass and Healy Pass. The presence of a gondola and seasonal bus service make this one of the easiest places in the Rockies for hikers to get above the tree line without chartering a private helicopter or expending copious gallons of sweat. No excuses – get up there and embrace it!

TOP TIP

Between late June and early September, the Sunshine Sightseeing Gondola whisks hikers from Sunshine's base station – located in a car park at the end of the Sunshine road – up to the ski 'village,' cutting out 6.5km (4 miles) of dull uphill hiking.

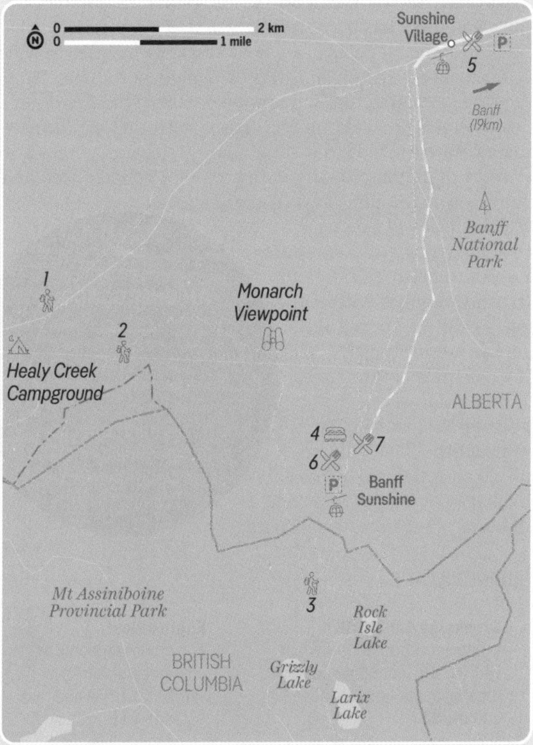

ACTIVITIES
1 Healy Pass
2 Simpson Pass
3 Sunshine Meadows

SLEEPING
4 Sunshine Mountain Lodge

EATING
5 Creekside Bar & Grill
6 Eagle's Nest
7 Mad Trapper's Saloon

Sunshine Village

0 ——————— 2 km
0 ——————— 1 mile

Banff
(19km)

Banff
National
Park

Monarch
Viewpoint

Healy Creek
Campground

1

2

4

7

6

P   Banff
Sunshine

ALBERTA

Mt Assiniboine
Provincial Park

3

Rock
Isle
Lake

BRITISH
COLUMBIA

Grizzly
Lake

Larix
Lake

87

THE VILLAGE

Clustered around the top station of the Sunshine gondola at an altitude of 2159m (7083ft), Sunshine Village consists of a handsome glass-and-wood hotel, the Sunshine Mountain Lodge, along with half a dozen cafes and restaurants, from the pub-like Mad Trappers Saloon housed in a 1928-vintage hunting cabin (that predates the ski resort) to the upscale Eagle's Nest.

In the summer, the village provides a gateway to a circuit of short alpine trails, accessed via the Standish chairlift, and a couple of longer hikes, most notably the backcountry excursions to Egypt Lake and Mt Assiniboine Provincial Park.

The Creekside lodge at the gondola base station sports a coffee shop and grill restaurant, and handles hotel check-in and ski rentals. It's also the summer trailhead for Healy Pass.

AUTUMN SKY PHOTOGRAPHY/SHUTTERSTOCK ©

Sunshine Village

Skiing on the British Columbia–Alberta Border

ONE OF CANADA'S SNOWIEST RESORTS

People have skied at **Banff Sunshine** (skibanff.com) since the 1930s and there has been the semblance of a resort here since the 1940s. The pioneers knew good terrain when they saw it. In a comparative study of Rocky Mountain ski resorts, Banff Sunshine comes out top for quantity of snow: it receives double Lake Louise's snow-dump and three times that of Norquay. The reason? Altitude. Sunshine's base village is perched at a height of 2159m (7083ft) at the top of a gondola ride and abutting a huge alpine bowl. There are very few trees in this neck of the woods and the views over toward the Continental Divide and British Columbia will have you skidding to regular stops in admiration.

Sunshine's stats are equally impressive, if not quite up to Lake Louise's in breadth. The 13.6-sq-km (5-sq-mile) ski area is divided between 137 runs and a 6-hectare (14.8-acre) terrain park.

A HIGHER GONDOLA

Of Banff's three gondolas, Sunshine has the largest cabins (eight-person) but it's not the highest. That honor goes to the **Banff Gondola** (p65) on Sulphur Mountain, with its top station perched at 2281m (7484ft).

 WHERE TO EAT IN SUNSHINE VILLAGE

Mad Trapper's Saloon
Pub grub in an ever-popular 1920s-era log cabin that is open year-round. **$$**

Creekside Bar & Grill
Winter-only hub for breakfast waffles and lunchtime poutine located in the gondola base station. **$$**

Eagle's Nest
The mountain's only fine-dining restaurant offers ski-in coq au vin and rack of lamb. **$$$**

The runs are spread over three mountains: Standish (the easiest), Lookout (intermediate) and Goat's Eye (the most challenging). The latter is accessed from the midpoint gondola station and some of its runs descend below the tree line. This is where to head in the mornings for shorter lines.

Not surprisingly, Sunshine's altitude can usher in occasional cold spells exasperated by the wind. To counter them, wrap up warm and earmark a ride on Canada's only heated chairlift – the Teepee Town TX – introduced in 2015.

Sunshine is the only ski area in the park with its own mountainside accommodations in the shape of the ski-in **Sunshine Mountain Lodge**. A good half-dozen eating joints surround it near the base.

Hiking Healy Pass & Simpson Pass

CLIMBING TO THE CONTINENTAL DIVIDE

For something more challenging than Sunshine Meadows, the 18.4km (11.4-mile) **Healy Pass and Simpson Pass** day hike traverses the lofty passes and lush meadows on the Alberta–British Columbia border. It's ideally undertaken from July onward, when the meadows are in flower and the weather's blissfully warm.

The trailhead is in the Sunshine Village parking lot, near the gondola base station, and ascends steadily along Healy Valley, canopied by spruce and fir trees. Look out for red squirrels, woodpeckers and chickadees in the trees. After the **Healy Creek Campground**, the forest falls away and the trail eases into a more gradual climb as it enters Healy Meadows by a gurgling stream. Wildflowers carpet the ground throughout July and August. Pass the junction for **Simpson Pass Trail** on the left and press on to **Healy Pass**. Standing at 2330m (7644ft) atop the escarpment of Monarch Ramparts, only 1km (0.6 miles) from the Great Divide, you'll be treated to some of the region's most dramatic sights, including the witch's-hat peak of Mt Assiniboine, glassy Egypt Lake, and the aptly named Massive Range. Grizzly and black bears aren't uncommon in the open meadows around the pass.

Descend the way you came back to the Healy Meadows junction and take the trail to Simpson Pass at 2135m (7004ft), a narrow meadow furnished with a couple of red bollards that mark the border between Alberta and British Columbia.

The path re-enters forest and traverses beneath a low escarpment before climbing to Wawa Ridge and the dramatic **Monarch Viewpoint** at the edge of Sunshine Meadows. From here it's a 1.6km (1-mile) descent to Sunshine Village and the gondola top station.

A O WHEELER: MOUNTAIN MAN

Between 1913 and 1925, Irish-born surveyor, Arthur O Wheeler (1860–1945) worked as a commissioner for the boundary survey mandated with mapping 970km (606 miles) of the British Columbia–Alberta border along the Continental Divide.

The Irishman was responsible for naming many of the peaks that guard the provincial boundary (or *renaming* them, as most already had long-established Indigenous names). He had a particular penchant for WWI generals – Joffre and Petain both feature – but, also, had the boldness to name a mountain after himself.

The 3336m (10,945ft) Mt Wheeler in Glacier National Park was first climbed by Wheeler and his Swiss guide in 1902. Wheeler's passion for climbing was deep-rooted and he was key in helping found the Alpine Club of Canada, becoming its first president in 1906.

GETTING AROUND

The base station for the Sunshine gondola is 18km (11.2 miles) from Banff Town along Sunshine Rd, which branches south off the Trans-Canada Hwy.

There's a free shuttle (banffsunshine meadows.com) from Banff Town to the base of the gondola that runs year-round, except for a few weeks in each shoulder season.

Sunshine Meadows Hike

Come July, the once-busy ski runs above Sunshine Village unveil a wilder, prettier face – a high-alpine heaven of blue-green lakes and jubilant flower meadows that feed energy back into the most exhausted of legs.

1 Mt Standish

Take the gondola to Sunshine Village and then the express chairlift to the top of Mt Standish on the cusp of the meadowlands on the Continental Divide. This is one of Banff Sunshine's three ski mountains and, at 2400m (7940ft), it's the highest lift in the park open to summer visitors.

The Hike: A short loop trail pitches 300m (984ft) south across open terrain into British Columbia and the wooden Standish Viewing Deck.

2 Standish Viewing Deck

The path deposits you at a rectangular platform divulging an extravagant panorama over the rooftop of the Rockies. Behold, three alpine lakes surrounded by clusters of diminutive larches and backed by steep, craggy peaks. You're now standing in Assiniboine Provincial Park, not Banff, but the views are just as epic.

The Hike: From the viewpoint, take the trail down to Rock Isle Lake.

MINH YUNG KIM/SHUTTERSTOCK ©

Sunshine Meadows

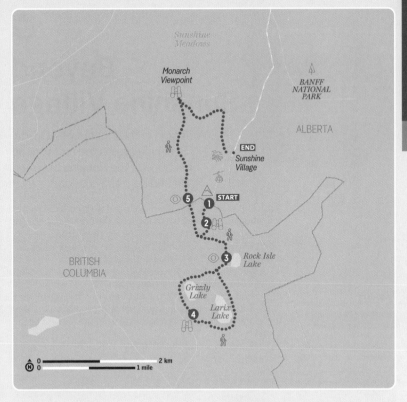

3 Rock Isle Lake

So called for the distinctive wooded islet that juts out from the middle of the water, this iconic lake has its own lookout with views of Standish Ridge, Quartz Hill and a distant glimpse of the Matterhorn-like pinnacle of Mt Assiniboine.

When the gondola and chairlifts close in September, you can still hike up to the lake via the Citadel Pass trail. It's one of the best places in Banff to see golden larch trees in the fall.

The Hike: From the lake, a path winds through larch trees and past pebble-filled streams to a junction with the 3.6km (2.2-mile) Grizzly and Laryx Lakes Loop.

4 Simpson Viewpoint

The loop is best tackled counterclockwise incorporating both lakes and the Simpson Viewpoint, named after George Simpson, governor of the Hudson's Bay Company, who made his first foray across this landscape in 1841.

The Hike: On completion of the loop, retrace your steps to the Rock Isle junction before branching northwest on the Twin Cairns to Monarch Lookout trail.

5 Twin Cairns Meadow

The meadows of Twin Cairns are replete with hardy wildflowers, including white Western anemones, yellow glacier lilies and purple moss campion. Beautiful as they appear, a beast lurks within in the form of ferocious bugs. Bring repellent!

Cross back into Alberta and plot your return via the Monarch Viewpoint, from where you can get an eyeful of the eponymous cleaver-shaped mountain. From here, the winding Meadow Park trail nosedives for 1.6km (1 mile) through forest to Sunshine Village, where you can catch the gondola back to the base.

Shadow Lake

Egypt Lake   Sunshine Village

Scarab Lake

Mummy Lake

Mt Assiniboine Provincial Park   Cerulean Lake

Lake Magog

Beyond Sunshine Village

Welcome to the Continental Divide. Sunshine sits on the metaphoric backbone of the Rockies between Banff and Kootenay national parks.

Beauty knows no borders. The fan-shaped wedge of backcountry that abuts Banff Sunshine to the west is where long-distance hikers go to lose themselves for days, or even weeks.

Beyond Healy Pass, the Egypt Lake area acts as a base for forays around and up to the Continental Divide.

Further south from Sunshine Village you'll quickly enter British Columbia and the remote confines of Assiniboine Provincial Park. Off-the-grid and bereft of roads, this is a taste of Banff pre-tourism where the only people you're likely to meet are backpackers on foot exploring the region like the pioneers of yore.

You'll need plenty of time to unlock this unbounded region and an aptitude for backcountry camping.

TOP TIP

Assiniboine Provincial Park has one mega-popular lodge and limited camping. Book well ahead at bcparks. ca/mount-assiniboine-park.

JAROMIR VANEK/SHUTTERSTOCK ©

Mt Assiniboine (p94)

Egypt Lake

Three Days Around Egypt Lake

BANFF'S ESSENTIAL BACKPACKING TRIP

Who knows what Alberta–British Columbia Boundary Commission surveyor Arthur O Wheeler had in mind when he started naming natural features around the Continental Divide between Banff and Kootenay after legends from ancient Egypt. But, while the lakes, mountains and meadows look nothing like the sphinxes, pharaohs and scarabs of Wheeler's imagination, they do exude a kind of prehistoric magnificence.

The three-day Egypt Lake hike is one of Banff's wilderness classics. Here, flush against the border with British Columbia, lies an irresistible network of high-altitude trails, supplemented by the park's largest backcountry campground (15 sites) and a rustic 'shelter' with six bunks.

Most people start at the base of the Sunshine gondola and hike up to the cusp of the Continental Divide at Healy Pass. Beyond, lie the high-mountain tarns that surround **Egypt Lake** and, if your timing's right, an impressionistic array of summer wildflowers.

Encircled by scattered forest and the craning Pharaoh Peaks, Egypt Lake is one of the most resplendent high-altitude lakes in the park. From its mega-popular campground, a couple of side trips beckon to **Scarab Lake** and **Mummy Lake**.

Beyond Egypt Lake, most long-distance hikers ascend Whistling Pass, named (more logically) for its resident hooting marmots, and continue for another 9km (5.6 miles) paralleling the Continental Divide to **Shadow Lake**, where they spend a second night at a secluded campground or the relatively deluxe Shadow Lake backcountry lodge.

SHADOW LAKE LODGE

One of two back-country lodges in Banff, Shadow Lake Lodge (shadowlake lodge.com) is 14km (8.8 miles) from the nearest road and usually reached on foot utilizing one of two trails: Redearth Creek that starts on Hwy 1 and the tougher but more striking Twin Lakes trail that branches off Hwy 93.

The lodge's ante-cedents lie in 1929 when it was founded as a Canadian Pacific Railway rest stop. Now overseen by the Alpine Club of Canada, the original cabin survives but has been joined by a dozen others fringing a pretty meadow a short walk from idyllic Shadow Lake.

The relatively deluxe cabins are spacious and private, and come with propane heating, solar-powered light-ing, and access to hot-water showers. Gourmet meals are included in the price.

 WHERE TO ENJOY LAKESIDE TRANQUILITY BEYOND SUNSHINE VILLAGE ——

Scarab Lake	Cerulean Lake	Shadow Lake
The quieter sibling of Egypt Lake is a steep climb to a high mountain heaven and a very bracing swim (if you dare).	Quiet, clear and secluded lake that lives up to its name in the tranquil folds of Mt Assiniboine Provincial Park.	Relax in a red national park Adirondack chair and admire the reflection of Mt Ball in the water.

From Shadow Lake, there are two options to return to civilization: northeast along the relatively straightforward Redearth Creek trail (13km/8.1 miles), or north over Gibbon Pass and via Twin Lakes to the Vista Lake trailhead on Hwy 93 (14km/8.8 miles).

A Foray into British Columbia

WILDERNESS WITH A CAPITAL 'W'

Sandwiched between Kootenay and Banff national parks, 39-sq-km (15-sq-mile) **Mt Assiniboine Provincial Park** was inaugurated in 1922 and later incorporated into the wider Rockies' Unesco World Heritage Site. Sitting wholly in British Columbia, it's dominated by the 3618m (11,870ft) pointed peak of Mt Assiniboine, often referred to as the Rocky Mountains' Matterhorn due to its colossal pyramidal shape.

Unlike its neighbor, Banff, Assiniboine is 100% wilderness. There are no roads in this neck of the woods. Hiking is the primary modus operandi and there is no shortage of trails. The park is also revered by experienced mountaineers. The tricky ascent of Mt Assiniboine is considered the holy grail for aspiring rock climbers.

Most of the terrain is sub- or high-alpine consisting of broad meadows, small lakes, rocky scree slopes, larch forests and scatterings of diminutive trees such as Engelmann spruce, lodgepole pine and scrubby willows. Fauna-wise, there's a very good chance of seeing grizzly bears (hopefully from a distance), along with mountain goats, elk and wolves.

The park's main hub is **Lake Magog** (pictured), which is reachable on a 27km (16.7-mile) trek from Sunshine Meadows or by helicopter from Canmore. Here you will find camping, several historic huts and the peerless Mt Assiniboine Lodge, North America's oldest backcountry ski lodge, built in 1928.

The 30-person accommodations offers all-inclusive packages with the added option of helicopter transportation. Since it's the only comfortable accommodations for miles around, you'll need to book months in advance.

Most visitors linger in the park for several days and sally forth on short hikes to hidden Edens nearby. Wonder Pass, Nub Peak and Sunburst Lake all feature.

BEST PLACES TO STAY IN MT ASSINIBOINE

Mt Assiniboine Lodge
Historic backcountry lodge with the option to fly in on a helicopter. Rates include food, accommodations and guiding services.

Magog Lake Camping
The park's largest campground is perched on a bench above the lake and has space for 40 tents, plus outhouses and a cooking shelter. If it's full, there are three smaller campgrounds in the park.

Naiset Cabins
Five wooden huts near Magog Lake, the oldest dating from 1925, with dorm facilities and communal cooking.

PUTTSK/SHUTTERSTOCK ©

GETTING AROUND

Mt Assiniboine Provincial Park is roadless. The most popular way in is on foot from Banff's Sunshine Meadows.

Other entry points are Kootenay National Park (via the Simpson River trail) or from the Bryant Creek trailhead in Kananaskis Country.

For considerably more money, you can book a helicopter ride from heli-pads in Canmore or Mt Shark in Kananaskis Country.

BOW VALLEY PARKWAY

Bow Valley
Parkway

While most Banff visitors rush along the Trans-Canada Hwy (Hwy 1) in the slipstream of the car in front, savvier souls divert serendipitously onto quieter Hwy 1A, also known as the Bow Valley Parkway, which parallels Hwy 1 for 51km (31.6 miles) between Banff Town and Lake Louise. This was the original road through the park, first opened in 1921 but replaced by the zippier Trans-Canada four decades later.

Constructed in the days before SUVs and high-velocity cars, the road was designed for slow meandering rather than speed. Despite the ubiquitous trees, there are regular viewpoints where drivers and cyclists can hit the brakes and gaze out across the Bow Valley and its forest-meets-mountain landscapes. This is a prime place to spot wildlife, especially elk, bighorn sheep and even the occasional moose. The obligatory stop is Johnston Canyon and its thunderous cascades, but there are plenty of other meadows, monuments and pull-overs to ponder.

TOP TIP

The parkway's regular speed limit is 60km/h (37mph), dropping down to 30km/h (19mph) at certain sections to avoid wildlife collisions. Consider tackling the road on a bike – traffic is light, the verges are wide and the terrain is mostly flat. Many outlets in Banff rent bicycles.

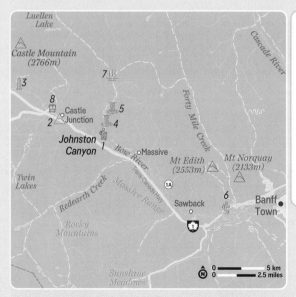

HIGHLIGHTS
1. Johnston Canyon

SIGHTS
2. Castle Mountain
3. Castle Mountain Internment Camp
4. Johnston Canyon Lower Falls
5. Johnston Canyon Upper Falls

ACTIVITIES & TOURS
6. Cory Pass Loop
7. Inkpots

TRANSPORT
8. Castle Junction

Bow Valley Parkway

Smooth, wide, mostly flat and equipped with a plethora of interesting excuses to pull over and explore, the Bow Valley Parkway might have been designed with road cycling in mind. No small wonder that, in a park with limited single-track opportunities, it's become one of the Rockies' great road rides.

1 Backswamp

One of the road's first bona fide pull-overs is Backswamp, on the left-hand side as you head north, which offers sweeping views over river and marshlands with opportunities to spot wildlife including bighorn sheep that stalk the roadside hereabouts. Detailed park information boards explain the local geography and wildlife.

The Ride: The road remains relatively flat as you head northwest past the Muleshoe picnic area toward Sawback.

2 Sawback

The open slopes around Sawback testify to a prescribed burn in the area in 1993 carried out by park authorities in order to rejuvenate the forest ecosystem. The small recuperating trees make it an ideal place for wildlife spotting.

The area was traditionally populated with lodgepole pines, but fire management has attempted to diversify the species and create grassy meadows in which flowers and wildlife can prosper.

BGSMITH/SHUTTERSTOCK ©

Castle Mountain

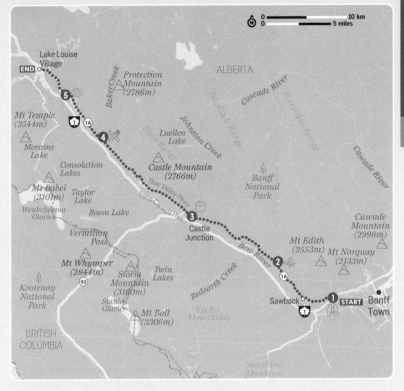

The Ride: The parkway splits in two soon after Sawback, reconnecting a few kilometers later. This section is punctuated by a couple of gentle hills. A small roundabout at the 17km (10.6 mile) mark guards the entrance to Johnston Canyon, the road's biggest lure.

3 Castle Mountain

The parkway's approximate halfway point is marked by Castle Junction, where you'll find an HI hostel, shop, chalet resort, several trailheads and a memorial to the erstwhile WWI Castle Mountain Internment Camp (p99) all within a kilometer (0.6-mile) radius. Be sure to stop at the Castle Cliff viewpoint to admire the mountain's lofty buttresses.

The Ride: Keep pedaling northwest, past the Castle Lookout trailhead and the Protection Mountain campground.

4 Baker Creek

The Baker Creek Mountain Resort is a deluxe cabin complex that's been around since the late 1940s. More recently, it's become a favored rest stop for parkway cyclists heading north with 37km (23 miles) under their belts, courtesy of its grab-and-go Creekside Cafe.

The Ride: Continue pedaling northwest alongside the river and railway.

5 Morant's Curve

Around 5km shy of Lake Louise, stop to take in the sweep of Morant's Curve where road, railway and river bend in unison against a backdrop of mountains. The site is named for the late Nicholas Morant, an esteemed Canadian Pacific Railway photographer whose images have graced magazines, promotional material and Canadian dollar bills. It's a short 15-minute ride from here to the parkway's terminus at Lake Louise. Total distance: 51km (32 miles).

MT EISENHOWER?

In 1946, swept up in the euphoria that followed victory in WWII, the Canadian prime minister Mackenzie-King decided to arbitrarily rename Castle Mountain in Banff Mt Eisenhower, after the distinguished US general.

The renaming came the day before Eisenhower was due to visit Canada on a whistle-stop tour and, while it might have helped curry favor in the corridors of power, it didn't please many ordinary Canadians who objected to one of their most illustrious peaks being named after a foreigner, heroic or not.

A vociferous campaign to reverse the decision ensued, but it wasn't until 1979 that prime minister Joe Clark yielded, changing the name back to Castle Mountain while electing, in a savvy act of diplomacy, to call its tallest eastern turret Eisenhower Peak.

MELISSAMN/SHUTTERSTOCK ©

Johnston Canyon

The Catwalks of Johnston Canyon

NARROW GORGE AND THUNDEROUS WATERFALLS

With the obvious exception of Lake Louise, nowhere else in Banff has as many admirers as **Johnston Canyon**. The reason? A short, easy hike to a couple of waterfalls that stuffs a lot of spectacular geology into a small area. Hidden from the road, the deep and narrow gorge is characterized by its dramatic limestone cliffs and two crashing cascades. To help negotiate it, a sturdy catwalk has been attached to the canyon wall offering a unique vertiginous perspective. Shrouded in foliage, the lofty cliffs are covered with mosses, lichen and ferns and, from late June to September, black swifts swoop to and from their moss-lined nests in the steep walls searching for flying insects.

There are three hiking options of varying lengths here with the crowds diminishing the further you penetrate. The 1.2km (0.7-mile) path to the **Lower Falls** is mostly asphalt and partly accessible to wheelchairs/strollers. For the last section, you'll need to descend some steps to get a view of the roaring cascade from inside a small cave. The trail heads further upstream

 WHERE TO EAT & DRINK ON THE BOW VALLEY PARKWAY ⸺

Creekside Cafe	**Blackswift Bistro**	**Market Cafe**
Woodsy emporium for Calgary-roasted coffee (Devil's Head) and Banff-distilled gin at Baker Creek Resort. $$	Serving the burger and fish-and-chips needs of the hungry hikers that amass at Johnston Canyon. $$	The casual cafe at Johnston Canyon is better suited to day hikers with its diner stools and perky coffee. $

– 2.5km (1.6 miles) from the start – to a taller **Upper Falls** cascade that's particularly beguiling in the spring when it cuts shapely holes in the ice.

If your best hiking years aren't yet behind you, it's worth pressing on a further 3.2km (2 miles) beyond the Upper Falls through coniferous forest to the **Inkpots**, a collection of half a dozen ultra-clear mineral pools with various inky hues that inhabit a wide meadow that contrasts sharply with the canyon below.

Johnston Canyon is open (and popular) year-round. Bring ice cleats if visiting in the winter.

Cory Pass Extreme Hike

A TEST OF FITNESS AND NERVE

Scree slopes, rock scrambling, boulder-hopping, spectacular traverses, springy forest paths, bear sightings and avalanche chutes – did we miss anything?

It might only be a mere 8km (5 miles) from Banff townsite, but this challenging hike amid some of the Rockies' most Gothic peaks is, arguably, the toughest in the national park. If it was a ski run, it would be graded a double black diamond.

The exhilarating 13km (8-mile) **Cory Pass Loop** begins as it means to go on, packing most of its 920m (3018ft) ascent into the first few kilometers. Soon after departing from the start point at the Fireside picnic area at the beginning of the Bow Valley Parkway, you'll find yourself toiling mercilessly uphill on a super-steep non-zigzagging path to a false summit where you can briefly catch your breath before the slog continues.

The next obstacle involves a steep down climb off a 15m (50ft) rock face, followed by a long traverse on a path that becomes increasingly narrow and exposed as it nears Cory Pass at 2350m (7710ft). Take a breather here (you've earned it!) and check you've still got enough nerve and energy left for the second act.

From Cory, the path drops into a barren moonscape of precipitous cliffs and rocky pinnacles, descending on loose scree that morphs into rock fall and, finally, larger boulders. A short ascent up a muddy slope brings you back into a dwarf forest bisected by several avalanche chutes. Make plenty of noise here – this is prime bear country. As the trees thicken, the route eases up at last, descending on ever-more-bouncy forest paths until you arrive exhausted and slightly spooked back at the start.

INTERNMENT CAMPS

Part of a regrettable chapter in Banff's history, the Castle Mountain Internment Camp was established in WWI when the Canadian government, invoking the 1914 War Measures Act, rounded up over 8000 so-called 'enemy aliens' and sent them to internment camps where they were forced to work in slave-labor conditions on national park building projects.

The prisoners were civilians whose only 'crime' was their ethnic background (mostly Austro-Hungarians allied with the Axis powers). Ironically, many of them had been enticed to immigrate to Canada only years before by a freedom-extolling government desperate for hardworking settlers.

A memorial entitled 'Why?' was installed next to the Bow Valley Parkway at the site of the original camp in 1995.

GETTING AROUND

The parkway branches off the Trans-Canada Hwy 8km (5 miles) west of Banff and tracks all the way to Lake Louise. The section between Banff and Johnston Canyon is closed to cars in May, June and September.

Roam Transit bus 9 runs between Johnston Canyon and Banff Town several times a day (weekends only October to May). The 8S summer bus runs along the parkway between Banff and Lake Louise, stopping at Johnston Canyon, Castle Junction and Beaver Creek.

Beyond Bow Valley Parkway

The parkway abuts the Continental Divide in the west, beyond which lies Kootenay National Park, a kind of mini Banff without the townsite.

From the intersection of Hwy 93 and the Trans-Canada Hwy at Castle Junction, it's only 10km (6.3 miles) to Vermilion Pass and the gateway to Kootenay. The road slowly crescendos with Storm Mountain drawing your gaze south and Mt Whymper tugging it north.

There are two good excuses to pull over. The Storm Mountain Lodge was conceived by the Canadian Pacific Railway in 1922 as one in a chain of eight bungalow camps, predating the highway by a year. The original log buildings remain in place, offering backwoodsy ambience in a drive-in front-country setting.

Just before you reach Vermilion Pass, the Boom Lake trail peels off to the north: an easy hike with satisfying mountain vistas.

TOP TIP

Unfortunately, Kootenay has no public transportation. The car-less can try tackling it as part of an adventurous multiday road-biking trip from Banff.

LEFT: AUTUMN SKY PHOTOGRAPHY/SHUTTERSTOCK © RIGHT: DAVEYNIN/FLICKR/CC BY-SA 2.0 ©

Kootenay National Park

Kootenay's Roadside Hikes

SHORT LEG-STRETCHING TRAILS

One-fifth the size of Banff, **Kootenay National Park** is a relatively small uncommercialized national park bereft of townsites, large lakes or downhill ski areas. It's feted mainly for its hot springs and climatic extremes, and is the only national park in Canada to harbor both glaciers and cacti.

Named for the Ktunaxa (Kutenai) people on whose traditional lands it stands, the park closely hugs Hwy 93, which meanders through a series of river valleys between Vermilion Pass and Radium Hot Springs. Various roadside pull-overs allow quick access to most of the main sights.

The short Fireweed trails on the Continental Divide loop through tracts of mixed forest at the north end of Hwy 93 in an area that's been left to naturally recover after a 1968 fire. Signboards explain the local ecology. Some 7km (4.3 miles) to the southwest, the Marble Canyon trail follows a milky blue river along the rim of a limestone gorge. Nearby is the easy 2km (1.2-mile) round-trip Paint Pots trail leading to muddy rust-red ocher pools that were important to Indigenous Peoples.

A Dip in Radium Hot Springs

POOLS AND A BATHHOUSE

The busiest and most commercialized attraction in Kootenay sits just inside the park's western entrance at the jaws of the soaring Sinclair Canyon. Radium Hot Springs (pictured) is a spa complex like Upper Hot Springs in Banff and Miette in Jasper that utilizes natural mineral water coming out of the ground at 44°C (111°F). The water is cooled to 39°C (102°F) and 29°C (84°F) before entering two different pools. Unlike its Rocky Mountain counterparts, Radium's water is odorless. You can walk to the bathhouse complex from the town of Radium Hot Springs along the 2.8km (1.7-mile) Juniper Trail.

BEST DAY HIKES IN KOOTENAY

Simpson River
Cross a river bridge beside Hwy 93 and proceed through one of Kootenay's fire-ravaged landscapes following a winding valley trail with access to Mt Assiniboine Provincial Park.

Stanley Glacier
With a trailhead only 15km (9.3 miles) west of Banff's Castle Junction, this intermediate 11km (6.8-mile) round-trip hike weaves through scattered forest and stony scree. It can be done solo or as part of a guided Burgess Shale hike.

Floe Lake
One of Kootenay's most popular hikes has a long, slow approach followed by a short, steep grind to dreamy Floe Lake, a worthwhile reward for your uphill endeavors.

GETTING AROUND

There is currently no public transportation in Kootenay National Park. Car rental is available in Banff and Lake Louise.

The park's eastern entrance is on Hwy 93, 41km (25.4 miles) northwest of Banff Town. Hwy 93 runs for 92km (57 miles) through the park, its only major road.

LAKE LOUISE

Lake Louise

There ought to be a rule in life that no one should depart this mortal coil without first visiting Lake Louise. It's hard to put into words exactly why. Just stand on the famous lakeshore at sunrise and soak up the spectacle around you. An icy amphitheater of steep-sided mountains, a deluxe lakeside hotel, two half-hidden alpine teahouses that serve hot beverages and crumbly scones, and the water in creeks that appears so clear you could almost solidify it and turn it into glass.

The village of Lake Louise is little more than a ho-hum shopping mall and a few hotels that nestles beside the Trans-Canada Hwy. The emerald-hued lake, 5km (3.1 miles) away, is the object of most people's longing. Outlying sights include the hikeable Larch Valley (at its best in autumn), gorgeous Moraine Lake and an extensive downhill ski area that becomes an important wildlife corridor in the summer.

TOP TIP

Parking is limited lakeside at Lake Louise. A better alternative is to walk up from the village to the lake on the pretty Louise Creek Trail. This 3.5km (2.2-mile) route roughly parallels the main road from Lake Louise village, reaching the lakeshore in less than an hour.

YUNSUN_KIM/SHUTTERSTOCK ©

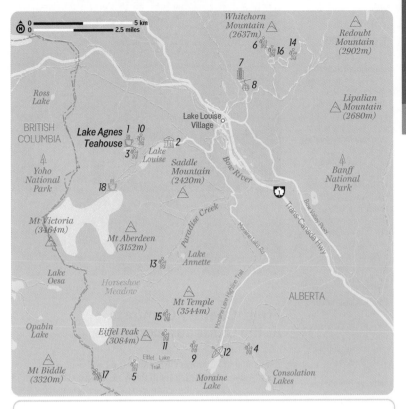

HIGHLIGHTS

1 Lake Agnes Teahouse

SIGHTS

2 Fairmont Chateau Lake Louise

ACTIVITIES, COURSES & TOURS

3 Big Beehive
4 Consolation Lakes Trail
5 Eiffel Lake
6 Kicking Horse Pass Viewpoint
7 Lake Louise Ski Resort
8 Lake Louise Summer Gondola

9 Larch Valley
10 Little Beehive
11 Minnestimma Lakes
12 Moraine Lake
13 Paradise Valley
14 Ptarmigan Valley Viewpoint
15 Sentinel Pass
16 Trail of the Great Bear
17 Wenkchemna Pass

DRINKING

18 Plain of Six Glaciers Teahouse

 WHERE TO STAY IN LAKE LOUISE

Chateau Lake Louise
The Versailles of Canadian hotels offers five-star accommodations in a six-star setting beside the lake. $$$

Moraine Lake Lodge
Mountain-inspired luxury with big picture windows that let in one of the world's greatest views. $$$

Post Hotel
A stately hotel with old-world charm and tranquil shaded gardens near the center of the village. $$

THE BEEHIVES

After you've re-caffeinated at the Lake Agnes Teahouse, you can detour to the top of the Little Beehive (105m/344ft elevation gain) before semi-circumnavigating the lake on your way to its taller sibling, the Big Beehive (135m/442ft elevation gain), which you'll reach after 1.6km (1 mile) of punishing switchbacks, every one of them worth it.

The lofty vantage point, equipped with an old weather shelter built by the Canadian Pacific Railway in 1916, offers an airplane-like view of Lake Louise, the Chateau and the surrounding valleys and mountains.

Descend on the same path, admiring the protruding nodule of Devil's Thumb and the reflective waters of Lake Agnes, before retracing your steps to the teahouse – you've earned a second cup.

LEONARD ZHUKOVSKY/SHUTTERSTOCK ©

Fairmont Chateau Lake Louise

Front-Country Comforts at the Chateau Lake Louise

ROOM WITH A VIEW

The opulent **Fairmont Chateau Lake Louise** dominates the eastern shore of Lake Louise in the same way that the glistening Victoria glacier dominates the west. Originally constructed in the 1890s but altered radically in 1924 after a serious fire, the hotel is a railway-era twin of the Fairmont Banff Springs (p63), whose Renaissance Revival style it closely mimics. A newer wing was added in 2004.

While the imposing multistory facade might not blend harmoniously with its natural surroundings, the soaring turrets and manicured gardens certainly add a dash of architectural panache to the Rocky Mountain landscape. Forks regularly drop in to the hotel's deluxe dining room as guests spy their first glimpse of the lake's sparkling turquoise water through the arched windows.

Like the Banff Springs, the accommodations was designed as a railway hotel to lure wealthy tourists to the area in the late

 WHERE TO EAT IN LAKE LOUISE

Bill Peyto's Cafe
The best joint in the village for big breakfasts, and economic burger and pasta dinners. $

The Station Restaurant
Maple-glazed salmon and braised bison ribs are given extra panache in Lake Louise's 1910 railway station. $$$

Fairview Dining Room
Expensive afternoon tea in the Chateau Lake Louise with Devonshire-style cream and priceless views. $$$

19th century. The plan triumphantly succeeded. In its first year (1890), the Chateau listed a mere 50 guests, but by 1912 it was welcoming 50,000. Film stars and royals were regulars by the interwar years and, in the 1970s, the hotel began opening year-round to service the growing number of skiers.

The oldest existing part of the hotel is the Painter wing, which dates from 1913 and survived the 1924 fire because it was made of concrete. The newest part is the Mt Temple wing, which curls away from the lake and displays an interesting collection of historical murals. The hotel's public areas – spa, dining rooms, lobby and shops – are lavishly grandiose and decorated with sumptuous chandeliers, thick patterned carpets and stained-glass windows.

Teahouse Hikes

TEA AND SCONES AT 2100M (6890FT)

When you've digested the beauty of Lake Louise's Chateau and the luminosity of the water, there are a couple of other surprises waiting. Hidden away in the amphitheater of mountains that surround Lake Louise are two backcountry teahouses, inaccessible by road, that serve up the kind of light, flaky scones (with strawberry jam!) normally confined to dainty tearooms in England.

The teahouses share a lot in common. Both were built using local materials by the Canadian Pacific Railway in the early 1900s and both serve delicious homemade food despite being unconnected to the electricity grid.

Hikers have been calling in at the **Lake Agnes Teahouse** since 1901, although the current building's a replica of the original. It started serving tea in 1905 and snacks soon after. The soup, sandwiches on homemade bread, and apple crumble are as spectacular as the scenery (which is drop-dead gorgeous). The scones go under the Americanized banner of 'tea biscuits.' Most of the staff are university students who carry up supplies daily; something you can ruminate on as you begin your own 3.5km (2.2-mile) ascent from the lakeside.

The **Plain of Six Glaciers Teahouse** is of newer vintage and involves a slightly longer 5.5km (3.4-mile) hike. Constructed in 1927 as a way station for Swiss mountaineering guides leading clients up to the summit of Mt Victoria, the twin-level stone chalet sits nestled in a quiet glade at 2100m (6890ft) and dispatches almost identical dishes to Lake Agnes to a steady stream of sugar-depleted hikers.

And the winner of this closely fought Lake Louise tearoom contest? Lake Agnes by a hair!

RESTRICTIONS WHEN HIKING AROUND LAKE LOUISE

The Lake Louise area is one of three key grizzly-bear habitats in Banff National Park, and supports a number of grizzly sows and their cubs. To avoid bear encounters, park authorities often impose group access restrictions in summer on several trails around Lake Louise, including the Consolation Lakes Trail, Larch Valley, Sentinel Pass, Paradise Valley and Wenkchemna Pass.

Under the rules, hikers are required to travel in tight groups of at least four people, and take the usual precautions to avoid bear encounters (make noise on the trail, carry bear spray etc).

The timetable varies every year according to bear activity and the berry season, but usually begins around mid-July and lasts until early September. Restrictions are clearly posted in park offices and at trailheads.

 WHERE TO GO FOR COFFEE & A SNACK IN LAKE LOUISE

Laggan's Mountain Bakery & Deli
Combine a steaming dark roast with a flaky pastry at this quick-service, busy deli.

Trailhead Cafe
Lake Louise's most popular specialty coffee shop backs up its java with cinnamon buns, pancakes and long queues.

The Guide's Pantry
The best grab-and-go in the Chateau Lake Louise does superb croissants, coffee and overnight oats.

BEST WHITEHORN MOUNTAIN HIKES

Kicking Horse Pass Viewpoint
Follow an unpaved service road along a ski run and then cut through larch and spruce trees to a 2185m (7169ft) viewpoint over the Bow Valley and Kicking Horse Pass.

Trail of the Great Bear
This hike allows group access to the protected wildlife corridor under the auspices of a qualified guide.

Ptarmigan Valley Viewpoint
The mountain's longest hike starts on the Pika Trail and finishes at a viewpoint that reveals views of the Skoki Valley.

Grandstand Views at Alberta's Largest Ski Area

CANADA'S THIRD-LARGEST SKI RESORT

The biggest of Banff's three ski areas and the third largest in Canada, Lake Louise's 17 sq km (6.5 sq miles) of skiable terrain grafted onto the slopes of Whitehorn Mountain ought to satisfy every standard and taste with 145 individual runs, the longest measuring a leg-numbing 8km (5 miles). But it's the views that steal the show. Lest we forget, this is Lake Louise, a guaranteed finalist in every Canadian beauty contest. Behold those snowcapped vistas!

While **Lake Louise Ski Resort** (skilouise.com) rarely lacks powder, its average snowfall is only around half that of Sunshine Village, meaning snow machines are often used to supplement the natural snowpack.

The main day lodge resembles a giant deluxe log cabin and is well equipped with ski schools and food outlets but offers no on-mountain accommodations. **Lake Louise Village**, 4km away, is the nearest hub and decidedly sleepy in the après-ski stakes.

Bear-Viewing on the Lake Louise Summer Gondola

WHERE GRIZZLIES ROAM

Whitehorn Mountain does a volte-face in the spring, switching from ski resort to summer activity center with a big focus on wildlife. The **Lake Louise Summer Gondola** still runs, with its cabins grafted onto the Glacier Express chairlift where they alternate with alfresco quad-chairs.

Lower Whitehorn, where skiers zigzag dexterously in winter, becomes a wildlife corridor that's closed to visitors. Aspiring hikers must ascend the mountain on the gondola/chairlift to a viewpoint halfway up where there's a restaurant, wildlife interpretive center and small trail network. Looking down as you're pulled heavenward, it's not unusual to see grizzly bears roaming on the grassy slopes below.

The gondola top station inhabits an enclosed area protected by an electric fence. Due to the presence of bears, guided hikes are popular and spotlight the region's fearsome fauna. Alternatively, you can strike out alone. The longest trail is 3.4km (2.1 miles) return.

GONDOLAS TO SUNSHINE

Banff Sunshine's gondola (p88) also does summer duty, ferrying hikers to the subalpine nirvana of Sunshine Village where they can catch the Standish chairlift to the Continental Divide.

WHERE TO FIND THE BEST LAKE LOUISE VIEWPOINTS

Big Beehive
Follow the grueling switchbacks above Lake Agnes to see the full expanse of Lake Louise emit its sapphire sheen.

Fairview
Short uphill grind through forest from the lakeshore to a tree-framed vista of Lake Louise and the Chateau.

Whitehorn Mountain
Take the summer gondola above a protected wildlife corridor to the Whitehorn Bistro and Michelin-star views.

Grizzly bear

Consolation Lakes Hike

EASY LAKE-TO-LAKE TRAIL

From one beautiful but decidedly crowded lakeshore (Moraine) to another almost as beautiful but notably less crowded (Consolation), the **Consolation Lakes Trail** is, arguably, the region's most instantly satisfying hike – easy, relatively short at 6km (3.7 miles) out and back, and logging a modest 65m (213ft) elevation change. After initially skirting the famous rock pile at the north end of **Moraine Lake**, the path crosses a wooden bridge and pitches east through pine forest, climbing gradually alongside Babel Creek. This section of the trail offers great views up the side of Mt Babel and back over the shoreline peaks of Moraine Lake.

For the next 1.6km (1 mile), the path winds alongside the banks of the noisy creek. Beware, some sections get very muddy after snowmelt and heavy rain.

Just before you reach the Consolation Lakes, the trees start to thin out and the path opens serendipitously into a small meadow. The lakes themselves are tucked into the base of a distinctive U-shaped glacial valley dotted with rough boulders, scree and smashed rocks, which can be tricky to negotiate when wet. Take extra care as you cross the rocks toward the shore of the Lower Lake, marveling at the hoary marmots that scurry nonchalantly between them.

SOLVING THE TRAFFIC ISSUE

Lake Louise and Moraine Lake are linked by an undulating 11km (7-mile) road that's only open from June to October due to heavy winter snow.

In the past, this short seasonal window caused Moraine Lake to be inundated with summer visitors, most of whom arrived in private cars. As a result, the local parking lot was often full by 5:30am and Parks Canada was forced to turn an increasing number of people away.

To alleviate the traffic jams and subsequent overcrowding, park authorities decided to close the road to private vehicles in 2023 and lay on shuttle buses instead. Shuttles run from the Park-and-Ride at the Lake Louise ski area May to October. Seats must be reserved online (parks.canada.ca/pn-np/ab/banff/visit/parkbus/louise).

WHERE TO CYCLE IN LAKE LOUISE

Bow River Loop
Family-friendly trail that loops around both sides of Banff's emblematic river starting at Lake Louise train station.

Great Divide
Relatively easy run on the old rough paved road (Hwy 1A) between Lake Louise and Yoho National Park.

Moraine Lake Road
Pleasantly paved but uphill grind between Louise and Moraine lakes with only buses for company.

GOLDEN SEASON

Larches are deciduous conifers found in mountainous areas with cool temperate climates. Although they sport needles like traditional pine trees, they shed their foliage in the autumn when their color changes from broccoli green to golden yellow.

In Banff, this remarkable natural metamorphosis creates a kaleidoscopic juxtaposition of flaxen larches, green conifers and blue sky etched against a moody backdrop of mountains and lakes.

Larch season in the park is only very fleeting usually, starting in mid-September and running for around two to three weeks.

The best places to view the spectacle is Lake Louise's Larch Valley and the ridges and slopes atop Sunshine Meadows and Healy Pass on the Continental Divide.

BRADLEY L GRANT/SHUTTERSTOCK ©

Minnestimma Lake, Larch Valley

The valley is guarded by Panorama Ridge to the east, Mt Bell to the southeast and the sharp four peaks of Mt Quadra at the northern side of the lake. Quadra has a distinctive hanging glacier draped across its upper reaches, and huge chunks of ice occasionally fall off and crash into the lake.

A Day at Moraine Lake

CANADA'S MOST FAMOUS VIEW

Emblazoned on calendars, dish towels, coffee-table books and 20-dollar bills, **Moraine Lake** is an eerily familiar sight even to first-time visitors. To say that the view from its rocky northern shore is cinematic would be an understatement: the water a deep teal, the surrounding forest a dark bottle-green, a rampart of 10 dagger-like peaks – the **Wenkchemna Range** – stacked up behind like a giant medieval fortress. Moraine Lake is often compared to nearby Lake Louise but it's a moot point. Both places are indescribably beautiful, although the former with its smaller lakeside hotel feels less overrun and commercial, despite the thousands of daily admirers who pile in from 7am onward (as of 2023, cars are banned; you must catch a shuttle bus).

This is superb hiking terrain. There are four main trails emanating from the lakeshore, plus a short punt to the top of

 WHERE TO STAY IN LAKE LOUISE

Lake Louise Campground
Wooded 395-site campground, accommodating RVs on one side of the river and tents, and soft-sided vehicles on the other. **$**

Lake Louise Inn
Large, sprawling resort near the village with indoor pool, three restaurants, and a free shuttle to the ski mountain. **$$$**

HI Lake Louise Alpine Centre
This rustic but comfortable lodge-style building with plenty of raw timber and stone is as close as you'll get to 'budget' in Lake Louise. **$**

the 400m (0.2-mile) 'Rockpile' on Moraine's north shore for a view that every single person who comes here wants (and *has*) to see. Two of the hikes are graded 'easy:' a weaving path that tracks the lakeshore for 1.6km (1 mile), and a slightly more adventurous trail to Consolation Lakes.

Larch Valley and **Eiffel Lake** are longer, harder treks. Both offer the option of even tougher add-ons, to **Sentinel Pass** and **Wenkchemna Pass** respectively.

For priceless views from the rippling confines of Moraine Lake itself, you can paddle forth on one of Canada's most expensive canoe rides. One-hour rentals can be procured at the lakeside boathouse. First-come-first-served.

Fall Hiking in Larch Valley

BANFF'S BEST AUTUMNAL HIKE

Banff has many memorable hikes, but there's only one contender for top spot in the fall. The wondrous **Larch Valley** comes into its own when the scent of autumn is in the air and its namesake trees blaze golden yellow.

The broad, well-signposted path into the valley branches off the Moraine Lake trail and travels up a set of switchbacks that gain over 350m (1148ft) in 2.5km (1.6 miles) before leveling out into alpine meadows interspersed with larch forest.

At the first junction, follow the right-hand turn and climb further through the fragrant forest, emerging after about 3.5km (2.2 miles) into the wide-open spaces of Larch Valley proper. The meadows hereabouts are famous for their wildflowers.

A little further on, the path breaks above the tree line and continues to the little **Minnestimma Lakes** at around the 4.5km (2.8-mile) mark. Here you can soak up a unique view of eight of the 10 Wenkchemna Peaks, as well as the white mass of the Fay Glacier.

Most hikers end the walk here, but if the weather's good and you had enough porridge for breakfast, it's possible to continue up and over 2611m (8566ft) **Sentinel Pass**, one of the highest maintained passes in the Canadian Rockies. It's a hard, tiring trail that crosses slippery areas of talus and scree; don't even think about tackling it in snow or heavy rain as the weather can turn suddenly.

From the top of the pass, experienced hikers can make a truly epic circle down into the adjacent **Paradise Valley**.

Larch Valley reaches its golden apex in the second half of September, with the colors usually fading by the second week of October.

SWISS GUIDES

Study the wall displays in the Chateau Lake Louise and you'll see numerous photos of craggy-faced European men dressed in natty cravats, thick jackets and heavy boots. In their hands they brandish coils of rope and ice axes, and between their teeth rests an obligatory pipe. These are the Swiss guides first hired by the Canadian Pacific Railway in 1899 to construct remote mountain huts and safely guide tourists and budding mountaineers through the more dangerous corners of the Rockies.

Adept and highly professional, the guides left a huge legacy in Banff in the early 1900s, igniting a local penchant for Swiss-style architecture and personally embarking upon hundreds of first ascents of lofty Canadian peaks.

Astonishingly, in over 50 years of climbing and mountaineering, Swiss-led expeditions never registered a single fatality.

GETTING AROUND

Roam transit bus 8X Express runs year-round between Banff Town and Lake Louise, stopping in the village and at the lake.

As of 2023, private vehicles are barred from the Moraine Lake area. Parks Canada shuttles run regularly along the Moraine Lake Rd from Lake Louise between June and September.

Beyond Lake Louise

The natural beauty doesn't end at Lake Louise. It stetches tantalizingly west into the mountain ranges of British Columbia.

Just north of Lake Louise, the Trans-Canada Hwy swings west to cross the provincial border between Alberta and British Columbia at Kicking Horse Pass, where John Hector of the Palliser expedition was rudely booted by his steed in 1858. The Ktunaxa (Kootenay) people had used the pass for eons as a seasonal access route to the prairies where they once hunted bison. In the 1880s, the Canadian Pacific Railway chose it over the lower Yellowhead Pass to link British Columbia with the rest of the nation.

On the western side of the pass, it's a steep drop to Field, the launchpad for Yoho National Park, a land of giant waterfalls, tempestuous rivers and rich fossil deposits.

TOP TIP

The Skoki Lodge hike can be turned into a three-day adventure by diverting to Baker Lake and hiking around Fossil Mountain to Merlin Meadows.

Takakkaw Falls

I VIEWFINDER/SHUTTERSTOCK ©

Emerald Lake

Embracing Emerald Lake

YOHO'S FAVORITE BEAUTY SPOT

Looking like Lake Louise's greener twin, serene **Emerald Lake** is **Yoho National Park**'s heavyweight attraction. Ringed by montane forest and silhouetted by impressive mountains, including the much-painted and photographed profile of Mt Burgess to the southeast, it's a gorgeous but often crowded spot – for obvious reasons. Toss a coin and either rent a canoe or hike around the lakeshore on a well-defined 5.2km (3.2-mile) trail. Hemmed in by slender evergreens, the Emerald Lake Lodge sits on a small peninsula on the lake's southwest corner and is accessed by a bridge. It was conceived in the early 1900s but completely rebuilt in the 1980s with throwback artifacts including an 1890s-era bar salvaged from the Yukon. The road to the lake is signposted off Hwy 1 just southwest of the park service-center of **Field**. Arrive early; it gets busy.

A Close-Up View of Takakkaw Falls

ULTIMATE ROCKIES WATERFALL

Yoho might be one of the smaller Rocky Mountain parks, but it counts on a couple of big-hitter attractions, including the second-highest waterfall in Canada, the magnificent **Takakkaw Falls** (Takakkaw rather aptly translates as 'magnificent' in the Cree language). The thundering torrent of water tumbles from its source in the nearby Daly Glacier over a sheer cliff face for a total drop of 373m (1224ft). From the parking lot at the end of Yoho Valley Rd, a short, paved trail leads across a bridge to the base of the falls. Longer tougher treks, incorporating the challenging Iceline Trail, can also be accessed from here. The road is open from late June to early October.

BURGESS SHALE FOSSIL DEPOSIT

Discovered by American paleontologist Charles Walcott in 1909, but not fully investigated until the 1980s, the 508-million-year-old Cambrian-age fossil bed on Mt Stephen and Mt Field is known as the Burgess Shale World Heritage Site.

Herein lie the well-preserved remains of marine creatures thought to be some of the earliest forms of life on earth. The rock is comprised of black shale and contains rarely seen soft-body imprints of over 200 species including the most primitive vertebrate known to science.

You can only get to the fossil beds by two long but rewarding guided hikes led by naturalists from the Burgess Shale Geoscience Foundation (burgess-shale.bc.ca) or Parks Canada (reservations.pc.gc.ca).

Rendezvous at the Yoho Visitor Centre in Field. Reservations are essential.

GETTING AROUND

Rider Express (riderexpress.ca) runs one daily bus between Banff, Lake Louise and Field in Yoho National Park. Field is a 20-minute drive from Lake Louise on the Trans-Canada Hwy.

Skoki Lodge Hike

Skoki Lodge is an important part of Banff's early history. Located 11km (6.8 miles) from the nearest road, it's remote enough to be deemed 'backcountry' but close enough to Lake Louise to be hiked or skied in a day (one way) if you're fleet-footed and start early. Most visitors stay overnight to savor the atmosphere of the 1930s-era lodge and its surrounding scenery. Book well ahead, it's mega popular.

1 Fish Creek
The trailhead for the lodge is signposted off the road to the Lake Louise ski resort. Drive a short way down a side road to a small parking lot.

The Hike: The first wooded section of the route follows the unpaved Temple Fire Rd steeply uphill for 3.9km (2.4 miles).

2 Temple Lodge
The original Temple Lodge was built in 1930 and was the first structure in what

would ultimately become the Lake Louise ski resort. It burned down in 1973 and was quickly replaced by the current log building.

The Hike: From the lodge, walk across an open ski run and pick up the signposted path that ascends to a meadowy area dotted with larches that turn gold in autumn.

3 Halfway Hut
Located at the 7km (4.3-mile) mark, this small log refuge was built as a day shelter

Halfway Hut

AUTUMN SKY PHOTOGRAPHY/SHUTTERSTOCK ©

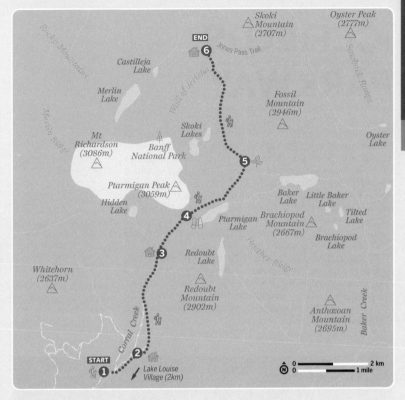

in the 1930s specifically for skiers heading to Skoki Lodge. Campers can make a small detour to the Hidden Lake Campground from here, although most push on deeper into the wilderness.

The Hike: The path heads northeast through ever-thinning trees toward Boulder Pass.

4 Boulder Pass

Perched above Ptarmigan Lake with a view of Ptarmigan Peak, Redoubt Mountain and Mt Temple to the southwest, Boulder Pass is marked by hardy dwarf trees and scattered boulders. Come prepared – the winds can be brutal up here.

The Hike: Leaving the lake behind, the trail crosses an open plateau reminiscent of a mini Tibet. A turnoff to the right heads toward Baker Lake, site of a campground and one of several loop trails that connects back to Skoki Lodge.

5 Deception Pass

Deception Pass, the highest point on the trail at 2485m (8200ft), is even bleaker and more exposed than Boulder Pass. Not long after summiting, you'll spy the rich greenery of the Skoki Valley on the other side.

The Hike: Descend toward the broccoli-green trees with Skoki Lakes glimmering to your left.

6 Skoki Lodge

Hewn from local logs, the lodge was built in 1931 and expanded in 1936. Originally conceived as a backcountry ski lodge – one of the first of its kind in Canada – Skoki has stood the test of time, and regular inclement weather, and remains a popular winter destination. In recent years, it has also amassed a sizable summer fan club. For nonguests, the lodge can provide drop-in afternoon tea. Camping is available at the Merlin Meadows Campground 1.2km (0.7 miles) to the northwest.

ICEFIELDS
PARKWAY

Icefields
Parkway

The Icefields Parkway, or the Promenade des Glaciers as it's more romantically known in French, is one of the most spectacular slices of asphalt in North America, maybe the world. Running just east of the Continental Divide, which it parallels for 233km (145 miles), between Lake Louise and Jasper Town, the highway is shared between Banff and Jasper national parks and studded with a sensory overload of scenery. Landscape-shaping glaciers, foraging wildlife and Gothic mountains will be your constant companions. When we say don't miss it, we mean *don't miss it!*

The Banff section of the parkway, rather like its Jasper counterpart, is littered with copious excuses to pull over and contemplate your speck-like importance in the vast natural universe of the Rocky Mountains. Some of the stops have accommodations (in campgrounds or rustic hotels and hostels) and simple eating joints. Others are the starting points for magnificent short trails.

TOP TIP

The speed limit on the parkway is 90km/h (56mph), with reduced speeds around Saskatchewan River Crossing and the Columbia Icefield. The road often becomes impassable in winter due to heavy snow, and chains or all-season tires are advisable between October and May. You'll also need a National Park Pass to drive the parkway.

LEFT: TRPHOTOS/SHUTTERSTOCK ©; RIGHT: BRADLEY L. GRANT/SHUTTERSTOCK ©

Icefields Parkway at Bow Lake (p119)

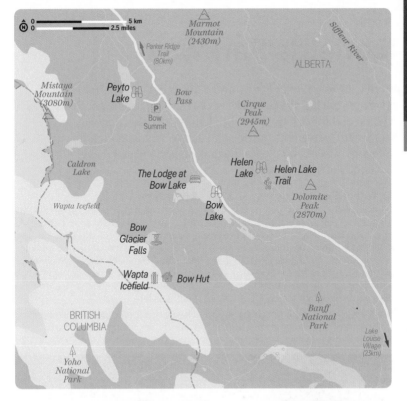

Magical Colors of Peyto Lake

SUMMERTIME BLUES

Every Rocky Mountain lake has its own distinctive hue, but none are quite as dazzling as **Peyto Lake** (pictured). It's almost as if the lake has invented its own color – Peyto blue – a luminous turquoise that takes a little green from the forest and a little blue from the sky and soaks it in frigid glacial waters for 10,000 years with psychedelic results.

The water is runoff from the Peyto glacier, an offshoot of the Wapta Icefield, which straddles the boundary between Banff and Yoho national parks. When it reaches the lake, the sunlight bounces off the glacial silt with vivid results.

 WHERE TO EAT ON THE ICEFIELDS PARKWAY

Hanging Glacier Cafe
New in 2023 on the shores of Bow Lake, this log cafe serves coffee, hot chocolate, sandwiches and beer. $

Mt Wilson Restaurant
The best of the three Crossing Resort eating options does decent breakfasts and lunch, and dinner buffets. $$

Laggan's Mountain Bakery & Deli
Grab quiches and sausage rolls from this Lake Louise deli before you hit the road. $

Icefields Parkway

What will likely turn out to be one of the most unforgettable drives of your life starts in Lake Louise and tracks the southern section of the extravagantly spectacular Icefields Parkway to Sunwapta Pass on the border with Jasper National Park. Set out early, ensure you have a full tank of gas, and savor every last spellbinding kilometer.

1 Crowfoot Glacier Lookout

After 33km (20.5 miles), pull over at the Crowfoot Glacier Lookout, to admire the icy giant spread across the rocky flanks of Crowfoot Mountain above super-reflective Bow Lake. If you have the time and energy, better views beckon if you take the 12km (7.5-mile) return trail on the opposite side of the road to Helen Lake.

The Drive: From Bow Lake, the road climbs toward Bow Pass, which at 2069m (6788ft) is the highest point on the parkway.

2 Bow Pass

Close to the parkway's loftiest point, the fourth-highest paved road in Canada, you'll find the turnoff to the busy Peyto Lake and Bow Summit Lookout, named after erstwhile park warden, Bill Peyto. A short wooded trail leads to an ultra-popular viewpoint over the luminous lake.

The Drive: Motor past green Waterfowl Lake and menacing Howse Peak.

SID0601/SHUTTERSTOCK ©

Ice-climbing, Weeping Wall

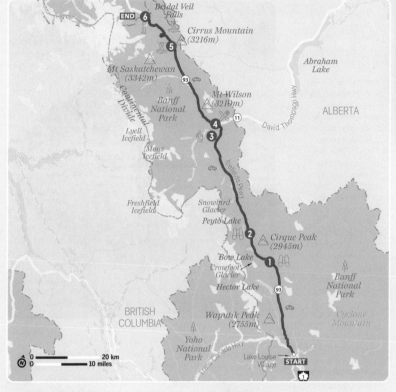

3 Mistaya Canyon

Stop for a short bang-for-your-buck stroll to a bridge over a narrow slot canyon where smooth rock contrasts with a rutted river.

The Drive: A short drive northwest brings you to Saskatchewan River Crossing.

4 Saskatchewan River Crossing

Established by 19th-century fur trappers who forded the North Saskatchewan River here on their way through the Rockies, the crossing is marked today by the junction of Hwy 93 (the Icefields Parkway) and Hwy 11 (the David Thompson Hwy). It's home to the only facilities between Lake Louise and the Columbia Icefield – a basic motel, cafeteria-style restaurant and gas station.

The Drive: From the crossing, the road traverses river flats (keep an eye out for wildlife) en route to Cirrus Mountain.

5 Weeping Wall

Snowmelt streams off Cirrus Mountain, creating a sheet of waterfalls known as the Weeping Wall, which freeze solid in winter. From here, the road negotiates a huge hairpin and ascends the aptly named Big Hill. At the summit, there's a superb viewpoint looking back down the North Saskatchewan Valley toward Mt Saskatchewan. Nearby are Bridal Veil Falls that cascades down a cliff.

The Drive: At 125km (78 miles) into the trip, you'll reach the subalpine Sunwapta Pass, 2023m (6637ft) above sea level with its dwarf trees and blustery winds.

6 Sunwapta Pass

In winter, this is the most avalanche-prone section of the parkway. The pass marks the boundary with Jasper National Park. A small stone monument denotes the watershed between the Athabasca and North Saskatchewan rivers.

SUNSET LOOKOUT TRAIL

The 9.4km (5.8-mile) Sunset Lookout Trail just inside Banff's northern border feels deliciously remote although it never strays far from the Icefields Parkway.

It's used mainly as an access route for backpackers on the Sunset Pass Trail to Pinto Lake and the wilderness beyond, but the first section gives you an opportunity to divert to the site of an abandoned fire lookout.

The launchpad is a parking lot 16.5km (10.3 miles) north of Saskatchewan River Crossing, from where the trail climbs sharply through lodgepole pine forest, roughly following the course of Norman Creek. After passing a dramatic canyon and waterfall it branches off to the lofty lookout site dangling high above the forest with the Graveyard Flats, crisscrossed by the Alexandra and North Saskatchewan rivers glimmering far below.

SIRAPHOB TATIYARAT/GETTY IMAGES ©

Bow Lake

Peyto Lake is 40km (25 miles) north of Lake Louise and one of the most popular stops on the Icefields Parkway. Only Moraine Lake makes it onto more magazine covers. Unlike other sights on the parkway, minimal hiking is required to see it. The viewing platform is a mere 15 minutes' walk from the **Bow Summit** parking lot.

It's a lofty vantage point perched several hundred feet above the water and best visited in early morning, between the time the sun first illuminates the water and the first tour bus arrives.

For more tranquility, it's possible to walk along a dirt road beyond the lookout, zigzagging up above the trees to a rocky bowl often frequented by sunbathing marmots. On the other side of the bowl, the path ascends further to the **Bow Summit Lookout** with views of the Mistaya Valley, Cirque Peak and the Crowfoot Glacier. Total distance is 6.2km (3.8 miles) round trip.

 WHERE TO STAY ON THE ICEFIELDS PARKWAY ──────────

The Crossing Resort
Standard motel units set around a central courtyard that's also home to the only cafe and shop around. **$$$**

The Lodge at Bow Lake
The historic Num Ti-Jah lodge on the edge of Bow Lake reopened under new management in 2023. **$$$**

HI Mosquito Creek Wilderness Hostel
Charming 34-bed backcountry hostel built to house German POWs during WWII. **$**

Jimmy Simpson & Bow Lake

LAKE, LODGE AND WATERFALL

Bow Lake, 33km (20.6 miles) north of Lake Louise, has multiple reasons to apply a little pressure to the brakes. Firstly, there's the distracting view of Crowfoot Mountain from a roadside pull-over with its craggy cliffs and scree-laden skirts perfectly reflected in the water. Then there's the eponymous glacier spread across the mountain's upper flanks. Decades of glacial retreat mean its name is no longer 100% accurate: the lowest toe has melted, making it look more like an ostrich's foot.

The four-story wooden structure on the lake's north shore was the erstwhile business and residence of one of Banff's most endearing legends, Jimmy Simpson. Gambler, cook, outfitter, trapper, guide and hotel proprietor, British-born Simpson was allegedly sent to Canada in his teens after embarrassing his family at a wedding. He first passed through the Bow Lake region on an expedition in 1898 and was so enamored with the scenery he vowed to return, a promise he fulfilled in 1922 when he fashioned a small shack for himself out of local logs. In 1937, with the opening of the Icefields Parkway, the shack was amplified into the Num Ti-Jah lodge, an iconic way station used by copious naturalists, climbers, hunters and wealthy tourists. Simpson died in 1972, aged 95, but the Num Ti-Jah continued to operate under the Simpson umbrella until 2020. It reopened with new management in 2023 in its original (refurbished) building as **The Lodge at Bow Lake** (lodgeatbowlake.com).

The lodge is the start of a 7.2km (4.4-mile) trail to the 100m-tall **Bow Glacier Falls**. When Simpson used to lead his guests along this well-worn path in the early 1900s, the Bow Glacier still filled much of the basin at the end of the trail. These days it is no longer visible, having shrunk back into the mountains leaving a boulder-filled valley fed by the frigid spray of the falls. The slender cascade emanates from a small lake at the snout of the glacier that sits above tall cliffs.

The trailhead for Bow Glacier Falls is just behind the lodge and follows the super-reflective lake on its north shore before cutting across a wide rocky river valley to a steep staircase beside a small canyon. From here you climb up through patchy forest to a huge moraine field, at the end of which lies the waterfall.

STILL GOT THE BLUES

If you're collecting photo shots of turquoise lakes, you'll want to gravitate to **Moraine Lake** (p108) near Lake Louise where the glacial waters glow a slightly different shade of blue.

WILD BILL PEYTO

You can't help logging Bill Peyto's face when you arrive in Banff. He's the rugged, steely-eyed gentleman who stares out from the 'Welcome to Banff' sign greeting visitors as they enter town.

Born in England in 1869, Peyto came to Canada as a teenager and found work as a railway laborer for the Canadian Pacific Railway. But it was the Rocky Mountains that gave him his vocation. Peyto built a log cabin by the Bow River and reinvented himself as an outfitter and mountain guide for the park's early visitors. Cultivating a mystique as a man who loved solitude and simple backcountry living, he graduated to becoming a park warden, a position he held for nearly 30 years. His no-nonsense spirit has since become part of Banff folklore.

The Crossing Resort
Standard motel units set around a central courtyard that's also home to the only cafe and shop around. **$$$**

The Lodge at Bow Lake
The historic Num Ti-Jah lodge on the edge of Bow Lake reopened under new management in 2023. **$$$**

HI Mosquito Creek Wilderness Hostel
Charming 34-bed back-country hostel built to house German POWs during WWII. **$**

About halfway up the staircase you'll pass a massive boulder jammed into the valley. This is the intersection with another trail to the 30-capacity **Bow Hut**, one of four lonely shelters in the region owned by the Alpine Club of Canada. It's perennially popular with mountaineers and backcountry skiers.

Hike to Helen Lake

CANADA IMITATING ITALY

Bow Lake guards a surfeit of journey-breaking sights. Almost opposite the Crowfoot Glacier Viewpoint is the trailhead for the 12km (7.5-mile) out-and-back **Helen Lake Trail**, an irresistible high-country hike that switchbacks its way above the Icefields Parkway into wildflower-strewn meadows with in-your-face views of Dolomite Peak (2860m/9383ft) and Cirque Peak (2993m/9819ft). The former mountain's brawny battlements – jagged even by Rockies' standards – were aptly named by early explorers for their close resemblance to the Italian Dolomites.

The trail starts as a rootsy forest path and climbs up via tree-speckled subalpine slopes to the more barren alpine heights that surround ice-blue **Helen Lake**.

Peering Over Parker Ridge

ICE FOR A LOW PRICE

A moderate walk to an exceptional viewpoint, **Parker Ridge Trail** is, arguably, Banff's best 'value-for-money' hike if you prefer measuring your costs in sweat. For only 2km (1.3 miles) of gradual uphill effort, you'll be rewarded with a grandstand view of Mt Saskatchewan, Mt Athabasca, and the gargantuan Saskatchewan Glacier dripping slowly into the North Saskatchewan River, which curls away to the east through a medial moraine. Bring warm clothing and a decent windbreaker, as the gusts on the ridge can be as icy as the glacier.

The trailhead is located 4km (2.5 miles) south of Sunwapta Pass, the last popular stop on the Icefields Parkway before Jasper. Since the path starts at a considerable elevation, it doesn't take long to break above the tree line switching back across an open hillside with the Icefields Parkway getting ever-smaller below. After around 40 minutes of climbing, you'll stumble up a last stony incline and crest a ridge to behold one of Banff's finest vistas.

 WHERE TO CAMP ON THE ICEFIELDS PARKWAY

Mosquito Creek Campground
Tucked under Mt Hector in a wooded creek-side setting, this primitive 32-site campground is wonderful for seclusion. **$**

Waterfowl Lakes Campground
Wedged between two beautiful lakes; wooded sites and plenty of hiking. **$**

Rampart Creek Campground
In Banff's northernmost campground, mountain views are grand and bighorn sheep putter past your tent. **$**

DAVID P. LEWIS/SHUTTERSTOCK ©

Helen Lake Trail

BREWSTER BROTHERS

Banff's largest and oldest tour company was founded in 1892 when brothers Bill and Jim Brewster, at the ages of 12 and 10, started offering guided fishing trips to guests at the new Banff Springs Hotel.

Within a decade, they had become the exclusive outfitters for the Canadian Pacific Railway and their horseback operations were vital in promoting early tourism in the park. Motor coaches were introduced in 1916 and the business was successfully passed down through generations of the Brewster family.

Rebranded as Pursuit (banffjasper collection.com) in 2017, the company today runs the Banff Gondola, the Minnewanka and Maligne lake cruises, the Columbia Icefield Snocoaches, over a dozen hotels, and Brewster Express shuttle services between Calgary Airport, Banff and Jasper.

To the west loom Mts Athabasca and Andromeda and, to the south, the glistening surface of the Saskatchewan Glacier lurking at the end of a deeply gouged valley. Although in slow-melting retreat, the Saskatchewan is still the largest of the half-dozen glaciers that slide off the Columbia Icefield, measuring 13km (8 miles) in length.

For the best views, turn left at the ridgetop and follow the trail southeast across open mountain slopes replete with foraging ground squirrels and bighorn sheep.

There are several unmarked viewpoints along the way where you can stop and savor the icy behemoth in all its glory.

GETTING AROUND

Sundog Tours (sundogtours.com) runs year-round buses along the parkway between Banff, Lake Louise and Jasper. In summer, you can do it as part of a guided tour with stops at Bow Lake, the Weeping Wall, the Columbia Icefield and Athabasca Falls.

If you're driving, start out with a full tank of gas. It's fairly pricey to fill up at Saskatchewan River Crossing, the only gas station in the 233km-long (145-mile) stretch between Lake Louise and Jasper.

JASPER NATIONAL PARK

THE ROCKY MOUNTAINS AT THEIR PUREST

When you've explored the well-trodden edges of the Canadian Rockies, the desire to delve deeper into the wilderness is hard to suppress. Head north. Jasper awaits.

Take Banff, stretch its borders, remove over half its tourists, sprinkle it with a bit more wildlife and endow it with a coarser, slightly more rugged edge and you've got Jasper. The less famous of the two main Rocky Mountain parks is sometimes (wrongly) regarded as a latecomer to the ball – it was designated 22 years after Banff but was still Canada's sixth national park when it was founded in 1907.

In some ways the park seems like a northern extension of Banff. The two conjoined areas have several communalities: sizable townsites, alpine ski resorts, hot springs and a rambunctious history connected to the transcontinental railroad. They also share the Columbia Icefield and the Icefields Parkway, the spectacular road that cuts through northern Banff and southern Jasper like a Rocky Mountain roller-coaster.

But overall, Jasper is a larger and wilder beast with expansive tracts of gritty backcountry demanding detailed exploration. While the park attracts all types of travelers, especially in the summer, it carries a special appeal for solitude-seekers and off-the-grid adventurers. Old-school and friendly, the well-organized town-site feels wholesome and blue-collar; a little less staged than Banff's. Amid the plethora of activities on offer, mountain biking, backcountry hiking and white-water rafting stand out.

Although public transportation is limited, much of the outdoor fun is easily reachable on foot from the townsite.

THE MAIN AREAS

JASPER TOWN	MALIGNE VALLEY	MIETTE HOT SPRINGS	ICEFIELDS PARKWAY
Shops, restaurants and a fabulous trail network.	Wildlife spotting, boat cruises and hiking.	Recuperative waters in a remote mountain setting.	A gorgeous drive past glaciers and waterfalls.
p128	p142	p152	p156

Sunwapta Falls (p162)

CAR

Private cars are the main means of getting around in Jasper, where distances are often long and public transportation scant. The main roads are the Icefields Parkway (Hwy93) and the Yellowhead Hwy (Hwy16). Secondary roads include the Maligne Lake Rd, Whistlers Rd and Miette Rd.

BUS

Unlike Banff, there are no regular public buses in Jasper. Private companies such as Sundog (sundogtours.com) offer daily schedules to Edmonton and via the Icefields Parkway to Banff. Summer shuttles link the town with Maligne Lake and the Jasper SkyTram aerial tramway.

BIKE

Jasper has an active mountain-biking community and a comprehensive network of single-track and paved trails directly accessible from town. Many of the sights within the vicinity of Jasper Town are easily reachable on a bike. There are numerous rental outlets.

Miette Hot Springs, p152

Key to the area's early development, the park's northeastern corner is littered with mining and fur-trading history, a handful of short hikes and a commercial hot springs.

Jasper Town, p128

More than just a townsite, Jasper is surrounded by a rich 'front-country' of lakes, forest, wetlands and river valleys readily accessible by foot or bicycle.

COLUMBIA

Whistlers Summit (2466m)

Peveril Peak (2679m)

Sorrow Peak (3020m)

Mt Edith Cavell (3363m)

Cavell Lake

Cavell Rd

Centre Mountain (2700m)

Curator Mountain (2624m)

Skyline

(2791m)

Little Shovel Pass (2240m)

Maligne Range

Trail

Lakes Trail

Gundl Riveders

Mt Hardisty (2700m)

Evelyn Pass

Mt Kerkeslin (2909m)

Helmet Mountain (2890m)

Leah Peak (2800m)

Opal Hills

Maligne Lake Samson Narrows

Maligne Mountain (3200m)

Mt Unwin (3268m)

Maligne River

Maligne Pass Trail

Moose Lake

Bald Hills Trail

ALBERTA

Maligne River

Maligne River

Athabasca River

93

93A

Moab Lake Rd

Athabasca Falls

Athabasca River

Brussels Peak (3161m)

Icefields Pkwy

Sunwapta Falls

Icefields Parkway, p156

Jasper's portion of the Rockies' greatest road trip is dotted with campgrounds, trailheads, waterfalls and the most colossal of several massive ice fields.

Maligne Valley, p142

Remote lake with a well-developed hub on its north shore that's a nexus for kayaking, hiking and backpacking. An interconnecting road offers excellent wildlife-spotting opportunities.

0   5 miles

0   10 km

N

Find Your Way

While Jasper has less public transportation provision than Banff, many areas are directly accessible by walking or cycling from the townsite. Elsewhere, a car will offer you more flexibility, particularly outside the high summer season.

125

Plan Your Time

Jasper is large and deserves at least a week, preferably two if you're keen on hiking. A comprehensive trail network close to town is ideal for those just passing through.

Maligne Lake (p144)

A Fleeting Visit

Get orientated in the townsite by navigating around the circuitous **Discovery Trail** (p130). Stop off at the **Jasper-Yellowhead Museum & Archives** (p131) to absorb some of Jasper's history, and the attractive **Jasper Park Information Centre** (p131) for up-to-date trail info. Grab lunch in **The Other Paw** (p134) opposite the train tracks and spend the afternoon exploring the Pyramid Bench on the **Mina and Riley Lakes Loop** (p136).

On day two sip a coffee in **SnowDome Coffee Bar** (p134) and hire a bike to take you around the easy trails that abut the Athabasca River Valley, stopping off at **Old Fort Point** (p132), **Lake Annette** (p135) and **Maligne Canyon** (p147) for short hikes.

Seasonal Highlights

Ninety percent of visitors arrive in the summer. If you hate crowds and like the snow, come in the winter. For a taste of both, try the late spring.

JANUARY

Jasper's atmospheric **winter festival** hosts plenty of family-friendly events: cross-country skiing, sleigh rides, a chili cook-off.

APRIL

Wrap yourself in a rainbow flag and hit the ski slopes for the four-day **Jasper Pride and Ski Festival**.

JULY

Colorful blooms blanket mountain meadows, and most trails are open. Long days of hiking, cycling and outdoor activity.

FROM LEFT: TETIANA MEZINA/SHUTTERSTOCK ©, CERI BREEZE/SHUTTERSTOCK ©, LIZ MILLER/SHUTTERSTOCK ©

A Busy Week

After a couple of days getting to know Jasper Town, pitch south for a day at **Maligne Lake** (p144). Take a boat cruise to Spirit Island and save enough time to complete the **Moose Lake** (p144) and **Mary Schäffer** (p144) hikes afterwards.

On day four, take the **Jasper SkyTram** (p135) up The Whistlers and spend the evening star-gazing at the **Jasper Planetarium** (p132).

Days five and six can be dedicated to cycling in the **Valley of the Five Lakes** (p140) and rafting the **Sunwapta River** (p159).

Round off the week by driving down to the **Columbia Icefield** (p160) and hiking on and around the **Athabasca Glacier** (p161).

The Park's Your Oyster

Build on a busy first week in Jasper by heading over to **Mt Edith Cavell** (p158) to hike the meadows and lakes around the Angel Glacier. Take in the immensity of **Athabasca Falls** (p162) before heading back to town.

Factor in three days to hike the backcountry on the **Skyline Trail** (p150), staying over at the Little Shovel and Tekarra campgrounds.

Spend a final day in the northeast, exploring the mining legacy at **Miette/Pocahontas** (p155) and recovering in the mineral waters of **Miette Hot Springs** (p152). Say goodbye to the townsite with a beer in **Jasper Brewing Company** (p133) and a last supper in **Raven Bistro** (p129).

AUGUST

The warmest month of the year coincides with a host of special events, as well as the Rockies' busiest tourist season.

SEPTEMBER

Fall brings a blaze of color to Jasper, making it one of the most spectacular seasons for hiking, especially with the crowds gone.

OCTOBER

Since 2011 the **Dark Sky Festival** (p132) has become one of the most important and anticipated events on Jasper's annual calendar.

DECEMBER

The ski season is getting underway, with snow descending from the mountaintops to the slopes of Jasper's Marmot Basin.

JASPER TOWN

● Jasper Town

Jasper Town is more 'blue-collar' and understated than Banff. While both places act as important national park portals and tourist hubs, Jasper's aura feels more authentic and low-key; a working railway town with one foot still in its industrial past. Elk graze calmly next to the rail line while half-mile-long freight trains rattle past against a spectacular backdrop of mountains.

The town's two main thoroughfares, Patricia St and Connaught Dr run parallel to the train tracks and are lined with enough businesses and outfitters to equip any type of backcountry adventure. Trails for hiking, biking and cross-country skiing lead out directly from the townsite accessing both the Pyramid Bench, a wooded plateau to the west, and the Athabasca River Valley with its necklace of small lakes to the east.

As a refueling stop, Jasper is amply stocked with a consortium of restaurants, unpretentious bars and midrange hotels.

TOP TIP

Jasper Town is significantly smaller than Banff with no capacity to expand. As a result, its limited hotel and hostel rooms fill up quickly in summer, as do the cabins, bungalows and campgrounds in the surrounding countryside. Book well in advance between May and September.

LEFT: TATSUO NAKAMURA/SHUTTERSTOCK ©. RIGHT: SHAWN.CCF/SHUTTERSTOCK ©

Jasper Town

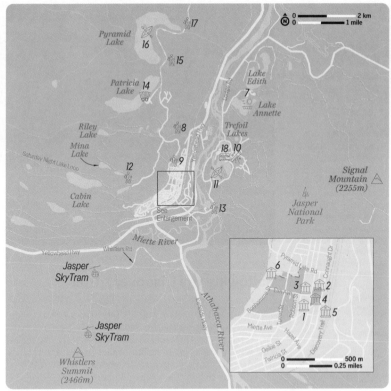

SIGHTS
1 Athabasca Hotel
2 CIBC Bank
3 Firehall
4 Jasper Park Information Centre
5 Jasper Train Station
6 Jasper-Yellowhead Museum & Archives
7 Lake Annette

ACTIVITIES & TOURS
8 Cottonwood Creek Trail
9 Discovery Trail
10 Jasper Planetarium
11 Lac Beauvert

12 Mina and Riley Lakes Loop
13 Old Fort Point Loop
14 Patricia Lake
15 Pyramid Bench
16 Pyramid Lake
17 Pyramid Trail

SLEEPING
18 Fairmont Jasper Park Lodge

Pyramid Lake (p134)

 WHERE TO EAT IN JASPER TOWN

Terra
Exceptional farm-to-table food in the Crimson Hotel offering gourmet dishes in a casual setting. **$$**

Spicy Joint Lounge
Jamaican-influenced products including jerk-chicken wraps, Red Stripe beer and Blue Mountain coffee. **$**

Raven Bistro
A small European-style bistro specializing in vegetable-forward dishes with a strong Mediterranean bias. **$$$**

FROM FITZHUGH TO JASPER

The original Jasper townsite, founded in 1911 as a siding on two nascent and competing cross-continental railroads, was called Fitzhugh under an alphabetical naming system then employed by Canadian railway companies.

For a while, it was eclipsed in size by Pocahontas, a budding mining community to the northeast, but by the 1920s the tables had turned.

The town's name was changed to Jasper in 1913 to match the national park, conceived as Jasper Forest Park six years earlier.

It was a curious choice. Far from being a well-known folk hero, Jasper Haws was a relatively low-ranking clerk who had manned an isolated fur-trading supply post for four years in the late 1810s. Little could he have known how profoundly his name would resonate over 200 years later.

Jasper Park Information Centre

Following the Discovery Trail

JASPER'S QUINTESSENTIAL ORIENTATION HIKE

Jasper's definitive 'urban' walking **Discovery Trail** circumnavigates the town on a part-paved, part-rustic path that's split into three sections focusing on the town's natural, historical and railroad legacies. A wealth of fact-packed interpretive boards dotted along the route provide an educational introduction to both the town and national park.

You can jump on the 8km (5-mile) loop at any point along its course, although the best place to start is the Discovery Trail info kiosk at the foot of Pyramid Lake Rd, north of the train station, where a map acts as a good orientation tool. The trail is numbered '11' and marked with a bear motif on trees.

The eastern portion of the trail runs adjacent to the railway for 3km (1.9 miles), tracking past the heritage station, a retired steam locomotive dating from 1923, and various railway sidings where elk graze with fearless indifference. It swings back on the west side of town on the cusp of the Pyramid Bench (with several interconnecting trails for those who want to penetrate deeper) gaining a little height as it dips in and out of montane forest offering excellent views over the surrounding mountains.

 WHERE TO STAY IN JASPER TOWN

Fairmont Jasper Park Lodge
Like a mini-village on the east side of the Athabasca, offering golf, boating, fine food and a planetarium. **$$$**

Tekarra Lodge
Riverside cabin resort with deluxe Rocky Mountain interiors and songs 'n' s'mores around the campfire. **$$$**

HI Jasper
New-build hostel with a clean-lined Scandinavian vibe and bright, welcoming common spaces. **$**

Blast from the Past

AN ARCHIVE OF HISTORY

Jasper's volunteer-run, pay-by-donation museum, officially known as the **Jasper-Yellowhead Museum & Archives**, does a fine job of squeezing several centuries' worth of anecdotes into a very tight space. A multitude of eras are eloquently evoked tracking through Indigenous Peoples, fur traders, hardy homesteaders, railway rivalries, early park outfitters and the more modern cash cow of tourism. To take the story back even further, stop by at the novel geology garden outside.

Jasper's History & Heritage

A TOWN BUILT AROUND THE RAILROAD

Most visitors probably don't come to Jasper for a history lesson, but the story of how the town was conceived and developed in the early 20th century is peppered with illuminating characters and pioneering tales of derring-do. Adding depth are the thousands of years of Indigenous history that preceded it.

On a morning when you're too knackered to face another mountain hike, it's worth lingering in town to absorb its numerous historical signboards and admire the handful of attractive buildings turned national historic sites.

Anchoring proceedings in Athabasca Park is the town's oldest surviving building, the **Jasper Park Information Centre**, a gorgeous rustic construction fashioned out of local wood and stone in 1914 in a style that would ultimately come to define national park architecture.

Of a similar ilk is the stone and timber **CIBC Bank** practically next door and the former **firehall** on Patricia St directly behind.

Not far away, **Jasper Train Station** conforms to the classic British arts-and-craft style in vogue in the 1920s. With its gabled roof, stucco walls and slender stone-finished chimney, it's arguably the most architecturally accomplished of all Canadian stations. Be sure to check out its retro interior, complete with old travel posters and plush wooden benches.

Founded a year before the park's super-posh Jasper Park Lodge, the **Athabasca Hotel** (or Atha-B as locals call it) has occupied its prime position on the corner of Miette and Patricia streets since 1921. The current brick building with its unsubtle taxidermy, patterned carpets and heavy drapes replaced the wooden predecessor in 1928.

Athabasca Hotel
No-frills centrally located hotel with shared bathrooms, decent prices and an on-site bar and restaurant. **$$**

The Crimson
Jasper's snazziest option is modern and sleek, with an indoor pool, gym and one of Jasper's best restaurants. **$$$**

Mt Robson Inn
A motel vibe with some plush Jacuzzi suites and substantial breakfasts on the western edge of town. **$$$**

**TWO BROTHERS
TOTEM POLE**

Towering over the rail
tracks next to Jasper's
train station is a
12m-tall (39ft) totem
pole that has long
been an important
symbol of the town.

For 94 years, the
spot was marked by
a so-called 'Raven
pole' carved in the
1870s in Haida Gwaii
and brought to Jasper
in 1915. It was one
of numerous poles
that used to line the
railway between
Jasper and Prince
Rupert.

Because of
deterioration, the pole
was repatriated in
2009 and replaced by
a newly commissioned
structure. The so-
called 'Two Brothers
Pole' raised in 2011
tells the story of the
special bond between
the Haida people and
the Rocky Mountains
through the fate of
two brothers.

Stargazing in a Dark Sky Preserve

STUDYING THE ROCKY MOUNTAIN SKIES

Stargazing in Jasper has a long history dating back to ancient
traditions practiced by Indigenous Peoples. David Thompson,
one of the area's earliest European explorers, was an expert
surveyor and astronomer nicknamed Koo-Koo-Sint, or
'stargazer' by the First Nations.

Interest in outer space was reignited in 2011, 200 years after
Thompson first passed through, when the park was named
a 'Dark Sky Preserve' by the Royal Astronomical Society of
Canada, earmarking it as a special zone where light pollution
is measured and controlled to enhance galactic vistas and
promote astronomical study. Jasper is currently listed as the
planet's third largest **Dark Sky Preserve** and, once you've
factored in accessibility and light pollution (or lack of it), there
are few better places in the world to observe the cosmos in
all its magnitude.

In the years since 2011, Jasper has held a **Dark Sky Festival**
every October, hosting a diverse schedule of events, including
visits from well-known astronomers and starlit musical
concerts.

The **Jasper Planetarium** (jasperplanetarium.com), a
novelty in such a small town, is bivouacked in an unusual
inflatable structure at the Jasper Park Lodge. The 40-capacity
auditorium runs regularly scheduled audiovisual shows about
Jasper's night sky and offers the opportunity to steal a glance
through the largest telescope in the Rockies.

Well-known places to go stargazing on your own are the
small island on Pyramid Lake, 6km (3.8 miles) northeast of
Jasper Town, the north shore of Maligne Lake, and Old Fort
Point. Backcountry camping presents an ideal opportunity to
contemplate the grandeur of the celestial world. The Tonquin
Valley is refreshingly free of light pollution.

Climb Old Fort Point

SHORT WALK UP A STEEP HILL

You won't find any old forts atop this *roche moutonnée* – a
bedrock knob shaped by glaciers – just south of Jasper Town.
Rather, the name refers to the likely site of an erstwhile fur-
trading post known as **Henry House**, thought to have been
built here in 1811 by William Henry, a colleague of Canadian–
British explorer David Thompson. It was abandoned soon
after and nothing visible remains today.

 WHERE TO GO FOR BREAKFAST IN JASPER TOWN

Sunhouse Cafe
Favorite local spot for
nourishing breakfasts. Expect
powerful porridge, and eggs
and avocado on sourdough. **$$**

Coco's Cafe
Diminutive cafe plying
excellent coffee and brunches
concocted with home-baked
bread and bagels. **$$**

Harvest
For late birds, this earthy
locavore restaurant opens
at 10am for both classic and
fancy brunch dishes. **$$$**

Pyramid Lake (p134)

DARK SKY PRESERVES

Dark Sky Preserves – protected areas that aim to minimize light pollution – are a relatively new phenomenon. The first was inaugurated in Michigan in the US in 1993, although most of the current crop of 200-plus preserves around the world date from the 2010s.

Canada has 21 Dark Sky Preserves, reserves, Star Parks and sanctuaries, eight of them within national parks, including the world's largest, 44,807-sq-km (17,300-sq-mile) Wood Buffalo.

On the Bortle scale, a nine-level ranking system designed to measure the sky's brightness, Jasper rates a very favorable 1–2, meaning zodiacal light is visible, the Milky Way is highly structured and the Triangulum galaxy, 2.73 million light years away, can be seen with the naked eye.

Instead, the hill has become one of Jasper Town's favorite local hikes, easily reachable on foot from the townsite and instantly rewarding with its broad mountain-studded vista across the Athabasca River Valley.

The 4km (2.5-mile) **Old Fort Point Loop** starts in a parking lot beside a truss bridge that spans a majestic bend in the braided Athabasca River. Take the wooden stairway that ascends a tall crag overlooking the river. At the top, next to a monument dedicated to the mighty Athabasca, a steep path with rough-cut steps leads up toward a grassy slope – perfect grazing ground for bighorn sheep – and on to Old Fort Point's summit where the views of Jasper Town, the river valley and the surrounding peaks are phenomenal. On a clear day, you'll be able to count off the handsome tops of Mt Edith Cavell, The Whistlers and Pyramid Mountain, along with the more distant peaks of the Continental Divide.

Beyond the summit, the path dips less precipitously into aspen forest and returns to the parking lot via trail 1, which is heavily used by mountain bikers accessing the Valley of the Five Lakes, the Holy Grail of Jasper's bike trails.

WHERE TO GET A DRINK IN JASPER TOWN

Jasper Brewing Company
The first brewpub in a Canadian national park when it opened, JBC fortifies its fine ales with glacial water.

Downstream Bar
The best-stocked bar in town with a wide array of whiskeys and vodkas in a subterranean setting.

Whistle Stop Pub
Salt-of-the-earth pub attached to the Whistlers Inn where you might even meet a local in the boisterous interior.

ASK A JASPER EXPERT

Recommendations from **Kim Weir**, Product Development Officer, Jasper National Park.

Favorite day hike in Jasper?
Wilcox Pass. Because you begin at such a high elevation, you get far-reaching views almost right away. The viewpoint over the Athabasca Glacier is only a few kilometers up. After that, you're hiking through alpine meadows. The flowers can be unreal.

See any wildlife?
We almost always see bighorn sheep. We've seen mountain goats a few times on this hike too.

Tips for first timers?
If you're not used to hiking or being at this elevation above 2000m (6562ft), pace yourself, especially at the start.

Where to eat?
A picnic at Mt Christie on the way back to town! Great peak views and the river is right below.

JOSH MCCULLOCH/GETTY IMAGES ©

White-tailed ptarmigan

Hike & Ride the Pyramid Bench

PLATEAU REPLETE WITH LAKES AND TRAILS

The elevated plateau immediately northwest of Jasper Town is often referred to as the **Pyramid Bench**, a lattice of forested trails, diminutive lakes and reedy sloughs (swampy areas) that's refreshingly accessible from the townsite without a car – just choose your preferred trailhead and keep walking.

This is Jasper's all-season playground, the cherished domain of mountain bikers, hikers, snowshoers and horseback riders all sharing the same mouthwatering landscapes.

The Bench's two major lakes are accessed via the winding 6km (3.7-mile) Pyramid Lake Rd, the area's only paved thoroughfare that dead-ends just beyond the deluxe Pyramid Lake Resort.

Patricia Lake, the lower of the two lakes, offers abundant aquatic activities including fishing and diving. In its shadowy depths lies the wreck of a prototype ice-based aircraft carrier called *Habakkuk*, designed as part of a top-secret British mission during WWII.

Pyramid Lake is the realm of canoers and kayakers in summer and ice-skaters in winter (procure equipment from

WHERE TO GO FOR COFFEE AND CAKE IN JASPER TOWN

The Other Paw
Go on a long enough hike and you can easily justify the epic cakes at this well-loved cafe opposite the train tracks.

Wicked Cup
Coffee, cake and more-substantial snacks can be savored on a pretty patio at the quiet end of Connaught Ave.

SnowDome Coffee Bar
The best coffee in Jasper is served in the unlikely confines of the local launderette.

the lakeside boat rental). From its eastern shore, a wooden pedestrian bridge leads out to tiny **Pyramid Island**, a protected nature reserve. Sufficiently detached from the lights of town, this is where budding stargazers congregate after dark for unobstructed views of the cosmos.

The network of trails that covers the forested 'bench' is well mapped with copious clearly numbered paths. A good first-day orientation hike is the 9km (5.6-mile) **Mina and Riley Lakes Loop** (trail 8) that leaves from the northwest corner of the Jasper-Yellowhead Museum parking lot and climbs into a lake-speckled mini-wilderness where you'll spot ptarmigan, Barrow's goldeneye ducks and loons gliding across the green surface of the water.

Be on your guard. The rootsy single-track trails are also used by mountain bikers and horseback riders – there's a stable complex 3km (1.9 miles) up the Pyramid Lake Rd – plus the odd elk and bear. Bikes can be rented from Pyramid Lake or in town.

Other top trails are the 10.4km (6.5-mile) **Pyramid Trail** that zigzags up to the lake mostly avoiding the road, and the short **Cottonwood Creek Trail** that meanders around a local stream.

Brave the Beach at Lake Annette

ALBERTA'S CUTEST BEACH

One in a necklace of diminutive lakes that grace the Athabasca River Valley east of Jasper town, **Lake Annette** is hailed for its beach – a godsend in landlocked Alberta – and numerous picnic spots that entertain the crowds in summer. Short and narrow and backed by a large grassy area, the thin sweep of yellowish sand is popular on hot days when foot-sore hikers drop by to cool off.

As this is Jasper, you might want to pack some bear spray alongside your blow-up raft: grizzlies are sometimes spotted in the area, while elk and mule deer provide more innocuous company.

For brave swimmers, Annette beckons like a giant ice bath. The glacier-fed water is invigorating even on the hottest days, although this doesn't stop plenty of masochists from wading in.

A multiuse 2.4km (1.5-mile) trail circumnavigates Annette's forested shoreline and is accessible to wheelchairs as well as hikers.

PROJECT HABAKKUK

Lying beneath the waters of diminutive Patricia Lake are the remnants of a wartime project to construct the largest aircraft carrier ever built – out of ice.

During WWII, ships were urgently needed in the hunt for German U-boats in the Atlantic. As steel was in short supply, British researchers, led by inventor Geoffrey Pyke, came up with an alternative material, pykrete (wood pulp and ice). Winston Churchill was enthusiastic about the plan and a scale prototype of a 600m (1969ft) pykrete ship was commissioned and built, in top secret, at Patricia Lake in 1944. However, with costs spiraling and the tide of the war turning, the project was ultimately scrapped. The remains of the ship still lie at the bottom of the lake and attract curious scuba divers.

The *Habakkuk* is one of two fascinating sub-aquatic ruins in the Rockies. The other is Minnewanka Landing (p84), the well-preserved remains of an old resort village that was flooded by the expansion of Lake Minnewanka in the early 20th century.

 WHERE TO REFUEL AFTER HIKING IN JASPER TOWN

Something Else	Cassio's Italian Restaurant	Papa George's
Casual restaurant that wears many hats (steakhouse, Italian, Cajun) but at its core remains authentically Greek. **$$**	Inside the long-standing Whistlers Inn, the Cassio family concentrates on presenting large filling portions of authentic Italian cucina. **$$**	Almost as old as the park, this stalwart has been in business since 1925 offering salt-of-the-earth comfort food with no surprises. **$$**

BEST OUT-OF-TOWN SLEEPING OPTIONS

Pyramid Lake Resort
Small resort complex overlooking Pyramid Lake with chalet-style rooms, rental canoes, kayaks and bikes, and a small beach to hang out on.

Alpine Village
Just outside the hubbub of town, but close enough to walk, these log cabins have plush, country-style decor, with mezzanine bedrooms, renovated bathrooms and stone fireplaces.

Patricia Lake Bungalows
Charming assemblage of family-owned bungalows that sits on the shores of Patricia Lake, 5km north of Jasper Town.

DOUGLAS CARR/ALAMY STOCK PHOTO ©

Fairmont Jasper Park Lodge

Legendary Jasper Park Lodge
SMART HOTEL BESIDE AN ATTRACTIVE LAKE

Within golf-putting distance of Lac Beauvert and surrounded by manicured grounds and rugged mountain peaks, the classic **Fairmont Jasper Park Lodge** (fairmont.com/jasper) is less showy than its Banff and Lake Louise counterparts. Eschewing the Renaissance Revival architecture of other grand railway hotels, its 1920s builders designed it as a diffused resort made up of individual log cabins surrounding a larger central lodge. The original, like so many of the era, burnt down in 1952, but was quickly replaced by a similar if better fire-proofed model. This is what you see today, a cluster of chic wooden cabins with a country-club-meets-upscale-holiday-camp air.

The lodge's centerpiece is the grand Emerald Lounge, open to all-comers and backed by stupendous Lac Beauvert views. Its rustic backwoods decor instills a cozy fireside ambience. Think log furniture, low-hung chandeliers, assorted taxidermy, and fireplaces hewn from local stone. Flop down on a sofa with a whiskey and shoot off some emails.

GRAND RAILWAY HOTELS

The Jasper Park Lodge is one of four grand railway hotels that remain in the Canadian Rockies. The others are **Chateau Lake Louise** (p104), **Banff Upper Hot Springs** (p67) and the **Prince of Wales Hotel** (p213) in Waterton.

The aptly named **Lac Beauvert** (literally 'beautiful green' in French) is an all-season recreation lake popular for boating in the summer and ice-skating in winter when it's smoothed over by a Zamboni. There's a boathouse beside the lake along with a challenging Stanley Thompson–designed golf course attached to the Jasper Park Lodge. Shoes and clubs can be rented at the hotel. Try not to whack a bear. Grizzlies and black bears are not unknown on the fairways.

The lake and hotel are easily hikeable from Jasper Town and a 3.4km (2.1-mile) path circumnavigates the water incorporating both forest and golf course.

GETTING AROUND

Jasper is toying with the idea of a local public transportation system like Banff's to serve the Pyramid Bench, the Jasper Park Lodge and the campgrounds immediately south of town. But,

as yet, it hasn't materialized. For the energetic, all of these places are currently linked by well-defined hiking and walking paths. The town center is highly walkable.

Beyond Jasper Town

Snake Indian Pass
Snake Indian Falls
Celestine Lake
Mt Robson
Jasper Town
The Whistlers
Valley of the Five Lakes

Using train, car, bike, aerial tram or your own two feet, there are many places to eke out an adventure around Jasper.

Jasper's ruggedness unfolds gradually as you sally forth from the townsite. Thanks to a network of well-marked, interconnecting trails, people with a measure of physical mettle can reach several outlying sights by bike or on foot. Other attractions require car or train travel.

To the west, the Yellowhead Pass, the lowest of the Rocky Mountain passes, marks the border with British Columbia and is overlooked by the region's highest peak, Mt Robson. To the south lie the park's largest campgrounds and its most legendary mountain-biking trails. To the northeast the Overlander Trail, which parallels Hwy 16 for 16km (10 miles), is dotted with the legacy of some of the region's original homesteads.

TOP TIP

Pop into the Parks Canada Information Centre on Connaught Dr for excellent maps of Jasper and its local trail network.

GALYNA ANDRUSHKO/SHUTTERSTOCK ©

Mt Robson (p141)

A MOUNTAIN-BIKING NIRVANA

Unlike more rule-ridden national parks, the majority of Jasper's trails are multipurpose and not just exclusively reserved for hikers.

Cyclists experience few limitations here and it's an open secret among mountain bikers that the park harbors some of the most panoramic, varied and technically demanding rides in Canada, nay North America.

Many trails emanate from the townsite, including challenging single-track on the Pyramid Bench, and easy forest paths around the Athabasca River Valley. Unless you're on a fat bike, the season runs from May to October, which is also when bears are most active. Ride with caution (and bear spray).

If you didn't bring your own bike, there are half a dozen rental businesses in Jasper Town offering a full gamut of makes and models.

Jasper SkyTram

Ascending The Whistlers

INSTANT ACCESS TO THE ALPINE

While Banff has three different gondola options, Jasper offers just one: an aerial tramway that utilizes a slightly different technology to its southern cousins, shunting two large passenger cabins up and down a fixed moving cable. The **Jasper SkyTram** (jasperskytram.com) is the largest and highest of its type in Canada and whips visitors up the steep slopes of **The Whistlers**, a 2470m (8100ft) mountain 7km (4.4 miles) southwest of Jasper Town, in a brisk seven minutes.

The SkyTram doesn't actually call at the summit. For that you'll have to hike 1.3km (0.8 miles) further up the rocky ridge where 75km (47-mile) views justify the energy expenditure. On a very clear day you can see Mt Robson – at 3954m (12,972ft), the highest point in the Canadian Rockies – to the northwest.

If you're poor, masochistic or simply love hiking, contemplate toiling *all* the way to the top. A 7.3km/4.5-mile (one-way) trail starts 1.6km (1 mile) east of the main SkyTram parking lot. The forest-shaded path – graded as 'difficult' – winds steadily

MOUNTAIN TWINS

Banff's version of The Whistlers is **Sulphur Mountain** (p65). Both peaks offer illuminating mountaintop activities, tough ascent trails and the option of gliding up or down on a gondola/aerial tram.

  WHERE TO STAY AROUND JASPER

The Whistlers Campground
Jasper's largest campground has undergone extensive refurbishing, with new showers and washrooms. $

Becker's Chalets
A complex of 118 riverside chalets with cute 1940s 'heritage' cabins and big modern four-plexes. $$

Wapiti Campground
Jasper's second-biggest campground, on the banks of the Athabasca River, is open year-round. $

uphill, roughly paralleling the route of the gondola and passing through various Rocky Mountain life zones – montane, subalpine and alpine – en route. There's a fun scramble halfway up courtesy of a recent rockslide.

The 'summit' **chalet** is equipped with a cafe/restaurant and obligatory gift shop, and is located well above the tree line in the alpine zone. Bring extra clothing, even in high summer.

The SkyTram was constructed in 1964 and has proved to be enduringly popular. It's open from late March to late October and online ticket reservations are recommended. Cars depart every nine minutes.

The Blank Points on the Map

BACKPACKING THE NORTH BOUNDARY TRAIL

Study a detailed map of Jasper and you'll notice the top third of the park is practically blank. Although this extensive region packs in plenty of spectacular scenery, it contains no roads, no facilities and warrants no mention in popular park brochures and trail guides. To all intent and purpose, it's off the radar.

Blanketed in dense mountains, the rugged north is composed of a bristling backcountry of bugs, mud and roaming fauna, where accommodations is at primitive campsites and a throne toilet is considered the height of luxury. For skilled adventurers, this is wilderness of the highest order, where you're often three or four days' walk from civilization, and a week can pass without encountering any of Jasper's other two million annual visitors. The main path through the region is the 192km (120-mile) **North Boundary Trail**, a demanding self-sufficient trek dotted with 20 primitive campgrounds and numerous river crossings (only some of which have bridges). Long stretches of shadowy forest and boggy marsh are punctuated by several reaffirming highlights, such as thunderous **Snake Indian Falls**, the ice-encrusted southwest face of Mt Robson (the tallest mountain in the Canadian Rockies) and the meadowed magnificence of **Snake Indian Pass**, the trail's highpoint at 2128m (6982ft).

Although lightly trafficked, the North Boundary Trail is relatively well maintained. It's usually tackled east–west over eight to 12 days starting at **Celestine Lake**, 53km (33 miles) northeast of Jasper Town, and finishing near Mt Robson on Hwy 16. Due to river levels, it's best attempted mid-August to early October. Careful trip-planning and a backcountry permit are essential.

BEAR IN MIND

Bear paranoia has dampened the thrill of many a Jasper adventure, but summer hikers would be foolish to tiptoe around in a state of perpetual fear.

Fatal bear attacks in Jasper are extremely rare. There have been just *three* in the national park's 120-year history. And while lesser attacks aren't unheard of, they still only occur at the rate of about one a year, invariably involving people who haven't followed the correct hiking etiquette (making noise, carrying bear spray).

In essence, bears are peace-loving beasts who shirk human contact and will far more likely run away from you than bristle for a punch-up.

The park has around 200 bears in an area covering over 11,000 sq km (4247 sq miles) meaning your chance of spontaneously meeting one is slim.

 WHERE TO MOUNTAIN BIKE AROUND JASPER

Overland Trail	Pyramid Trail	Saturday Night Loop
This popular historic trail parallels Hwy 16 and is refreshingly flat, passing an early-20th-century homestead.	A speedy downhill jaunt from Pyramid Lake to Jasper Town on bumpy forest paths.	A technical 27km (17-mile) ride through a root-ridden and some-times swampy forest, with plenty of nature-watching.

TWO BECOME ONE

In the early 20th century, two railway companies began layng steel across the Canadian prairies in a bid to cement a new transportation corridor.

The Grand Trunk Railway (GTR) and the Great Northern Railway (GNR) reached Jasper almost simultaneously in 1911, forging parallel lines through the region's seemingly impenetrable valleys and mountains.

But WWI put an end to any ideas of quick profits and, by the end of the 1910s, both companies were in financial difficulties.

To remedy this, the Canadian government intervened in 1919, amalgamating the GTR and GNR into one federal enterprise, the Canadian National Railway. One of their earliest actions was to build a magnificent new train station in Jasper.

Jasper by Train

A SPECTACULAR ARRIVAL

Arguably the best way to see the landscapes beyond Jasper Town is on a train – be it on a day trip, a deluxe multiday package from Vancouver, or a full-blown cross-continental journey.

Despite the late arrival of the railway in the northern Rockies, Jasper has always been more of a train town than Banff. The line runs directly through the town center where kilometer-long freight trains regularly hold up traffic and a cross-continental passenger service operated by VIA-Rail (viarail.ca/en) still stops at the historic station twice a week. Jasper is also the terminus for a separate thrice-weekly service to Prince Rupert on the British Columbia coast.

Arriving in Jasper by train is still an enjoyable experience, particularly if you're coming from Vancouver. The iconic *Canadian* train runs east overnight equipped with large comfy seats and deluxe sleeper compartments. You can fall asleep somewhere around Kamloops and wake up in time for an early-morning view of snowcapped Mt Robson, weather permitting.

For a more substantial fee it's possible to ride with the private **Rocky Mountaineer** (rockymountaineer.com) along the same route but in a ritzier train that stops overnight in Kamloops to maximize mountain-viewing time. The Vancouver–Jasper route, called 'Journey Through the Clouds,' offers a specially curated package with professional guides and fine dining.

A third option is to take an organized train tour on the Jasper–Prince Rupert Skeena line as far as McBride, British Columbia, before returning in a bus. Several Jasper agencies offer this as a day trip.

COMPETING RAILWAYS

In the early 1900s, the Canadian Pacific Railway that ran through Banff was more successful than its northern counterparts. Today, it only offers **private train tours** (p78) while Jasper, thanks to the Canadian National Railway, still maintains a public transportation service.

Mountain Biking the Valley of the Five Lakes

ONE OF CANADA'S BEST SINGLE-TRACKS

If Jasper does one thing better than Banff – and every other Canadian national park – it's off-road mountain biking.

WHERE TO HIKE AROUND JASPER —————————————

Wapiti Campgrounds Trail
An easy trail that interacts with the Athabasca River, passing campgrounds between Jasper Town and Wapiti.

Dorothy & Christine Lakes Trail
An uphill hike to small lakes from the Yellowhead Hwy through quiet forest.

Wabasso Lake Trail
A connector to the Skyline Trail, the Wabasso tracks from the Icefields Parkway over low ridges to an idyllic lake.

Views from the Rocky Mountaineer

The park's intricate network of trails fanning out from the central hub of Jasper Town is extensive, well maintained and incredibly varied. Its crowning glory? A scenic two-wheeled odyssey known as the **Valley of the Five Lakes**.

This technically challenging 27km (17-mile) loop is not for beginners. Get ready to be taken on a hair-raising journey over sinuous single-track, bone-rattling rocks, sudden drops, abrupt inclines and twisted roots.

Like most of Jasper's best bike trails, the Five Lakes loop is easily accessible from the townsite via trail 1 that cuts around the back of the mega-popular Old Fort Point.

Linking up with path 9 after a few kilometers, the ride gathers pace as you glide on a narrow but nontechnical path through quiet tracts of sun-dappled forest to the lakes themselves, approximately 10km (6.2 miles) to the south. Here, things get decidedly trickier, and your bike-handling skills will be given a thorough evaluation with sharp turns and even sharper rocks. Good luck if you can make it around all five lakes without losing your balance.

Save time during your bike-beasting to take the pace down a notch and enjoy the tranquility of the sleepy, ultra-clear lakes with their resident loons and shimmering emerald coloration.

To get back to the townsite, you can double back on the opposite side of the lakes and reunite with trail 9, or cross a plank bridge over the Wabasso Creek Wetlands and return along asphalt Hwy 93.

MT ROBSON

Measuring just shy of 4000m and sitting wholly in British Columbia, Mt Robson is the highest peak in the Canadian Rockies and its spine-chillingly steep southwest face is a sight to behold.

While located just outside Jasper, it is visible from many places from within the park and dominates the drive west along the Yellowhead Hwy to the Continental Divide.

Mighty Robson is protected in a provincial park of the same name that abuts Jasper and marks the start of the equally mighty Fraser River that flows 1375km (854 miles) to the sea at Vancouver.

There's a visitor center aside the main road extolling the virtues of the park's steep glaciers, prolific wildlife and superb hiking spearheaded by the Kinney Lake and Berg Lake trails.

GETTING AROUND

The Valley of the Five Lakes can be easily reached from the townsite on two wheels.

A daily shuttle bus operated by Sundog (sundogtours.com) runs between Jasper Town and the SkyTram when it's open. You'll need your own wheels or a taxi to get to the trailheads for the North Boundary Trail.

MALIGNE VALLEY

The Maligne Valley runs from Maligne Canyon to the northern tip of Maligne Lake, a small but busy hub for numerous water- and land-based activities, especially in the summer. It's accessed by the 43km (27-mile) Maligne Lake Rd that begins at the HJ Moberly Bridge just outside Jasper Town and dead-ends on the lake's north shore, where there are a couple of eating joints, a boathouse and trailheads for a quintet of paths.

On the way, you'll pass seasonally shrinking Medicine Lake and the launchpad for a backpacking route to smaller Jacques Lake. The paved road bisects a wildlife corridor and is one of the easiest places in the park to see moose, bears and other big fauna.

Beyond its busy north shore, Maligne Lake quickly dissolves into burly wilderness. There is no road loop. The only access is via mega-popular summer boat cruises or with your own oar-power.

TOP TIP

There are six bridges at Maligne Canyon with several trails threading between them. The further you wander from the main parking lot by First Bridge, the more the crowds thin out. By the time you hit the riverside trail between Fifth and Sixth bridges, you'll practically have the path to yourself.

LEFT: ELENA ELISSEEVA/SHUTTERSTOCK ©; RIGHT: ANNA DUNLOP/SHUTTERSTOCK ©

Medicine Lake (p146)

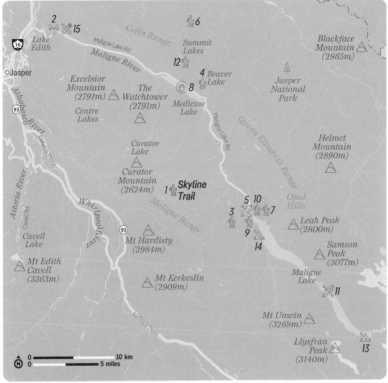

Maligne Lake (p144)

HIGHLIGHTS
1 Skyline Trail

SIGHTS
2 Maligne Canyon

ACTIVITIES & TOURS
3 Bald Hills Loop
4 Beaver Lake
5 Curly Phillips Boathouse
6 Jacques Lake
7 Mary Schäffer Loop
8 Medicine Lake
9 Moose Lake Loop
10 Opal Hills

11 Spirit Island
12 Summit Lake

SLEEPING
13 Coronet Creek Campground
14 Hidden Cove Campground

EATING
15 Maligne Canyon Wilderness Kitchen

 WHERE TO MOUNTAIN BIKE AROUND THE MALIGNE VALLEY

Overland Trail
From Sixth Bridge, this trail heads north for over 15km (9miles) past forests, meadows, and an early-20th-century homestead.

Lower Canyon Trail
The section of trail 7 between Fifth and Sixth bridges is quiet and relatively flat as it tracks alongside the wide, fast-flowing Maligne River

Trail 7h
From the Canyon parking lot, this trail climbs to a viewpoint and then tumbles steeply downhill fully testing your brakes.

OTHER MALIGNE LAKE TRAILS

Opal Hills
This tough relentless climb incorporates a loop above the tree line on the slopes opposite the Bald Hills – a hike it closely mirrors.

Moose Lake Loop
There's a genuine chance of spotting a moose bull on this short meander around the shores of a heavily forested lagoon close to the north shore of Maligne Lake.

Mary Schäffer Loop
View the lake through the eyes of one of Jasper's earliest 'tourists' on a flat 3.2km (2-mile) circuit with interpretive signs that relate her fascinating story.

MIKE SMITH/SHUTTERSTOCK ©

Spirit Island

A Watery Wilderness

CRUISING OR KAYAKING ON MALIGNE LAKE

CONTINUE CRUISING

The tour company Pursuit, also known as Brewster, operates similar boat cruises on **Lake Minnewanka** (p82) in Banff National Park.

Maligne Lake is the largest natural lake in the Rocky Mountain parks and only slightly smaller than artificially enhanced Lake Minnewanka in Banff.

Its appeal is legendary. The classic photo shot of **Spirit Island** situated two-thirds of the way along the lake's course is world-famous. The sapphire hue of the water and the craning circle of glaciated mountains in the background only adds to the romance.

WHERE TO HAVE A PICNIC IN THE MALIGNE VALLEY

Sixth Bridge
Lovely spot by the river at the quiet end of the Maligne Canyon trail network.

Mary Schäffer Loop
Popular lookout aside Maligne Lake equipped with picnic tables and the park's classic red Adirondack chairs.

First Bridge
Buy a snack at the superb Maligne Canyon Wilderness Kitchen and plonk down for an alfresco picnic lunch.

Although the north end of the lake gets busy with the summer tour-bus brigade, the rest of the shoreline is wilderness, accessible only by kayak or boat. There aren't even any recognizable hiking trails beyond the short Mary Schäffer and Moose Lake loops, both within 15 minutes of the day lodge parking lot.

Further south, several off-the-grid lakeside campgrounds prick the curiosity of adventurous kayakers. The closest is **Hidden Cove Campground** (a doable 4km/2.5 miles). The furthest, **Coronet Creek Campground** (21km/13 miles), sits at the lake's southern tip. Beware: moose and bears frequent the lakeshore.

The easiest way to see the lake is on summer boat cruises run by Pursuit (banffjaspercollection.com), which also manage Banff's Lake Minnewanka cruises. There are a couple of tour options ranging from 1½ to two hours. Neither are cheap.

For the more physically inclined, canoes, kayaks and rowboats can be rented from the historic **Curly Phillips Boathouse**, dating from 1928. To get to Spirit Island, you'll need at least two days and camping gear.

Much of the lake's early tourist development was thanks to the pioneering spirit of Mary Schäffer, whose story can be gleaned from various interpretive boards scattered around the north shore.

A Tough Hike in the Bald Hills

STEEP CLIMB ABOVE MALIGNE LAKE

There's nothing 'bald' about the first two-thirds of the **Bald Hills Loop** hike that ascends steadily through forest on a wide, well-maintained fire road from a parking lot on the northwest corner of Maligne Lake. But as you gain altitude and the trees begin to diminish in both stature and number, the hike starts to live up to its name, shedding foliage until the hillside's thinning pate starts to look decidedly smooth.

At the 2.5km (1.5-mile) mark, the trail splits in two with an easier fire road swinging north in a long broad loop and a rougher, steeper trail (marked black for 'challenging') heading directly uphill. The two paths reunite a few hundred meters higher up next to an old fire lookout. By taking the black route, you'll save 1.5km (0.9 miles) in distance but not sweat.

From the convergence point, it's 400m to the start of the loop proper, all of it conveniently above the tree line. Views quickly unfold in all directions. Particularly dramatic are

MARY SCHÄFFER, TRAILBLAZER

History has taught us that most Rocky Mountain pathfinders were men. But, in the case of Jasper, much of the credit for opening up the region to tourism goes to Mary Schäffer, an American–Canadian naturalist who was the first non-native person to lay eyes on Maligne Lake in 1908.

Accompanied by her trusty mountain guide, Billy Wilson, Mary undertook extensive travels around the Canadian Rockies in the early 1900s and first got wind of a magical lake long known to Indigenous Peoples as 'Chaba Imne' from a map drawn by a Stoney First Nation trail-setter called Samson Beaver.

She returned to the lake in 1911 to survey the area for the Canadian government and was responsible for naming many of the surrounding peaks.

WHERE TO SPOT WILDLIFE IN THE MALIGNE VALLEY

Moose Lake
This small aptly named lake is the ideal place to view Jasper's giant ungulates peacefully feeding in the water.

Medicine Lake
Head to the north end of the lake where it's relatively easy to spot black bears where the Excelsior Fire has cleared thick foliage.

Maligne Canyon
Bighorn sheep are occasional visitors in the craggy confines of the park's deepest canyon.

BEAVER, SUMMIT & JACQUES LAKES

This is a 'long' hike with an abundance of saving graces including broad paths, little elevation gain and three turn-around options at three equally handsome lakes: Beaver Lake, Summit Lake and Jacques Lake.

The popular trail kicks off at the southern end of Medicine Lake and manages to navigate its way out of the Maligne Valley and into a narrow side-valley with minimal climbing.

Thanks to its low altitude, the hike is accessible year-round (in winter it becomes a cross-country ski trail). It's notable for its glorious views of the Colin and Queen Elizabeth ranges around the lakes and ample possibilities for spotting wildlife.

Moose are often seen foraging in the lakes and signs of bear activity are everywhere – if not the bears themselves.

It's 12.2km (7.6 miles) one way to Jacques Lake, where there's a much-loved eight-tent campsite.

the perspectives to the east over Maligne Lake and north toward the **Skyline Trail** and the Queen Elizabeth Range.

Turn right and head uphill at the start of the loop and you'll soon be standing on the summit. Weather permitting, the rest of the route is clearly visible. First track down to a viewpoint over the wilderness Evelyn Creek Valley. Then climb briefly to a rocky ridge, before descending and looping through alpine meadows back to the trail junction just below the summit. From here you can retrace your steps to Maligne Lake.

Disappearing Medicine Lake

GOING UNDERGROUND

A geological rarity, **Medicine Lake**, 20km (12.5 miles) south of Jasper on the Maligne Lake Rd, is not technically a lake at all, but the point where the Maligne River disappears underground for several kilometers as a 'losing stream' before converging with the Athabasca River. The water is absorbed into the ground through a series of small holes. When glacial meltwater is high in summer, the holes aren't large enough to absorb all the water and the broad river valley clogs up like a slow-draining sink in need of some bleach.

The back-up of water results in the formation of Medicine Lake, a shallow body of water that can measure 7km (4.4 miles) in length when it appears in late spring. In October, as water flow eases again, the lake starts to disappear leaving a series of featureless mudflats that are quickly covered by snow.

The sporadically disappearing lake was a constant source of bewilderment to early visitors who couldn't find any visible water outlet on the muddy lakebed. In reality, the water filters into a complex underground cave system before re-emerging downstream near Maligne Canyon.

Due to these peculiarities, Medicine Lake is a popular stop for visitors. There's a pull-over with explanatory signage at the northern end where you can contemplate the rippling water backed by the destructive signs of the 2015 Excelsior fire. The lack of thick forest means it's also a good place to spot animals, including bears, marmots and eagles.

A trail for the undemanding but lengthy hike to **Beaver Lake**, **Summit Lake** and **Jacques Lake** departs from the southern shore.

WHERE TO CAMP IN THE MALIGNE VALLEY BACKCOUNTRY

Jacques Lake
At the end of a 12.2km (7.6-mile) trail from the Maligne Lake Rd. Great place to overnight before retracing your steps. **$**

Hidden Cove
This four-site campground is a 4km (2.5-mile) paddle from Maligne Lake's north shore, making it viable for novice kayakers. **$**

Coronet Creek
Maligne Lake's most distant campground; over 21km (13 miles) from civilization and the pinnacle of a multiday kayak adventure. **$**

Maligne Canyon

THE CANYON IN WINTER

In summer, Maligne Canyon is a maelstrom of wild water carving its erosive path through a narrow weaving gorge. In winter, the water in the upper sections of the canyon freezes, enabling hikers to walk through its murky depths, admiring surreal icy formations and frozen waterfalls.

The winter freeze usually occurs between December and early April, giving a radically different perspective of the canyon's steep walls from below rather than above.

Because of falling ice and other safety issues, it's best to explore with a guide. Several companies in Jasper Town offer daily winter tours lasting around three hours. Cleats and boots are provided and experienced guides can lead you into hidden caves not visible to the summer hordes.

Maligne Canyon

STEEP CLIFFS AND GUSHING WATER

One of Jasper's signature sights, **Maligne Canyon**, 8km (5 miles) northeast of Jasper Town, is a year-round attraction with two very different faces. From May to December, it's an attractive riverside hike that threads over half a dozen bridges with sheer drops into the abyss below. From December to May, it's an eerie stroll through a gorge full of ice sculptures and frozen waterfalls that are beloved by ice climbers.

As a natural feature, the canyon is made from Devonian limestone shaped by the torrential waters of the Maligne River. Measuring 1.2km (0.75 miles) in length, it's only a few meters wide at its narrowest point and disappears a stomach-flipping 65m (213ft) beneath your feet.

 WHERE TO SEE THE BEST VIEWS IN THE MALIGNE VALLEY

Spirit Island
One of the most famous views in the Rockies can be snapped from a cruise boat on Maligne Lake.

Bald Hills Summit
Look down on Maligne Lake on one side and the forested green baize of the Evelyn Creek Valley on the other.

Jacques Lake
The trees part to reveal mountains and maybe a moose above the reedy waters of this hike-in lake.

GOURMET IN THE WILDERNESS

One of Jasper's finest restaurants isn't in the town at all, it sits 10km to the northeast, guarding the entrance to Maligne Canyon.

The so-called Wilderness Kitchen opened in 2019 to much local acclaim serving fancy cocktails and Albertan meats cooked in an old-school smokehouse method favored by early European explorers.

The plush interior, which includes a coffee bar, gift shop, and riverside patio warmed by firepits, epitomizes what is known as 'rustic-chic' where rough backwoods architecture has been given a smooth designer touch. It's a comfortable and idyllic perch to sink a sundowner or three after an afternoon spent admiring the canyon and its bridges.

Ice climber, Maligne Canyon

The canyon is crossed by six bridges. The first was built in 1914. The newest, Fifth Bridge, opened in 2015 replacing an older model damaged in a flood.

The area is most easily accessed from the parking area on Maligne Lake Rd, near First Bridge, where you'll find the **Maligne Canyon Wilderness Kitchen**, a well-appointed eating joint on the site of a former teahouse.

However, for a more gradual approach to the canyon's most dramatic section, pull into at the Fifth Bridge parking area off Maligne Lake Rd and stroll east.

The family-friendly hike traces the banks of the Maligne River through the gorge, passing a series of waterfalls and incorporating a landscape that feels surprisingly wild given its proximity to town.

The bridges get more densely packed as you continue upstream. Third and Second bridges cross directly above dramatic cascades. Soon thereafter you'll reach First Bridge where you can loop back on trail 7f.

GETTING AROUND

Maligne Lake is 45km (28 miles) south of Jasper on a good paved road.

Aside from a June to September shuttle primarily orientated toward Skyline Trail hikers, there is no regular bus service.

If you don't have your own car, your best bet is to join one of the many guided tours offered in town, most of which include transportation from Jasper hotels to the lake.

Beyond Maligne Valley

Dramatic mountains line the west side of the Maligne Valley and are best explored on one of Canada's finest alpine trails.

Jasper

Skyline Trail • • Maligne Valley

Aside from its one arterial highway, there are no side roads leading off the Maligne Valley. To get out you have to hike. In the east, a moderate 12.2km (7.6-mile) path threads up a side valley to Jacques Lake. In the west, the solid slopes of the Maligne Range, reaching their highest point at 2956m (9698ft) Mt Kerkeslin, block easy passage. To walk among their treeless summits, you must take one of Canada's most famous multiday hikes, the peerless Skyline Trail that runs between Maligne Lake and Maligne Canyon along the rooftop of the Rockies. Equipped with six campgrounds and one rustic lodge, this area, along with the Tonquin Valley, is the park's most popular slice of backcountry.

TOP TIP

A summer shuttle bus run by Maligne Adventures (maligneadventures.com/shuttle) allows hikers to start the Skyline Trail at one trailhead and finish at the other.

JOSH MCCULLOCH/ALAMY STOCK PHOTO ©

Hiking the Skyline Trail (p150)

Skyline Trail

For many, the Skyline is the crème de la crème of backcountry hiking in the Canadian Rockies; a North American classic that hovers at or above the tree line for nearly two-thirds of its 45km (28-mile) course. Some hikers spread the expedition over three days, others tackle it in two, or even one. It's imperative to book well in advance: the hiking season is short and campground spots are limited.

1 Maligne Lake

Almost all hikers track the Skyline south–north starting by the lakeside. The first section, including the Evelyn Creek campground, is in forest.

The Hike: You'll hit the tree line at Little Shovel Campground after 8.5km (5.3 miles) and enjoy mostly wide-open vistas for the next 25km (15.5 miles).

2 Little Shovel Pass

This pass at the 10.2km (6.3-mile) mark offers views back over Maligne Lake and to the gray Queen Elizabeth Range, to the east. The pass was named by park pioneer Mary Schäffer in 1911, when she and her guides were forced to dig their way through the snow with shovels hastily fashioned out of nearby trees.

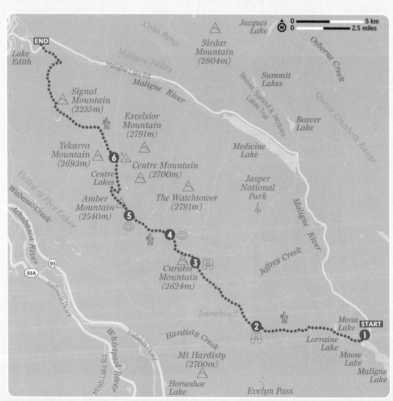

JAMES HAGUE/SHUTTERSTOCK ©

Skyline Trail

The Hike: From Little Shovel the trail dips down into the Snowbowl, a lush if somewhat boggy meadow that stretches for over 7km (4.3 miles) before starting a short climb up to Big Shovel Pass.

3 Big Shovel Pass

Perched at the 17km (10.5-mile) point, Big Shovel is replete with rugged, treeless high country and fabulous wide-open views.

The Hike: Soon after, the Skyline passes two main trail intersections. The first is with the Watchtower Trail branching off east, the second is with the Wabasso Trail branching off west. Descend 1km (0.6 miles) along the Wabasso to overnight at the Curator Campground or the backcountry Shovel Pass Lodge. Both trails can be used as escape routes in the event of inclement weather.

4 Curator Lake

Begin the day with a brisk climb up to tiny Curator Lake, which is surrounded by vast, windswept terrain.

The Hike: The trail now becomes even steeper as it climbs across bald stony slopes to the Notch, which almost feels as if you're walking on the moon.

5 The Notch

At 2510m (8733ft), this is the high point of the trail, with 360-degree views along the Athabasca Valley. The barren lunar-like pass looks almost lifeless save for the odd scavenging bighorn sheep.

The Hike: Continue on to the summit of Amber Mountain, below which the trail switchbacks down to Centre Lakes. After threading through a small valley to Tekarra Lake and traversing the north side of Tekarra Mountain, you'll hit Tekarra Campground.

6 Tekarra Campground

From Tekarra detour briefly to the Signal Lookout for a final above-the-tree-line vista before a rather long and uninspiring descent of 800 vertical meters (2625ft) over 9km (5.6 miles) through forest on an old fire road to the finish at a car park on the north end of the Maligne Lake Rd.

MIETTE HOT SPRINGS

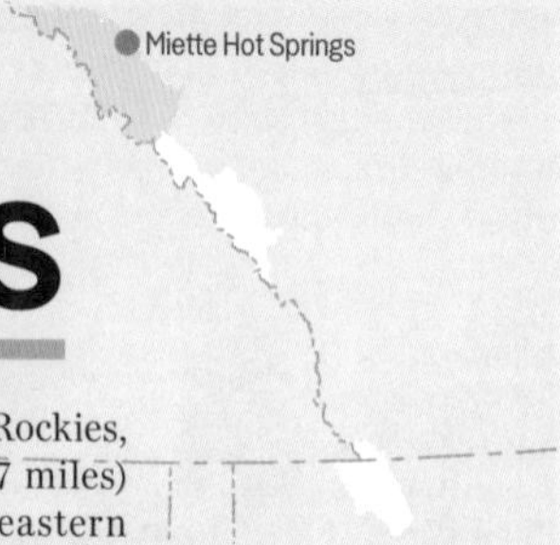

Of the three commercial hot springs in the Canadian Rockies, Miette is by far the most remote, situated 60km (37 miles) northeast of Jasper off Hwy 16, near the park's eastern boundary. There's no other settlement here and the only food and accommodations can be found at the Miette Hot Springs Bungalows, which offers cabins dating from the 1930s and chalets of a slightly newer vintage. Bears and bighorn sheep roam the grounds, phone coverage is non-existent, and everything shuts down for the season between October and May.

The springs are nestled amid mountains at the end of a 17km (10.6-mile) road that branches off Hwy 16 and winds gently through the Fiddle Valley. Aside from the medicinal waters, there are a couple of interesting hikes in the area: one easy ramble alongside Sulphur Creek to the source of the springs, and another tougher climb above the tree line to the stormy peak of Sulphur Skyline.

TOP TIP

Unlike the other two Rocky Mountain spas, Banff and Radium, Miette Hot Springs is only open seasonally between mid-May and mid-October. The approach road to the site is also closed outside of these times due to snow.

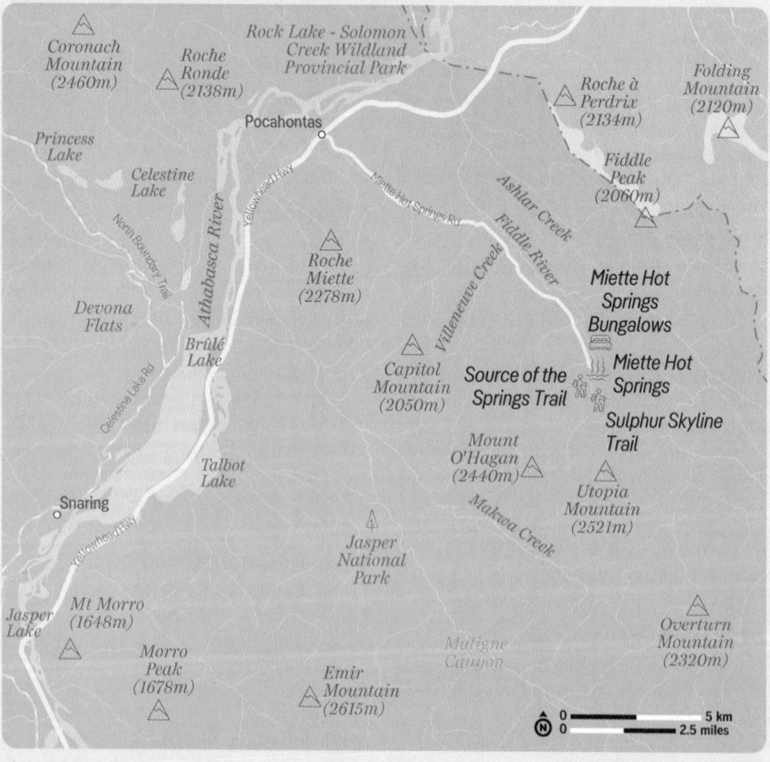

Miette Hot Springs

Getting in Hot Water

KEEPING WARM IN THE WILDERNESS

The hottest springs in the Canadian Rockies, **Miette Hot Springs** (hotsprings.ca/miette) are ejected from deep beneath the Sulphur Skyline at a scalding 54°C (129°F) before being cooled to a more bearable 40°C (104°F) in the pools of Miette's modern aquacourt. There's a warm pool, a hot pool and a couple of icy ones to get the heart racing – it's a good idea to test the water first before attempting a belly plop. Swimsuits and towels can be rented at the complex.

Long known and utilized by Indigenous Peoples, the springs were revealed to the wider world in the early 20th century and a rough trail was cut through the forest from the coal-mining community of Pocahontas in 1910. Hardy miners were the first regular bathers, nailing together a rudimentary bathhouse in 1913, but tourists only started arriving a couple of decades later after work gangs during the Great Depression constructed a road and aquacourt at Miette in the style of the facilities at Banff.

The aquacourt was replaced in the 1980s by a newer complex a little to the north, but the overgrown ruins of the original can still be seen approximately 1.2km (0.8 miles) along the **Source of the Springs Trail**.

The modern facilities have pleasantly undone ambience and are generally less crowded than Banff. On balmy summer days, the craggy mountains opposite look resplendent and close enough to touch. In fall, the pools are equally pretty when snow drifts in and steam envelops the assembled bathers. There's an on-site gift shop and cafe with wraps and paninis.

SULPHUR SKYLINE HIKE

The harder of the two hikes that lead out from Miette Hot Springs, the energetic 8km (5-mile) round-trip scramble up to Sulphur Skyline is notorious for its sudden-onset thunderstorms and scorching sun – often experienced in the same day.

The Sulphur Skyline Trail starts on a wide, paved path, which soon narrows to a less crowded single-track and continues to a clearly marked junction with the Shuey Pass trail. From here, a sharp climb ensues as the trail switchbacks through scattered forest and grassy slopes to emerge above the tree line. The final summit push cuts through a moonscape of loose rock to the windy 2050m (6724ft) Sulphur Skyline, where a sea of mountaintops stretches out in all directions.

Look south to see the Fiddle River disappearing into remote backcountry.

GETTING AROUND

There is no reliable public transportation in the Miette Hot Springs area. Car or taxi – or, at a push, bicycle – are the only practical ways of getting there. The springs are 60km (37 miles) from Jasper townsite by road.

Beyond Miette Hot Springs

Less-visited today, Jasper's eastern boundary was once a busy hub propelled by coal mining and a fur-trading post.

The Miette Hot Springs Rd branches off Hwy 16, 45km (28 miles) north of Jasper at a place traditionally known as Pocahontas. Once a thriving mining community, the junction today is marked by a bungalow resort, a campground and some scanty industrial remains. A couple of trails thread through the trees incorporating negligible mining ruins and a pretty waterfall.

Known as Pocahontas until 2020, the area's facilities, including the accommodations and campground, have been rebranded 'Miette' by an Advisory Group of the Jasper Indigenous Forum. The name Pocahontas (which you may still hear) was deemed problematic due to its sometime-use as a racial slur and the fact that Pocahontas, as a historical figure, had no regional connection with Jasper.

Pocahontas
(Miette)

Jasper House

TOP TIP

The Jasper House Viewpoint on Hwy 16 is an excellent spot to stretch your legs and get an overview of the park's early history.

AMANDA TO/SHUTTERSTOCK ©

Yellowhead Highway

Miette coal mine

When Coal Was King

AN INDUSTRIAL LEGACY

A one-time mining community, optimistically named after a lucrative colliery town in Virginia, Jasper's Pocahontas was less successful than its US counterpart, surviving for just 11 years between 1910 and 1921 when it produced tons of poor-quality, smokeless coal, much of it destined for the Allied war effort during WWI. For a short while, Pocahontas was the park's largest settlement – more populous than the budding Jasper townsite – with around 2000 inhabitants. Renamed **Miette** in 2020, all that remains today are some overgrown ruins, the old superintendent's home and a set of low-key tourist facilities, including a campground and a cabin resort conceived in the 1940s.

You can investigate the historical background on a 1km (0.6-mile) wheelchair-accessible interpretive trail that meanders around the erstwhile mining site that thrived in the days when the Canadian government encouraged resource extraction in national parks in return for handsome royalties. To widen your experience, pitch uphill on trail 32 for sweeping views of the Athabasca River Valley before pressing on to the pretty torrent of Punchbowl Falls that drops down a narrow cleft into a pool.

After a brief surge spurred by war demand, Jasper's coal industry declined as quickly as it had arisen, hindered by unprofitability and the spread of lethal gas in the mines.

The miners left a more lasting legacy at Miette Hot Springs, 17km (9.4 miles) to the south. In search of a relaxing spa on their days off, they were the first 'tourists' to exploit the recuperative waters, building a bathhouse in 1913.

JASPER HOUSE NATIONAL HISTORIC SITE

Around 35km (22 miles) northeast of Jasper on Hwy 16, a pull-over guarded by a memorial stone marks the one-time location of Jasper House, an isolated fur-trading post that once stood close by between 1829 and 1884. The 'house' was the descendant of an 1813 Northwestern Company provision depot moved here from Brûlé Lake, 20km (12.4 miles) away, and named for its one-time manager, Jasper Haws, who worked at the wooden cabin from 1817 to 1821. After 20 years refueling exhausted fur-trading parties, the post fell into decline and was mostly abandoned by the 1860s.

A short 0.8km (half-mile) trail leads through flowery foliage to the banks of the Athabasca River where a small wooden lookout equipped with interpretive panels explains the history and scenery.

GETTING AROUND

Miette (Pocahontas) is 45km (28 miles) northeast of Jasper Town on Hwy 16. There is no regular public transportation service, so you'll need your own wheels.

ICEFIELDS PARKWAY

● Icefields Parkway

As the magnificent Icefields Parkway crests Sunwapta Pass and enters Jasper National Park, you get your first real taste of the road's largest and most dramatic feature, the mighty Columbia Icefield, that makes its presence felt in the form of the Athabasca Glacier flowing off Alberta's tallest mountains to nearly kiss the asphalt. A whole industry has grown up around this dazzling spectacle; a hectic hub that includes a hotel, two restaurants, a glass 'skywalk,' and special 'Snocoaches' that drive tourists onto the glacial surface. Of all the stops on your journey, this is the busiest but most all-encompassing.

Beyond the Columbia Icefield, Jasper's section of the parkway – all 108km (67 miles) of it – quietens down and continues where Banff left off; a spectacular conveyor belt of Gothic mountains, isolated campgrounds, trailheads for remote backpacking adventures and sporadic pull-overs where you can admire waterfalls, lakes and majestic animals.

TOP TIP

With no commercial trucks, a generous shoulder throughout, and plenty of accommodations along the route (campgrounds, hostels and the occasional lodge or hotel), the parkway is a spectacular bike adventure. It's considered slightly easier to cycle from north to south, starting in Jasper and finishing in Lake Louise.

LEFT: CHANTAL DE BRUIJNE/SHUTTERSTOCK ©; RIGHT: COMSTOCK/GETTY IMAGES ©

Glacier Skywalk (p161)

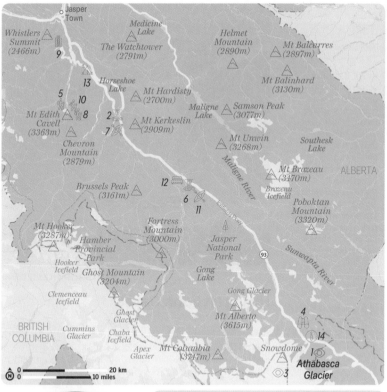

Mt Edith Cavell (p158)

HIGHLIGHTS
1 Athabasca Glacier

SIGHTS
2 Athabasca Falls
3 Columbia Icefield
4 Columbia Icefield Skywalk
5 Mt Edith Cavell Hike
6 Sunwapta Falls

ACTIVITIES
7 Athabasca River
8 Cavell Meadows Trail
9 Marmot Basin
10 Path of the Glacier Loop
11 Sunwapta River

SLEEPING
12 Sunwapta Falls Lodge
13 Wabasso Campground

INFORMATION
14 Columbia Icefields
   Discovery Centre

 WHERE TO PAUSE ON THE ICEFIELDS PARKWAY

Tangle Falls
Multilayered waterfall beside the highway with excellent views of the Stutfield Glacier looking west.

Wilcox Pass
The trailhead for one of Jasper's most beloved alpine hikes is 2km (1½ miles) north of Sunwapta Pass and the border with Banff.

Honeymoon Lake
A small lake and campground at the parkway's km 50 mark is good for a very cool late-summer dip.

THE WONDER TRAIL

By 1911, Banff and Jasper were both busy national park hubs equipped with railway stations. But to travel between the two towns still entailed a grueling three-week journey on horseback along the so-called 'Wonder Trail,' a rugged route first mapped out by surveyors marking the British Columbia–Alberta border in the 1880s.

A long dream about a road link through the mountains started to take shape in 1931 when Depression–era work gangs fashioned a 233km (146-mile) single-lane dirt road in a project that took nine years to complete.

Opened in 1941, the pioneering 'parkway' served its purpose for 20 years before an increase in car traffic necessitated the building of a two-lane asphalt replacement. Laid on top of the original route, the modern Icefields Parkway cut travel time down to 2½ hours.

THE WORLD TRAVELLER/SHUTTERSTOCK ©

Angel Glacier, Mt Edith Cavell

Hiking Mt Edith Cavell

JASPER'S MOST MONUMENTAL MOUNTAIN

Easily visible in the mid-distance from Jasper Town, **Mt Edith Cavell** (3363m/11,033ft) is one of the park's most distinctive and oft-visited peaks. The tallest mountain that's entirely in Alberta, it is known for its intimidating quartzite north face softened by the presence of the so-called **Angel Glacier**, whose icy 'wings' fan out above the floral extravaganza of Cavell Meadows.

It's the meadows and the cracking (literally) glacier views that are the mountain's biggest attraction, all accessible via a winding, precipitous road that branches off the Icefields Parkway 7km (4.4 miles) south of Jasper.

Edith Cavell, then known as Mt Fitzhugh, was first summited in 1915. It was renamed the following year in honor of a humanitarian British nurse who was executed by a German firing squad during WWI after helping to smuggle over 200 wounded Allied soldiers into neutral Holland.

There are two hikes that depart from the end of the road, both starting at the same trailhead. The 1.6km (1-mile) **Path of the Glacier Loop** takes you through stunted trees on a

 WHERE TO CAMP ON THE ICEFIELDS PARKWAY

Honeymoon Lake	**Wilcox Creek**	**Mt Kerkeslin**
Rustic first-come-first-served campsite with lake access and a restaurant nearby. $	Mostly wooded campground just north of Sunwapta Pass with a dry toilet and cooking shelter. $	A 42-site campground with drinking water and dry toilets; some plots overlook the Athabasca River. $

well-built path to a viewpoint over small milky-blue Cavell Pond, normally chock-a-block with icebergs, which nestles beneath the impressive north face of the mountain, the wings of the Angel Glacier spread celestially above it. Approaching the famous ice caves here is extremely hazardous. Keep your distance and beware of falling ice.

The 8km (5-mile) **Cavell Meadows Trail** is longer and tougher, leading to two more precipitous viewpoints.

After branching off the Path of the Glacier trail, the path begins a steep ascent north before leveling off with clear views of the glacier to the right. This area is strewn with boulders up to 4m (13ft) high, left behind by the glacier. After crossing a stream, switchbacks take you north into the forest, crossing two more streams before entering an open, flowery meadow, beyond which lies the Lower Viewpoint.

The way to the Upper Viewpoint is steep and rock-strewn, with the trail becoming fainter and slippery. It delivers you to a high subalpine meadow with an explosion of flowers where the path becomes incredibly steep and rather treacherous.

You'll know you've reached the Upper Viewpoint by the yellow marker and the sight of Angel Glacier suspended to the west revealing its wings in all their glory.

Rafting the Sumwapta & Athabasca Rivers

SHOOTING THE RAPIDS

White-water rafting is a Jasper specialty. There are two main rivers inside the park boundaries deemed rough enough for adrenaline-charged boat trips, both abutting the Icefields Parkway. The **Athabasca River** is usually tackled downstream of Athabasca Falls, where the mildly choppy water is graded as class II and deemed safe for beginners and families with kids. The **Sunwapta River**, a tributary of the Athabasca, is an altogether wilder beast. Between its headwaters on the Athabasca Glacier and turbulent Sunwapta Falls, the river throws up class III rapids at its roughest point. Previous experience and an adventurous spirit are recommended in this neck of the woods. Rafting trips can be organized in Jasper Town with several agencies who charge generic prices. The season runs from May to September, with June and July the best months.

GLACIER VIEWS

For another drone-like view of a glacier on the Icefields Parkway, ascend to **Parker Ridge** (p120), in Banff National Park, for a glimpse of the humongous Saskatchewan Glacier.

WITH THE BEETLES

Mountain pine beetles (p258) are small insects native to North America that infest a variety of pine trees with fungus by laying eggs under their bark. Once attacked, the trees' needles turn from red to gray as they slowly die.

The current epidemic began in British Columbia in the 1990s and slowly spread east into Alberta. Infestations started in Jasper in 2014 in a few spots around the townsite before growing progressively worse. Driven by warmer weather, the crisis reached a peak in 2019 when around 2300 sq km (888 sq miles) were affected by the blight.

Fortunately, a trio of cold winters have put the insect on the back burner and tests in late 2022 showed that pine-beetle infestation inside the park had dropped 94% in three years.

 WHERE TO EAT ON THE ICEFIELDS PARKWAY

Sunwapta Falls Rocky Mountain Lodge
Breakfast or dinner with a locally driven menu that includes bison bolognese. **$$$**

Altitude
Gourmet food served overlooking the Athabasca Glacier at a lofty altitude of 1993m (6539ft). **$$$**

Chalet
Cafeteria-style restaurant in the Discovery Centre for those short on time between activities. **$$**

159

© VIEWFINDER/SHUTTERSTOCK ©

Scan this
QR code for prices
and opening hours.

TOP SIGHT

Columbia Icefield

Looking magnificent from the road, the fanning snout of the Athabasca Glacier is like the protruding tail of a hidden dog. Behind it and out of sight lies a much vaster frozen plateau known as the Columbia Icefield that covers an area the size of Vancouver and feeds five more glaciers. Isolated and protected by mountains, the icy giant wasn't officially 'discovered' until 1898.

DON'T MISS

Crossing the moon-like moraine field of the Forefield Trail on foot.

Walking on thick ice in an organized hike.

Looking through the glass floor of the Glacier Skywalk.

Wrestling with the power of nature on a Snocoach tour.

The Icefield

The Columbia Icefield is the largest icefield in the Rockies, feeding five major river systems: the North Saskatchewan, Columbia, Athabasca, Mackenzie and Fraser. The vast crucible of ice is guarded by a ring of gigantic peaks, including 3747m (12,293ft) Mt Columbia, the highest mountain partially in Alberta, and the second-highest in the Canadian Rockies.

With antecedents going back a quarter of a million years, the icefield is a remnant of the last ice age and up to 365m (1198ft) thick in places. Though topped up with around 7m (23ft) of snow a year, its six major glaciers have been in retreat for nearly 200 years.

Athabasca Glacier

The most famous and accessible of the Columbia Icefield's tentacles is the Athabasca Glacier (pictured) that slides stealthily off the slopes of Mt Andromeda and Snow Dome to within walking distance of the Icefields Parkway opposite the Discovery Centre. You can hike toward its icy snout on a couple of trails that get slightly longer each year as the glacier retreats. Alternatively, jump in an Ice Explorer all-terrain Snocoach and get driven up.

The glacier itself is 6km (3.7 miles) long and has retreated about 2km (1.2 miles) from its peak flow in the 1840s when it reached the rock moraine on the north side of the parkway.

The Forefield Trail leads out to a car park from where the Toe-of-the-Athabasca-Glacier Trail loops close to the fringe of the behemoth itself.

Discovery Centre

Situated next to the Icefields Parkway, close to the 'toe' of the Athabasca Glacier, the green-roofed Columbia Icefield Discovery Centre is the hub for all activities and a mini-museum to the Icefield's scientific significance. Decamp here to purchase tickets and board buses for the Snocoaches and Glacier Skywalk. You'll also find a hotel, cafeteria, restaurant, gift shop and Parks Canada information desk.

Ice Walks

The most intimate and – let's face it – environmentally friendly way to access the Columbia Icefield is to walk on it with the help of a professional guide who knows the terrain and can navigate you around the various cracks and crevasses. Athabasca Glacier Icewalks (icewalks. com), a company with nearly 40 years of experience, can supply you with both gear and guides for an illuminating ice walk. They offer a basic three-hour tour, a six-hour option for those wanting to venture further out on the glacier, and an Indigenous-led tour that shines a light on the icefield's significance to First Nations people. Book in advance. Tours convene in the Discovery Centre parking lot.

Ice Explorers

The most popular way to get on the glacier is via the Columbia Icefield Adventure tour, which uses 56-seater 'Snocoaches' to access the ice. The large hybrid bus-trucks grind a track onto the ice, where they stop to allow passengers to study the surface and take a billion selfies for around 20 minutes. Entertaining drivers offer jocular narrations. Tickets can be bought at the Discovery Centre or online; tours depart every 15 to 30 minutes.

GLACIER SKYWALK

Opened in 2014 to ripples of architectural acclaim, this glass-floored, glass-sided, open-air lookout and walkway is suspended high above the Sunwapta River opposite Mt Kitchener, giving you the feeling of floating in midair over the valley. Numerous outdoor panels divulge the details of the surrounding geology, wildlife and architecture. The Columbia Icefield Skywalk must be visited via tour bus from the Discovery Centre, 6km (3.8 miles) to the south.

TOP TIPS

- Dress warmly in layers and wear good shoes for the Snocoach tours. Conditions on the glacier are usually colder and windier than on the parkway.
- Take an empty bottle if you want to sample the glacial water.
- Do not attempt to cross the warning tape on the glacier – it's riddled with crevasses and there have been fatalities.
- Drive 3km (1.9 miles) south of the Discovery Centre to the Wilcox Pass trail for a fabulous 3.4km (2.1-mile) alpine hike to a splendid viewpoint.
- Tours last 2½ to three hours with no bathroom breaks. Use the Discovery Centre facilities before you embark.

SNOW DOME: THE APEX OF AMERICA?

Snow Dome, a 3456m (11,339ft) mountain that marks the border between British Columbia and Alberta and the boundary of Banff and Jasper national parks, is a hydrological apex – it stands on a triple divide.

Water from its slopes finds its way into three major river systems – the North Saskatchewan, the Columbia and the Athabasca – and ultimately flows into three different oceans – the Atlantic (via Hudson Bay), the Pacific and the Arctic.

This makes it unique in the world. Well, almost. Some geographers claim Triple Divide Peak in Montana is North America's true hydrological apex. It all depends on whether you define Hudson Bay as part of the Arctic or Atlantic oceans. With no official agreement, both peaks continue to make rival claims.

SOPOTNICKI/SHUTTERSTOCK ©

Athabasca Falls

Two Wild Waterfalls

VIEWING ATHABASCA AND SUNWAPTA FALLS

Icefields aren't the only behemoths on the parkway. There's a duo of ferocious waterfalls too. The most dramatic is **Athabasca Falls** located on the namesake river, 30km (18.6 miles) south of Jasper Town. This thunderous maelstrom of angry water cuts deeply into the surrounding limestone rock, carving out an ever-changing patchwork of potholes, canyons and channels. Not surprisingly, the falls' easy accessibility means it's super-popular with road-trippers and bus tours. Expect plenty of company.

Around the parking lot, interpretive signs explain the basics of the local geology, while winding pathways direct you toward multiple lookout points with views of the water in graphic close-up. Although only 24m (79ft) in height, the falls are immensely powerful, especially in late spring when the river is engorged with glacial runoff.

Immediately downstream, the waterfall kicks up choppy class II rapids popular with rafting companies. Trips can be organized in town.

Sunwapta Falls, the parkway's other waterfall, is located just off the main highway, 25km (15.5 miles) south of Athabasca Falls. While the Athabasca is more famous, Sunwapta – the name means 'turbulent water' in the native language of the Stoney First Nations – is more voluminous when measured on

WHERE TO STAY ON THE ICEFIELDS PARKWAY

Sunwapta Falls Rocky Mountain Lodge
Comfortable mix of suites and lodge rooms with fireplaces or wood-burning stoves. **$$$**

HI Beauty Creek Wilderness Hostel
As basic as it gets, with two small bunkrooms and a communal kitchen. **$**

Glacier View Inn
Revamped hotel on the top floor of the Icefield Discovery Centre with panoramic glacier views. **$$$**

the international Beisel scale (class 6 compared to Athabasca's class 5). The impressive upper falls drop 18m (59ft) from a hanging valley into the deeper, U-shaped Athabasca Valley. There's a hotel here, the **Sunwapta Falls Lodge**, and an affiliated restaurant. The falls are also the start of a 15km (9.3-mile) biking and hiking trail to remote Athabasca Crossing near Hamber Provincial Park.

Skiing Marmot Basin

JASPER'S SKI CENTRAL

While Banff sports three ski areas, Jasper has just one: the loftily perched **Marmot Basin** located 19km (11.9 miles) southwest of Jasper Town, up a twisting road that branches off Hwy 93A. A daily shuttle runs between the resort and the townsite in winter only. The season normally starts in November and stretches into early May.

Measured statistically against other Rocky Mountain ski resorts, Marmot holds its own. Although not incredibly snowy (Banff Sunshine gets twice as much powder), there are 95 varied runs and regular equipment upgrades: the longest high-speed quad-chair in the Rockies was added in 2009.

Marmot has been in operation since the early 1960s and a proper road was first built up the mountain in 1970. Thanks to its relative isolation, it gets much shorter lift lines than the Banff resorts. The downside: it can get cold this far north and there's no on-mountain accommodations.

Tracking the Old Highway

QUIET ALTERNATIVE TO ICEFIELDS PARKWAY

Rather like the Bow Valley Parkway in Banff, Jasper maintains an old section of the Icefields Parkway as a quiet spur road that's little-used by through traffic. **Highway 93A** runs parallel to Hwy 93 for 24km (15 miles) just south of Jasper Town on the opposite side of the Athabasca River.

As well as marking junctions with the Marmot ski road and the road to Mt Edith Cavell, Hwy 93A passes a British military camp, the tranquil **Wabasso Campground** and the confluence of the Athabasca and Whirlpool rivers at the so-called Meeting of the Waters, a once busy trading post where heavily laden expeditions would forge west to Athabasca Pass. It rejoins the Icefields Parkway at Athabasca Falls. The road is great for cycling but closed in winter.

DAVID THOMPSON

Born in the UK in 1770 to poor Welsh parents, David Thompson became one of the lions of 19th-century exploration and, arguably, the finest cartographer who ever lived.

Employed as a fur trader for the Hudson's Bay Company and, later, the Northwest Company between 1792 and 1812, he traveled over 90,000km (55,923 miles) under his own steam mapping out 3.9 million sq km (1.5 million sq miles) of North America (an area larger than India) using just a sextant, drawing instruments, a telescope and two thermometers.

Jasper was pivotal in his travels and, guided by Indigenous Peoples, Thompson became the first European to cross Athabasca Pass in 1811.

His maps were so accurate they continued to be used for over 100 years until the advent of satellite technology in the 1950s.

GETTING AROUND

Most people drive the parkway in a car but there are other options.

Sundog (sundogtours.com) runs summer tours along the parkway all the way down to Lake Louise and Banff, stopping off at major sights en route, including Athabasca Falls and the Columbia Icefield.

Cycling is another possibility and there are various campgrounds, hostels and lodges to break the journey.

If heading south from Jasper, bear in mind it's mostly uphill until you cross into Banff National Park.

Beyond Icefields Parkway

West of the Icefields Parkway, Jasper quickly dissolves into wilderness as you approach the lofty ramparts of the Continental Divide.

Various routes penetrate Jasper's mountainous western boundary, none of them paved. An undemanding introduction is the 10km (6.3-mile) romp to Geraldine Lakes, a rocky scramble through a staircase-like valley brimming with lakes and waterfalls. Going up a notch is Athabasca Crossing, a 30km (18.6-mile) out-and-back haul with a couple of reclusive campsites. A more challenging trail to Athabasca Pass, an old fur-trading route and national historic site, is 55km (34 miles) and for expert hikers only.

The joker in the pack is the Tonquin, a wild and beautiful valley, sufficiently trafficked by adventurers to make it feel accessible. There are no roads in this unspoiled Eden but seven secluded campgrounds.

TOP TIP

It is wise to book Tonquin campsites several months in advance through Parks Canada (reservation.pc.gc. ca). Reservations normally open in late March.

Amethyst Lake

LEFT & RIGHT: TOBIN AKEHURST/SHUTTERSTOCK ©

Off-the-Grid in the Tonquin Valley

OVER THE HILLS AND FARAWAY

Of all Jasper's brawny backcountry, the roadless **Tonquin Valley**, 25km (15.5 miles) west of the Icefields Parkway, is the most accessible and rewarding; an uncultivated wilderness in the shadow of the aptly named **The Ramparts** mountains that on a good-weather day can feel a bit like a lost world.

To protect important caribou and grizzly-bear habitat in the area and help balance the park's ecological integrity with the demands of visitors, the Tonquin was significantly 'rewilded' in 2022 when Parks Canada closed two longstanding backcountry lodges that once hosted ski-tourers and horseback riders.

Lodges or not, it's still viable to hike into the Tonquin backcountry between mid-May and October with the valley retaining seven campgrounds and one rustic 26-capacity backcountry hut. While out-and-back trips are possible, most tramp the valley in a horseshoe-shaped curve between two trailheads just off the Icefields Parkway: **Portal Creek** trailhead near the Marmot Basin and **Astoria** trailhead on the Mt Edith Cavell Rd. The total distance is 43km (27 miles) although it's perfectly feasible to prolong your adventure with side trips. The hike is best done counterclockwise from Portal Creek, entering the valley via 2157m (7077ft) Maccarib Pass from where the Ramparts slowly reveal their splendor.

The valley's main nexus is broad **Amethyst Lake** overlooked by the Continental Divide and surrounded by flat, boggy meadows where you'll encounter the region's two main annoyances: mud and mosquitos. Boardwalks help curtail the mud; repellent will thwart the insects. Thanks to the rewilding, you're far more likely to spot bears, caribou (pictured) and other creatures great and small. Don't travel without bear spray.

WOODLAND CARIBOU

Jasper's most iconic fauna is also one of its most threatened. The woodland caribou is a subspecies of the more common tundra-roaming caribou.

Rather like the bison, the elegant animal was once ubiquitous in much of North America but hunting and habitat loss has seen its numbers drastically diminished. The woodland caribou live in smallish herds in subalpine regions where they subsist on a diet of lichen.

Jasper has two endangered herds in the Tonquin and Brazeau Valleys numbering less than 60, and a more stable northern group in the park's remote mountains numbering around 140.

To protect their habitat, authorities schedule seasonal trail closures and the Tonquin Valley was permanently shut to horse traffic in 2022.

GETTING AROUND

There are no roads in the Tonquin Valley and only two routes in – from the Astoria trailhead 13km (8.1 miles) up the Mt Edith Cavell Rd next to the HI Wilderness Hostel, and from the Portal Creek trailhead on the Marmot Rd just below the ski resort.

Most people do the hike as an anticlockwise circuit starting at Portal Creek and concluding at Astoria.

Hiker, Glacier National Park

GLACIER NATIONAL PARK

GLACIALLY CARVED NATURAL WONDERLAND

Peaks that will leave you gasping at their magnitude, 700 (1126km) miles of trails, 2000 lakes and an abundance of nature converge in this seemingly endless wilderness.

This high-country nirvana is home to some of the most spectacular scenery in North America. Two thousand glassy lakes, hulking granite peaks, rushing waterfalls, untamed forests and huckleberry-scattered slopes straddle a million acres along the border of the United States and Canada.

Glacial forces molded this epic rugged landscape and its immense valleys over two million years, and visitors are allowed to peek inside a biodiversity time capsule, where big-horn sheep (pictured), mountain goats, and black and grizzly bears roam free.

Glacier's accessible and authentically wild boundaries exist thanks to American naturalist and conservationist George Bird Grinnell, who had the foresight to protect these ancient lands. Uniquely, Glacier is one of few national parks you can

easily visit without a car, riding the route used by the Great Northern Railway, built in the early 20th century before automobiles took off. From train stations, shuttles whisk visitors into the park and to shudder-inducing Rocky Mountain vistas, while those with vehicle reservations can drive the spectacular Going-to-the-Sun Road, which bisects the park, crossing the Continental Divide along a windy, vertiginous, mountain-hugging 50-mile (80-km) stretch of asphalt.

Glacier has adventures suited to everyone, from multiday backpacking hikes for hard-core mountaineers to atmospheric nature boardwalks for families and wheelchair users, but this decade could be the last chance to see the remaining, and rapidly diminishing, 25 named ice glaciers. If there was ever a time to visit this epic natural wonderland...this is it.

THE MAIN AREAS

WEST GLACIER
The park's
largest lake.
p170

TWO MEDICINE
Nature-rich east
park entrance.
p186

**POLEBRIDGE &
THE NORTH FORK**
Lesser-visited area,
for wild adventures.
p196

ST MARY & MANY GLACIER
Home to the park's
most accessible glacier.
p199

Find Your Way

Glacier National Park is one of the few parks in the US where you don't need to have a car to explore. During the summer months, trains stop near multiple park entrances and shuttle buses whizz park-goers to trailheads. If you do want to drive the epic roads in peak times, you will need a reservation.

Polebridge & the North Fork, p196

The place for solitude, with charming hikes, glassy lakes and off-grid stays. Plus free camping along the Flathead River.

St Mary & Many Glacier, p199

Start or finish of the Going-to-the-Sun Rd and the best chance to spot bears.

West Glacier, p170

Home to the park headquarters, the largest lake in Glacier, a historic lodge and the start or finish of the iconic Going-to-the-Sun drive.

Two Medicine, p186

A less-visited area of the park, once the hub of east-side activities, with trails aplenty and an abundance of wildlife.

(Map labels) Red Rock Pkwy · Waterton Park · North Fork Flathead River · MONTANA · Belly River · CANADA / USA · Kintla Lake · Kintla Glacier · Agassiz Glacier · Bowman Lake · Kootenai Lakes · Mt Cleveland (10,466ft) · Ptarmigan Tunnel · St Mary River · Duck Lake · Babb · Many Glacier Rd · Quartz Lake · Glacier National Park · Lake Sherburne · Lower St Mary Lake · Polebridge · Logging Lake · Grinnell Glacier · St Mary · Heavens Peak (8987ft) · Logan Pass · Mt Siyeh (10,014ft) · St Mary Lake · Rising Sun · Divide Mountain (8665ft) · Lake McDonald · Going-to-the-Sun Rd · Camas Rd · Jackson Glacier · Blackfoot Glacier · Pumpelly Glacier · Rising Wolf Mountain (9513ft) · Kiowa · Apgar · West Glacier · Harrison Lake · Mt Stimson (10,142ft) · Two Medicine Lake · Whitefish · Coram · Nyack

TRAIN

Amtrak *Empire Builder* trains stop at the feeder towns of Whitefish and West Glacier (near a park entrance), plus East Glacier Park (near a park entrance) and the feeder town of Browning. The line starts in Seattle and finishes in Chicago.

CAR

A reservation system has been implemented for cars from May 26 to September 10, between 6am and 3pm. Many drive to do the mesmerizing 50-mile (80km) Going to the Sun Rd, bisecting the park from west to east. Expect congestion during peak times and queues at parking lots.

0 | 20 km
0 | 10 miles

Hikers, St Mary (p205)

Plan Your Time

Glacier National Park is enormous and seasonal. Plan before you go, prioritizing preferred activities and their locations, whether it's white-water thrills and solitude hikes or nature spotting and snowshoeing.

If You Only Have One Day

Get your bearings and take in staggering Rocky Mountain views, lakes and waterfalls with a century-old sightseeing tour on a vintage **Red Bus** (p177). Or try **Sun Tours** (p194) with Blackfeet guides for an Indigenous perspective on the park. Finish with a short hike – the **Rocky Point Nature Trail** (p176) is an awesome wander through Douglas fir and lodgepole pine to stunning western-shore views of Lake McDonald.

Two Days to Travel Around

Drive the **Going-to-the-Sun Road** (p178) past soaring Rocky Mountain vistas, waterfalls and wonderful hikes like the **Avalanche Lake Trail** (p172). Drive to the highest point in the park, **Logan Pass** (p176), before catching a star party at the **St Mary Visitor Center** (p201). Sleep in the historic **Many Glacier Hotel** (p204) before hitting the **Grinnell Glacier Trail** (p202) to see a glacier up close.

Seasonal Highlights

SPRING	SUMMER	AUTUMN	WINTER
The park slowly wakes from hibernation. Closed businesses open their shutters, wildflowers pop and wildlife gets active.	Trails are busy, traffic jams are common, but all trails and attractions are open and it's just warm enough to lake swim.	The landscape is awash with fall colors, and trails and attractions have fewer visitors.	Lakes are frozen over, the trails are empty, and cross-country skiers and snowshoers are in their element.

WEST GLACIER

West Glacier

The most accessible area of Glacier National Park (25 miles/ 40 kilometers) from Glacier Park International Airport and the popular feeder town of Whitefish) is home to the park's headquarters at Apgar Village. Here, a cluster of guesthouses and shops sit on shimmering Lake McDonald. Visitors can find amenities – information, coffee, backcountry permits and outdoor equipment rentals – before exploring the nearby trails, craggy peaks, waterfalls, lakes and immense wildflower-carpeted valleys. It's also the gateway to Going-to-the-Sun Road – the mind-bogglingly scenic 50-mile (80km) road through the park, and the most popular attraction in Glacier.

During the low season (November to May) it's not possible to drive from west to east due to snowfall and avalanche risk, but eastern sections can be accessed via Hwy 2, which skirts the southern boundaries of the park before connecting with Hwy 89 in the east.

TOP TIP

Apgar Village is the place to get wi-fi (at the visitor center), and download maps and audio tours – the rest of the park has very little cell signal.

LEFT: TUSHARKOLEY/SHUTTERSTOCK ©; RIGHT: KELLY VANDELLEN/SHUTTERSTOCK ©

Going-to-the-Sun Road (p178)

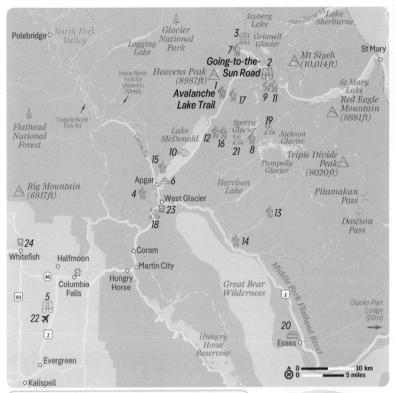

Granite Park Chalet (p181)

HIGHLIGHTS
1 Avalanche Lake Trail
2 Going-to-the-Sun Road

SIGHTS
3 Granite Park Chalet

ACTIVITIES & TOURS
4 Apgar Lookout Trail
5 Glacier Aviation Services
6 Glacker Park Boat Company
7 Granite Park Trail
8 Gunsight Pass Trail
9 Hidden Lake Nature Trail
10 Lake McDonald
11 Logan Pass
12 Mt Brown Lookout Trail

13 Nyack Creek/Coal Creek Loop
14 Nyack Ranger Station
15 Rocky Point Nature Trail
16 Snyder Lake Trail
17 Trail of the Cedars

SLEEPING
18 Glacier Campgound
19 Gunsight Lake Campground
20 Issak Walton Inn
21 Sperry Chalet Campground

TRANSPORT
22 Glacier Park International Airport
23 West Glacier Station
24 Whitefish Depot

 WHERE TO CAMP IN WEST GLACIER

Apgar Campground
The park's largest tent site is close to Apgar Village amenities on the southern tip of Lake McDonald. $

Glacier Campground
West of West Glacier, sites are surrounded by woodland. Basic wooden cabins offer heaters and fans. $

Avalanche Campground
Camping among old cedar trees. Heavy foot traffic because of popular nearby trails. $

The Avalanche Lake Trail

Just north of Lake McDonald Lodge, off Going-to-the-Sun Road, the awesome morning or afternoon Avalanche Lake Trail hike offers ancient woods, a narrow gorge and a charming amphitheater lake at its finale, clasped by mountains. It's an ideal introduction to what the park has to offer, and the one to do if you only have time for a few attractions (note: it can get busy in summer season).

1 Trail of the Cedars

Starting at an elevation of 3047ft (928m) and climbing 596ft (181m), this 3.6-mile (5.8km) out-and-back trail (taking roughly 2½ hours) starts at the Trail of the Cedars trailhead.

Get the shuttle or park at Avalanche Campground and meander through a stretch of the Trail of the Cedars (roughly 0.4 miles/0.6km), where half-a-century-old cedar trees rise to 100ft (30m) with trunks up to 7ft (2m) wide before the Avalanche Creek trailhead. Or tackle the full (1-mile/1.6km) wheelchair-accessible loop, which is great for children, with signs pointing out Rocky Mountain maple, western hemlock, Pacific yew, black cottonwood and a fallen tree with its intricate spiderweb of roots intact.

The Hike: From here it's a short, but steep climb through humid fairytale-like woods, with moss-covered boulders and bracken-fern-strewn floors.

JOHN REDDY/ALAMY STOCK PHOTO ©

Trail of the Cedars

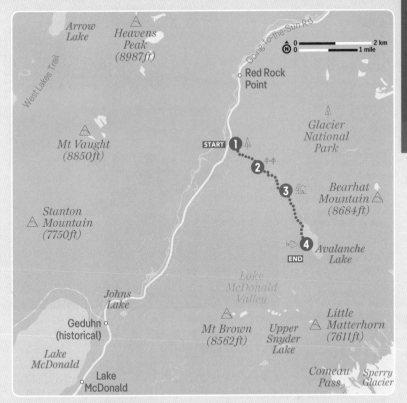

2 Avalanche Creek

Through the damp, mysterious trees listen out for birdsong as the majestic banks of a smooth, narrow gorge appear like a scene from an *Indiana Jones* flick. A bridge crossing the water offers the perfect vantage point to snap a photo of the bubbling indigo-blue waters in the center of purple argillite-layered bedrock and a blanket of deep-green moss above.

The Hike: The sounds of rushing glacial waters draw nearer as walkers get closer to the banks of Avalanche Creek, traversing densely wooded pathways.

3 Follow the Creek

Valley views appear in the clearings between the trees. In spring, meltwater will be cascading down the snow-tipped mountains. Keep your eyes peeled – the lake will come into view.

The Hike: A mile-long (1.6km) path skirts the western shore of Avalanche Lake with many entry points to the pebbled beach, where hikers can sit and picnic.

4 Avalanche Lake

Formed 12,000 years ago by glaciers, the half-mile (0.8m), 60ft-deep (18m) Avalanche Lake sits at the bottom of the looming Bearhat Mountain, rising up 8690ft and reflected in the emerald-green mirror of water below. Anglers come here for the abundance of westslope trout discovered in the lake, which scientists found are a genetic match to fish that existed here hundreds if not thousands of years ago.

WINTER ADVENTURES

Exploring the park in winter months is an entirely different experience. While many campgrounds and roads are closed, the wilderness turns into a desolate frozen dreamscape ripe for cold-weather pursuits, from snowshoeing and cross-country skiing trails to ice climbing and igloo building.

Glacier Adventure Guides runs day and multiday trips involving sleeping in quinzees (snow shelters) at Fish Creek, frozen waterfall viewing at Snyder Basin, and thousands of acres of open snow to explore at Firebrand Pass.

ROBERT PAULUS/SHUTTERSTOCK ©

Kayaking, Lake McDonald

Dip into Lake Life

FISHING, KAYAKING, PADDLEBOARDING, EXPLORING

Lake McDonald is the first of Glacier's magnificent bodies of water, flanked by towering mountains, that many visitors clap eyes on. This also happens to be the largest lake in the park – it's a mile (1.6km) wide and some 10 miles (16km) long, and was formed during the last ice age.

Fishers can enjoy this beautiful setting while catching gullible trout, either on the shore or in a small boat. The **Glacier Park Boat Company** rental shack sits on the south side of the lake, and offers hour-long tours of the emerald waters on historic vessels, some dating back to the 1920s. Meanwhile, **Glacier Outfitters** hires kayaks and paddleboards for those wanting to explore the shores and beaches of the lake by paddle power. It's possible to drive to the west side of the lake via the Going-to-the-Sun Road and over to its eastern shore as the road descends into St Mary.

 WHERE TO STAY IN WEST GLACIER

Village Inn at Apgar
Country-style motel rooms with terraces or balconies facing Lake McDonald with mountain views. **$$**

Glacier Homestead
Rustic lodge rooms, cabins, and hostel with shared bathrooms on a family-owned ranch in Coram. **$**

West Glacier KOA Resort
Sprawling campground with all the frills: wi-fi, sauna, laundry, playground, pool, dog park and cafe. **$$**

Boulder Down the Rapids

SCENIC AND THRILLING RAFTING TRIPS

Go deep into the park without having to hike by taking a rafting tour. Choose between a family scenic rafting tour (simply floating among spectacular views) or some thrilling but unintimidating rapids (graded class I to III).

Tours take place on the boundary of the park, with several rafting centers including the **Glacier Raft Company** and **Glacier Guides and Montana Raft** located in West Glacier. Tours mostly visit the glacially fed and incredibly clean North and Middle Forks of the Flathead River, but custom trips are also possible. Ask about overnight stays, where rafters camp in remote areas with their group (equipment provided) for greater wildlife-spotting opportunities – often seeing deer, mountain goats, osprey, eagles, beavers and bears, and hearing howling wolves. **Wild River Adventures** offers overnight tours with fly-fishing experiences.

Bird's-Eye Glacier Views

CONTINENTAL DIVIDE HELICOPTER TOURS

Scenic half-hour flights leave from **Glacier Park International Airport** with knowledgeable guides from **Glacier Aviation Services** and offer unparalleled views of West Glacier's big sights including the park's largest lake, Lake McDonald, and the imposing Continental Divide to the east. They also get within hundreds of feet of Stanton and Grant Glaciers and the towering monsters of Mt Stimson, Glacier's second-highest peak at 10,147ft (3092m), plus Mt Jackson, Glacier's fourth-tallest mountain, rising over 10,000ft (3048m) in elevation, and the 9381ft (2859m) Mt St Nicholas.

Ride the Train to Glacier

RAILWAY ADVENTURES THROUGH A NATIONAL PARK

Glacier National Park has a deep connection to the railway. In fact, it probably wouldn't exist if it weren't for the Great Northern Railway train line, which ran from St Paul in Minnesota to Seattle in Washington, and was developed in the 1890s by legendary railroad director James J Hill. The Amtrak *Empire Builder* train (named in honor of its creator) still spans the breadth of the US from Chicago to Seattle and transports plucky park-goers along the track on a 1½-hour journey between **West Glacier Station** (also known as Belton) and East Glacier Park Station (summer-

HOW TO IDENTIFY GLACIER'S BEARS

Researchers have estimated that there are roughly 1000 bears living within the boundaries of Glacier National Park, including black bears and grizzly bears.

However, size and color are not reliable enough indicators to determine each species, as black bears can be brown or blond, and grizzlies can also have dark coloring.

The easiest way to distinguish between them is by checking for a shoulder hump, prominent on grizzlies, which also have shorter rounded ears and light claws that are two to four inches long. Black bears don't have shoulder humps, but do have taller ears and dark claws that are around an inch and a half (3.8cm) long.

Belton Chalet
Swiss-style chalet opened in 1910 overlooking the railroad tracks in West Glacier. Rooms are elegant. **$$**

Sperry Chalet
Off-the-grid lodging in Glacier's backcountry; private rooms without lights, heat or water. Stays are full-board. **$$**

Lake McDonald Lodge
One of Glacier's century-old lodges with Western decor, taxidermy details and a huge fireplace in the lobby. **$$**

SADDLE UP

Cover more ground via mule with Swan Mountain Outfitters, which offers beginner-friendly horseback rides from Apgar and Lake McDonald, taking between one and three hours, through lush forests and along the flathead river.

The ride from Apgar climbs 1850ft (563m) to the Lookout Fire Tower for awesome 360-degree views of Lake McDonald and the mountains beyond. Swan also offers a number of trail rides outside the park entrance, but with equally impressive terrain, through larch trees and cottonwoods and Glacier Park mountain views, just off Hwy 2.

only stop). It's an atmospheric scenic route into the park with staggering views of the Rocky Mountains.

Train fanatics can stop (by request) in the tiny town of **Essex**, home to the Tudor–revival-style Izaak Walton Inn (p195). It has a footbridge over train tracks, for locomotive spotting, and offers sleeps inside remodeled railcars, from cabooses to a diesel locomotive. Guests can also dine in a restaurant surrounded by train memorabilia.

From Essex, the *Empire Builder* travels through to the 5220ft (1591m) Marias Pass and over the Continental Divide before arriving in East Glacier – a gateway to the sublime Two Medicine area and home to East Glacier's historic Glacier Park Lodge (p193), built with towering Douglas fir logs in 1913 by the Great Northern Railway.

Many choose to do the journey as a day trip, staying in the smart outdoorsy mountain town of Whitefish and boarding at **Whitefish Depot**, a charming Tudor-style station designed by renowned railroad architect Thomas McMahon in the 1920s.

Quick Hikes to Conquer

SHORT WALKS IN WEST GLACIER

Rambles under two hours are a way to get a taste of the sheer beauty the park has to offer, requiring little to no hiking experience. Some of Glacier's short trails are accessible for wheelchair users and most are family-friendly; visitors will likely see babies in backpacks and small children.

The flat 0.8-mile (1.28km) **Trail of the Cedars** loop (off Going-to-the-Sun Road) is an excellent place to start, on a wooded boardwalk through giant ancient cedar trees. The short but punchy **Rocky Point Nature Trail** is a terrific 1.9-mile out-and-back hike beginning at the Rocky Point trailhead and going to the western shore of **Lake McDonald**, through Douglas fir, lodgepole pine and fire-scorched forests to mind-blowing views of the lake. Stretch the legs a little more on the active-family-friendly 2.8-mile (4.5km) out-and-back **Hidden Lake Nature Trail**, climbing 540ft (164.6m) from **Logan Pass Visitor Center**, along an initial boardwalk through alpine meadows and lingering snow (even in the summer months) for staggering views of Garden Wall, Bearhat Mountain, Mt Reynolds and Heavy Runner Mountain. Look out for mountain goats and bighorn sheep, and grizzlies are sometimes seen in this area.

 BEST PLACES TO SHOP IN WEST GLACIER

Glacier Outfitters
Outdoor gear in Apgar, everything from waterproof bags and SPF lip balm to bear spray.

School House Gifts
A wall of Stetson–style hats, indigenous-style blankets and Glacier–themed T-shirts.

West Glacier Gifts
T-shirts, souvenirs, water cups and locally made body products plus huckleberry jam.

KELLY VANDELLEN/SHUTTERSTOCK ©

Red Bus Tours

Jump Aboard a Red Bus

A CENTURY-OLD SIGHTSEEING TOUR

Glacier's vintage rides, known as the 'Rubies of the Rockies,' are iconic emblems of the park. Many of the buses have been in service since the 1930s.

Red Bus Tours were introduced in 1914, becoming the first authorized motor vehicles in any US national park. The elongated Model 706s have open tops for unobstructed views of the park, but can be covered when rain showers occur. A dozen shuttles and tours whizz visitors around the park in style and hit the big attractions and jaw-dropping views – they range from a few hours to nine-hours long and run from mid-May to late September. Longer tours cover both the east and west sides of the park. Trips depart from Apgar Village and Lake McDonald Lodge in the west, and Swiftcurrent Motor Inn, St Mary Lodge and Many Glacier Hotel in the east (bookable via glaciernationalparklodges.com).

WHAT TO DO IF YOU SEE A BEAR

Glacier is one of the few places left where it's possible to see bears in their natural habitat.

Be bear-safe by hiking in a group, which will reduce your chance of an encounter, and make noise along a trail. Call out or clap if you are approaching a blind bend where a bear may be startled by your presence. Carry bear spray (and learn how to use it in advance); it can be rented and bought from all out-door stores and some grocery stores in the area.

If camping, do not leave food or anything with an odor in your tent. If camping in the backcountry, use a bear canister and hang your food away from your tent. If you see a bear on a trail, stay calm, pick up any children you are with, and move out of the way and let it pass.

If it is unsettled, stop moving and speak to it in a calm voice. Do not drop your pack. Do not run. As the situation allows, leave the area or take a detour.

 BEST FOR SUPPLIES IN WEST GLACIER

West Glacier Camp Store
Camping supplies from camp stoves to rehydrated meals, sleeping bags and hiking boots. Before park entrance.

The Cedar Tree
Good selection of gifts and books in Apgar for adults and children, such as how to identify animals by their poo.

Camp Store
The final shop before Logan Pass next to Lake McDonald Lodge. Groceries, drinks, gifts and books.

Going-to-the Sun Road

Cutting through the center of Glacier National Park, connecting West Glacier with St Mary in the east, this epic rollercoaster ride over the Continental Divide is one of the most spectacular roads in the US. Spanning 50 miles (80km), it climbs up to Logan Pass (6646ft/2025m) and is bursting with soaring vistas, hiking opportunities, glacial melt spewing down the rocks, and rushing waterfalls. The entire road is usually open June to October.

1 Apgar Village

Start here for sublime views from the south of Lake McDonald. Rent a kayak and go for a paddle before the drive.

The Drive: From Apgar Village drive 9 miles (14.4km) northeast to Lake McDonald Lodge, through pine trees around the east side of the lake.

2 Lake McDonald Lodge

Stop at the oldest lodge in the park, built in 1895 as the Glacier Hotel, but replaced by a Swiss-style building in 1913. Step inside the grand hunting lodge lobby, adorned with deer heads, atmospheric lanterns, and a huge fireplace.

The Drive: From Lake McDonald Lodge, drive 6 miles (9.6km) to the small parking lot near Avalanche Campground – it can be full in peak season so come early.

3 Avalanche Creek

Park here for a gentle meander up to Avalanche Lake (4.5 mile/7km round trip) – a punchy bang-for-your-buck trail starting at the Trail of the Cedars trailhead.

Hiking above Going-to-the-Sun Road

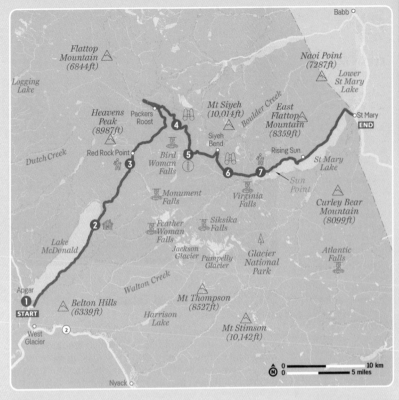

The Drive: From Avalanche Creek drive 8 miles (12.8km), through the 192ft (58.5m) West Tunnel, to The Loop – a giant switchback at an elevation of 4400ft (1341m) – and a further 3 miles (4.8km) past Garden Wall.

4 Bird Woman Falls Overlook

Stop to take in the highest waterfall on the drive, plummeting from 492ft (150m) in between Mt Oberlin and Mt Cannon, and formed by a glacier that melted around 12,000 years ago.

The Drive: Climb the switchbacks a further 5 miles to Logan Pass, the highest point of the road at 6500ft above sea level.

5 Logan Pass

Named after Glacier's first superintendent, Major William R Logan, the highest part of the park accessible by car sits at 6500ft (1981m). The visitor's center is open between mid-June and mid-September, exhibiting alpine plants and animals.

The Drive: Descend (8km) toward St Mary past staggering valley views and the trailhead to the challenging 25-mile (12.8km) Piegan Pass Trail to Jackson Glacier Overlook.

6 Jackson Glacier Overlook

Pull over to spy one of the remaining 25 glaciers in the park on the side of Mt Jackson, and the fourth-tallest mountain soaring to 10,052ft (3063m).

The Drive: Drive 3 miles (4.8km) through dense forest past St Mary Falls trailhead toward Sunrift Gorge.

7 Sunrift Gorge

Stretch your legs with a 1-mile (1.6km) round-trip hike to Baring Falls, tumbling 25ft (7.6m) over a rocky ledge, and continuing on to reach the rushing St Mary Falls (a further 2 miles/3km). Snap an iconic photo of the tiny Wild Goose Island before finishing the drive at St Mary Visitor Center.

BEST PLACES TO DRINK

Belton Chalet Grill & Taproom
Microbrews and craft cocktails inside a historic West Glacier building, opposite the train station.

Packer's Roost
Classic Western road-side dive bar in Coram, decorated with bank notes and license plates. Cheap beer and burgers.

Glacier Distilling Company
Craft whiskey distillery in Coram, offering flights of liquor and cocktails in its tasting room.

Freda's Bar
Outside the west entrance of Glacier, serving microbrews on outside tables for a post-rafting crowd.

Paul Bunyan Bar and Grill
Decorated with chain-saws and lumberjack decor. Friendly spot with a pool table, cheap beer and great burgers.

THEJUSTINMUELLER/SHUTTERSTOCK ©

Granite Park Chalet

Day Hikes in West Glacier

MODERATE TREKS OVER TWO HOURS

A good orientation hike for those spending plenty of time in the park is the 6.6-mile (10.6km) **Apgar Lookout Trail**, climbing a calf-pounding 1950ft (594m) along switchbacks to views over southwest Glacier and the Flathead River to the south, although for much of the trail views are blocked by lodgepole pine and Douglas fir.

Avalanche Lake Trail (see page 172) is a terrific 4.6-mile (7.4km) round trip that half-day hikers shouldn't miss, with ancient moss-covered forest, a waterfall and a magnificent glacial lake at its finale. The 8.8-mile (14km) out-and-back **Snyder Lake Trail** offers the opportunity to camp at the end of the trail (at 4.4 miles/7km), turning it into an overnight excursion. However, it's very doable as an afternoon or leisurely day hike, with a steep 2360ft (719m) elevation gain through dense forests and opening onto terrific views of Little Matterhorn and Mt Brown before the trout-rich lake appears (look out for the waterfall at its far end).

For a strenuous day-hike workout, conquer one of the toughest hikes in the park: the steep **Mt Brown Lookout**

WHERE TO GO FOR SNACKS IN WEST GLACIER

Russells Fireside Dining Room
In Lake McDonald Lodge; local huckleberry-elk burgers and Rocky Mountain cheeses. **$$**

The Cedar Tree
In Apgar, serving the best coffee around, Montana Coffee Traders roasts, plus sweet and savory snacks. **$**

West Glacier Cafe
Canteen-style joint, just outside the park entrance, serving burgers and huckleberry ice cream. **$**

Trail (8.8-mile/14km round trip) starts at Lake McDonald and climbs 4260ft along dozens of switchbacks but the payoff is big – epic panoramic views of the whole Lake McDonald Valley. Hiking to **Granite Park Chalet** (either 8.4 miles /13.5km from The Loop or 15.2 miles/24.4km out and back via the Highline Trail from **Logan Pass**) offers soaring bird's-eye views of Heavens Peak, Garden Wall and Swiftcurrent Mountain. The shorter trail climbs 2450ft through fire-devastated woodlands before entering healthier foliage, areas of regeneration and countless wildflowers. Some choose to stay overnight at the **Granite Park Chalet**, dating back to 1915 and built by the Great Northern Railway from stone for backcountry hikers. It's a friendly and basic spot with a dozen rooms for hikers, and a communal kitchen (book in advance).

Backcountry Hiking & Camping

WILDERNESS CROWDS-FREE TREKKING

The two-day **Gunsight Pass Trail** is a great intro to backcountry hiking in West Glacier. Covering 20 miles (32km) round trip and climbing 3280ft (999m), it has views of glaciers, brilliant peacock-colored alpine lakes and plenty of wildlife-spotting opportunities. Stay at the basic backcountry **Sperry Chalet** campground or **Gunsight Lake Campground** with an advanced reservation.

For information on wilderness hiking and camping before you set off, pay a visit to one of the wilderness offices, such as the **Apgar Backcountry Permit Center** next to Glacier Outfitters, which offers details on current trail conditions, packing and planning tips, and issues wilderness permits for overnight stays in the backcountry at 65 designated wilderness campgrounds. It also lends free bear canisters to hikers, for proper food storage when in remote campgrounds. Roughly 30% of all sites are reserved for walk-in campers, but multiday backpackers can take walk-in sites in advance.

One of the most primitive and demanding hikes in the park is the multiday **Nyack Creek/Coal Creek Loop**, a rewarding 42-mile (67.5km) rugged hike, often covered in fallen trees and requiring multiple river crossings; hikers are guaranteed solitude and it's the only place in the park offering the chance to camp without a reservation anywhere off the trail, rather than in a designated campground. Find the Nyack Creek/Coal Creek Loop trailhead along Hwy 2, near the **Nyack Ranger Station** – hikers have to cross the Middle Fork of the Flathead River to access the next section of trail.

 GETTING AROUND

Affordable shuttles run from the nearby communities of Whitefish, Columbia Falls and Kalispell (home to Glacier Park International Airport).

Free park shuttles (in summer only – check updated schedules) run around the park to the most popular trailheads, and from stations to the park entrances (for a small fee).

Bikes can be rented in Apgar Village.

Beyond West Glacier

Towns and attractions ouside the park

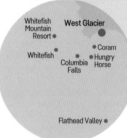

Beyond West Glacier are the feeder towns of   (for Glacier Park International Airport) and Whitefish, plus the tiny communities of Coram, Hungry Horse and Columbia Falls are packed with accommodations options and amenities.

Originally known as Stumptown, thanks to the timber that had to be cleared to build it, the walkable town of Whitefish (30 minutes from Glacier) has become a de facto adventure base (trains to the park leave from the town's historic station). Its close proximity to an underrated ski resort, a huge lake, and biking and hiking trails ensures there's an easygoing outdoorsy crowd here all year-round.

TOP TIP

Rent camping equipment, bear spray, walking poles and more 24/7 from the lockers at the Wilderness Edge by inserting your credit card.

DANITA DELIMONT/ALAMY STOCK PHOTO ©

City Beach, Whitefish

KARIN HILDEBRAND LAU/SHUTTERSTOCK ©

Fly-fishing, Moose Lake (p145)

Cast Some Lines

RIVER AND LAKE FLY-FISHING

The rivers around Whitefish, as its name would suggest, are ripe with the swimming morsels, plus other species including wild trout and northern pike. There's something very special about spending the day on one of the area's bodies of water doing what people have done for thousands of years here.

Justin and Kim Lawrence, owners of **Lakestream Fly Shop** in Whitefish, offer fly-fishing tours on the lakes and rivers in the area, including all equipment, plus lunch – beginners welcome. The **Montana Fly Fishing Experience**, run by Chris and Tara McCreedy, offers off-the-beaten-path trips. Their custom-built itineraries range from floats on big classic rivers to wading through tall grass to little spring creeks.

Lounge About at City Beach

SANDY SHORES, PADDLEBOARDING, KAYAKING

On the southern shore of the 7-mile (11km) glacially fed **Whitefish Lake** is City Beach, a sandy lake edge and a shaded grassy area where Whitefish town residents cool off on their lunch breaks in the summer months. There's a designated swimming area plus picnic tables, and kayak and paddleboard rentals are available. You'll find limited free parking, restrooms, and a refreshments hut on the beach selling gourmet hot dogs and ice cream.

MORE THRILLS

Need a break from hiking? Entertain the kids a short drive from the west park entrance here...

Big Sky Waterpark
In Columbia Falls, this is the place to cool down on hot summer days. Montana's largest waterpark has 10 waterslides and a whirlpool.

Glacier Highline
Not to be confused with the trail of the same name, this treetop adventure park (in Coram) has a vertigo-inducing aerial park, five zip lines, a climbing wall and Tarzan swing.

Amazing Fun Center
Numerous outdoor games from mini golf, bumper floats, a maze, go-karts, cornhole and the Bankshot Basketball challenge. In Columbia Falls.

THE GUIDE

GLACIER NATIONAL PARK BEYOND WEST GLACIER

BEST PLACES TO DRINK IN WHITEFISH

Spotted Bear Spirits
Locally distilled whiskey, vodka, gin and agave paired with secret herbs and spices to create original cocktails.

Bonsai Brewing Project
Welcoming microbrewery with plenty of craft brews and a nice outdoor garden area northeast of City Beach.

Great Northern Bar & Grille
Probably the hippest spot in town in a classic saloon setting with bar games and good vibes.

BEST WHITEFISH LUNCH SPOTS

Swift Creek Cafe
Low-key family-run cafe, serving freshly made doorstop farm-to-table sandwiches chock with fillings like blackened chicken thigh with pineapple oregano aioli, or bacon with basil mayo. $

Buffalo Cafe
Neighborly joint with hearty breakfasts served until 2pm (try the 'Buffalo Pies' hash browns) and terrific lunch sandwiches, salads and craft burgers using locally sourced meats and greens. $

Piggyback Barbeque
Pit barbecue joint that smokes meat with Flathead cherry wood. Pulled-pork sandwiches hit the spot. Large portions. $

Skiing, Whitefish Mountain Resort

Visit an Old-School Ski Resort

SCENIC SUMMIT TOURS, ZIP LINING, ALPINE SLIDES

Only 4 miles (6.4km) from Whitefish, the fun and friendly **Whitefish Mountain Resort**, which originally opened as 'Big Mountain' in 1947, has 12 chairlifts and two T-bars whizzing powder hounds to 14 runs. Local snowboarders often play hooky from work and hike up to the summit on fresh powder days. The mountain gets an average snowfall of 300 inches (762cm) per year and is suitable for both expert skiers and novices. Gear rental is available at Village Rentals.

Views from the 6800ft (2072m) summit are breathtaking on clear days, but it's often cloudy in winter. Summer days are the best bet for views – visitors can buy a ticket for a scenic ride, while mountain bikers use the lift for easy access to dirt trails. Zip-line tours are also available in the warmer months, with rides up to 1900ft (579m) long, and rising 300ft (91m) above the valley floor. At the self-guided **Aerial Adventure Park**, adventurers can cross cable bridges, climb ladders and swing on a trapeze. Kids love riding the luge-like Alpine Slide, traveling around half a mile down the mountain on a sled via dips, bridges and through a tunnel.

Many choose to stay in the center of Whitefish (it's only a 20-minute drive up the mountain), but there are plenty of overnight options on the Upper Village Boardwalk – **Morning Eagle** has spacious studios and one- to three-bedroom condos;

 BEST PLACES FOR DINNER IN WHITEFISH

Loula's Cafe
Inventive dishes in a former Masonic temple, from huckleberry Brie to pork with peach jalapeño glaze. $$

Latitude 48 Bistro
Fusion dishes from elk tenderloin to Asiago-stuffed gnocchi. Basement cocktail lounge. $$

Jersey Boys Pizzeria
Best pies in Whitefish, plus slices, huge calzones and more than a dozen sandwich varieties. $

don't miss a soak in the hot tub overlooking the mountain. Head to **Hellroaring Saloon & Eatery** after a day on the slopes for its legendary loaded mountain-high stacks of nachos or sink a pint at the mountain's lively timber lodge, and the first après-ski venue, **Bierstube** (or just 'The Stube'), which is packed by 4pm and hosts rock and blues musicians.

Learn About Railway History

MUSEUM IN A TRAIN STATION

At **Stumptown Historical Society Museum** in Whitefish, visitors can learn about the area's grand locomotive and logging history inside the Tudor–revival-style Great Northern Railway Depot, built in the 1920s. The on-site free museum has stacks of train memorabilia and black-and-white photos of Whitefish back in the early days. Don't miss the telegraph exhibition, where you can attempt a Morse code message on an antique telegraph.

Rest Your Hiking Legs

MASSAGE, STEAM AND SAUNA

Great for a rainy day or after a busy few days of hiking, the community-oriented **Whitefish Wave Aquatic & Fitness Center** has a lap swimming pool, sauna and hot tub for a minimal entry fee, plus a range of massages, from sports to acupressure and Swedish relaxation treatments (book in advance for an extra fee). Kids will enjoy the mini waterpark. Finish with a smoothie or fruit juice from the counter.

Explore the Flathead Valley Wilderness

HIKING, BIKING, HORSEBACK RIDING

A superb network of a dozen hiking, biking and horseback-riding trails, spanning 47 miles (75km), snake the borders of Whitefish Lake on public land in the **Flathead Valley**. Whitefish Legacy Partners have been a driving force in creating and maintaining them in an attempt to protect the 6100-acre (2468-hectare) wild space.

The 3-mile (4.8km) Swift Creek Trail is a fine ramble through old-growth forests and wildlife habitat, with sweeping views of craggy peaks. The Reservoir trailhead connects with the Whitefish Trail, climbing 1.5 miles (2.4km) to the Valley Overlook for stellar views over Whitefish Lake and across to Blacktail Mountain. Those wanting to cover more ground can rent a fat bike, cruiser or hybrid (with a car rack) at **Glacier Cyclery** in the center of Whitefish. It also rents cross-country skis in the winter months.

WHERE TO SHOP IN WHITEFISH

Whitefish Thrift Haus
The place to pick up vintage hiking boots, a sun hat or pre-used camping equipment, while helping volunteer service for women Soroptimist.

Columbia Falls Community Market
Some 100 vendors tout their wares in summer at this Thursday-evening market, selling jewelry, art and local farm produce.

Bookworks
Maps, wildflower and bird identifiers, wilderness survival and foraging guides plus other useful books.

Slow Burn Records
Independently owned with 3000 collectibles on sale, plus listening stations and open-mic nights.

Big Sky Antiques
Truly unique items from stuffed buffalo heads and an antique phone booth to a pre-Prohibition roulette wheel.

Voyageur Booksellers
Secondhand bookstore, stocking outdoor and travel tomes, plus Westerns and local hiking guides.

GETTING AROUND

Arrive at Whitefish by Amtrak *Empire Builder* train, which travels from Seattle to Chicago, or by private vehicle. Whitefish is easily bike-able. Rent one at Glacier Cyclery.

TWO
MEDICINE

Two
Medicine

Before Going-to-the-Sun Road was constructed, this lesser-visited corner was the hub of eastern activity in the park, as it was only a dozen miles by horseback from the Great Northern Railway. It has a glorious lake in the shadow of Rising Wolf Mountain, named for Hugh Monroe, a Canadian-turned–Piegan Native American who was the first non-native person to explore the region in the mid-19th century. President FD Roosevelt famously gave 'fireside chats' here at the former Two Medicine Chalet and although these days the area is less visited, its natural grandeur is no less striking than in its 1930s heyday. Reduced footfall means the wildlife-spotting opportunities are excellent. Walk the area's many scenic trails for big-mammal spotting.

TOP TIP

Amtrak's Empire Builder train stops at East Glacier Park station, then the East Side Shuttle (glacierparkcollection.com) will whisk you to the park, 30 minutes away.

Empire Builder (p195)

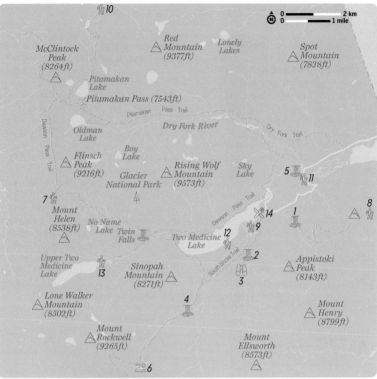

Mountain goat, Dawson Pass (p190)

SIGHTS

1 Appistoki Falls
2 Aster Falls
3 Aster Park Overlook
4 Rockwell Falls
5 Running Eagle Falls

ACTIVITIES & TOURS

6 Cobalt Lake
7 Dawson Pass
8 Mt Henry Trail
9 Paradise Point Spur Trail
10 Pitamakan Pass
11 Running Eagle Falls Trail
12 Two Medicine Lake
13 Upper Two Medicine Lake

EATING

14 Two Medicine General Store

 CURIOUS BIRDS TO SPOT IN TWO MEDICINE

Harlequin Duck
Spy these rare, regal birds
with slate-blue plumage
and white strips.

Black Rosy-Finch
Native to alpine areas above the
tree line, with pinky feathers.

Gray Jay
Aka the Canada jay
– this songbird lives
around the Rockies.

HIKE THE DAWSON–PITAMAKAN LOOP

This epic overnight backcountry adventure starts from the north shore of **1 Two Medicine Lake** and crosses the Continental Divide twice while on the 18.8-mile (30km) Dawson–Pitamakan Loop. The strenuous hike has many payoffs, including spectacular scenes of the exposed mountain ridges, solitude, plenty of wildlife- and wildflower-spotting opportunities, plus the chance to stay overnight (although it is possible as a long day hike, taking around eight hours).

Go clockwise up to Dawson Pass for a punch-packing 3000ft elevation gain into grizzly bear territory. The first major sight is the emerald green **2 No Name Lake** (4.9 miles/7.8km in) – an idyllic fishing spot beneath the walls of Pumpelly Pillar and Mt Helen, soaring to more than 8500ft (2590m). There's primitive camping here for those who start their loop later in the afternoon (get a backcountry permit before you set off).

The next section of the trail is a steep calf-flexing ascent up 1200ft in only a couple of miles to the exposed **3 Dawson Pass**, where it gets windy. The pass is, named after Thomas Dawson, of Blackfoot heritage was one of the early guides of the national park. The sheer path north skirts the Continental Divide and is filled with stunning high-country views. Continue on to **4 Cut Bank Pass** before descending to **5 Pitamakan Pass** along narrow ledges carved into the mountainside – be aware that it can be blustery here.

The conditions become far more sheltered further down at deep-blue **6 Oldman Lake** where backpackers can camp for the night, under the jagged peaks. The final 6.5 miles (10.4km) go through **7 Dry Fork** with forest and meadow sections and prime bear territory. Scan the ground for bear droppings and check the trees for bear claws while making the final descent back to the trailhead.

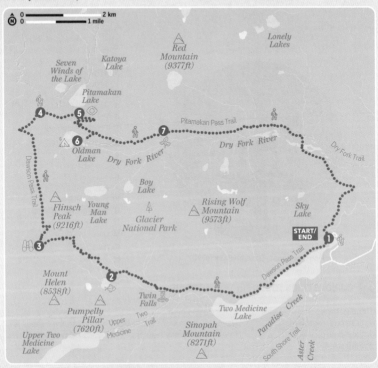

888

SMALL WORLD/SHUTTERSTOCK ©

Running Eagle Falls

Behold Running Eagle Falls

WALKING, WATERFALL SPOTTING, INDIGENOUS HISTORY

One of the most accessible hikes in the Two Medicine area is not to be missed. The short (0.8-mile/1.3km) wheelchair-accessible **Running Eagle Falls Trail** meanders through Engelmann spruce and black cottonwoods along Two Medicine Creek and crosses Dry Fork, an exposed gravel area subject to spring floods, where a unique rushing waterfall appears. In summer, the flow thins out to create a smaller waterfall at the top, which runs into a larger flow below as water pours through a cave.

This waterfall within a waterfall led to the moniker 'Trick Falls,' but the official name of this sacred site, **Running Eagle Falls**, honors a respected Indigenous female leader from the Pikuni Blackfeet tribe. Running Eagle was a fierce and knowledgeable warrior in the 1700s; a great horsewoman who conducted many war parties and raids, she was eventually killed by the Flathead during an attack. She's buried in a tree on the mountain above Upper Two Medicine Lake overlooking the falls.

A bridge (which may be out in the winter, depending on floods) crosses to the other side of the river for a close-up view of the mighty natural phenomenon and its aquamarine pool below. The trail returns to the parking lot where a short

TWO MEDICINE GENERAL STORE

Housed inside a historic chalet, built by the North Eastern Railway in 1914, the rustic and sturdy Two Medicine General Store, constructed with giant logs, provided meals and accommodations for early visitors to the area. President Roosevelt famously did a radio broadcast from here in 1934.

While it no longer offers lodgings, the building still serves basic meals (soup, chili and sandwiches), and hot drinks and ice cream. It's also well stocked with camp supplies and gifts. However, it's only open during the peak summer season.

THE GUIDE

GLACIER NATIONAL PARK TWO MEDICINE

 WHERE TO CAMP IN TWO MEDICINE

Two Medicine Campground
Three miles (4.8km) beyond the park entrance are 100 mostly shaded sites with potable water and restrooms. **$**

Cobalt Lake Campground
Backcountry primitive campsite at Cobalt Lake, with solitude and awesome views. Pit toilet, no water. **$**

Upper Two Medicine Campground
Four backcountry campsites share a pit toilet and food-prep area on the lake. **$**

BEST PLACES TO SPOT BIG MAMMALS

Bighorn Sheep and Mountain Goats
Search the rugged Rising Wolf Mountain slopes for sure-footed beasts including bighorn sheep and mountain goats.

Moose
These majestic cold-weather mountain animals are often seen at sunset along the road into Two Medicine.

Black and Grizzly Bears
Look out for bear tracks in prairie environments and flower fields plus Dawson Pass and Scenic Point Trail.

nature trail explores the native plants of the area, and their traditional uses – including spy cow parsnip, used in salads; the dark purple serviceberry fruit, a sugary treat enjoyed by the Blackfeet peoples of the area; and mountain ash, which was boiled and its steam used for relieving headaches and sore chests.

Climb to Appistoki Falls

EASY WATERFALL HIKE WITH EPIC VIEWS

Following the **Mt Henry Trail**, which sits a third of a mile before the ranger station on the left, it's a short and easy but rewarding 1.2-mile (2km) round-trip hike uphill to **Appistoki Falls**, rushing out of Appistoki Peak in spring and thinning out in summer. Continuing on the trail another 2.5 miles (4km) leads to Scenic Point (6.2 miles/10km round trip from the parking lot), climbing 2300ft (2300m) and turning it into a moderate to strenuous hike with soaring mountain views above a sea of dense emerald green forest below. This trail also runs along the Continental Divide Trail, starting at the town of Waterton Park in Canada and going all the way to the Mexican border in New Mexico.

Hike the Lake Shores

TRAILS, VIEWS AND WILDLIFE

There are a number of thrilling hikes of varying lengths to do from the south and north shores of **Two Medicine Lake** (pictured). South trails leave from the two parking lot areas and include the 1.2-mile (2km) round trip **Paradise Point Spur Trail** leading to a magnificent lakeside view. At Aster Creek another spur trail leads to **Aster Falls**, a lovely spot for a picnic, before the main trail climbs to outstanding panoramic views of the valley at the **Aster Park Overlook** (3.8 miles/6km round trip). The main trail continues to the tumbling **Rockwell Falls** (6.6 miles/10.6km round trip from the parking lot) and then on to the beautiful alpine **Cobalt Lake** (11.2 miles/18km round trip) where you can swim, fish and backcountry camp.

On the north shore of Two Medicine Lake hikers can access longer trails, including **Upper Two Medicine Lake** (9.6 miles/15.4 round trip), which some hikers combine with backcountry camping. **Dawson Pass** (13 miles/21km round trip) and **Pitamakan Pass** (15.6 miles/25km round trip), can be combined for an adventurous overnight 18.8-mile (30km) loop.

GETTING AROUND

There's one road into the park, which is accessible by car or prebooked shuttle from East Glacier Park.

A boat shuttle runs along Two Medicine Lake. Otherwise, set off on two feet on the main trails. Private vehicles will need a reservation between July 1 and September 10, from 6am to 3pm.

Blackfeet Indian Reservation •

• Browning

Two Medicine •

• East Glacier Park

Essex •

Beyond Two Medicine

Life just outside the park.

The feeder towns of Browning and East Glacier Park lie just beyond the Two Medicine entrance. East Glacier Park, a small village with a population of around 350 people, was once the main base for east-side park activity thanks to its train stop on the Great Northern Railway (Amtrak *Empire Builder* trains still stop here in summer).

There's a faded glory about the place, with vintage signs, quirky buildings and friendly locals. The upmarket crowd stays at the historic Glacier Park Lodge, set among manicured lawns, while backpackers bed up at the welcoming Brownies Hostel. The slightly run-down town of Browning, 12 miles (19km) east, is the headquarters of the Blackfeet Indian Reservation and has a terrific Indigenous museum.

TOP TIP

Travelers passing through in need of a hot shower can visit the log cabin on the south side of Brownies Hostel, which has a public coin-operated laundry and shower facilities.

Glacier Park Lodge (p193)

ATTEND A POWWOW

Blackfeet rancher, campground owner and native cowboy **Doug Fitzgerald** (liksikoyiitahta) explains why you should visit the annual North American Indian Days powwow in Browning, in the second week of July.

Indigenous Peoples come from all over the country and lots of tourists attend the powwow. It's such a good way for people to increase their awareness about our community and Indigenous history.
 At the annual Browning powwow, there's dancing, stick games, drum contests, Indian horse relay races and other traditional events. It's a peaceful and empowering atmosphere, showing that song and dance are powerful and important traditions to preserve for future generations.

North American Indian Days Powwow

Learn About Indigenous History

MUSEUM DEDICATED TO NEARBY TRIBES

Honoring the culture of the Crow, Northern Cheyenne, Sioux, Assiniboine, Arapaho, Shoshone, Nez Perce, Flathead, Chippewa, Cree and of course the Blackfeet tribes, the must-visit **Museum of the Plains Indian** in **Browning** has a sizable collection of horse gear, weapons, household goods and historic clothing, plus baby carriers and toys.

The attached gallery features prominent artists in the area. Check the website for upcoming exhibitions. Fascinating recent ones include Connections: The Blackfeet and Winold Reiss, with portraits of tribal members and leaders by German American artist Winold Reiss, who had a decades-long relationship with the Blackfeet tribe. Some of his iconic works, including the 1943 *Chief Wades in the Water*, were

 BEST PLACES TO EAT IN EAST GLACIER PARK

Brownie's Bakery
Terry Chase home-bakes huckleberry bear claws, cinnamon rolls, brownies, pizzas and sandwiches. **$**

Serrano's Mexican Restaurant
Giant enchiladas served on steaming skillets. Wicked chili margaritas. **$$**

Great Northern Dining Room
Upmarket plates in an unfussy dining room inside Glacier Park Lodge. Wild game, trout and chef-inspired specials. **$$$**

bought by the Great Northern Railway Company and these works reconnect the portraits with their community and families.

Another exhibition included the paintings of Ernest Marceau, who was raised on the **Blackfeet Reservation** – he paints on stretched canvas and creates vibrant tribal scenes that portray the warriors of the past on the Northern Plains. Plan on spending an hour or so here; the staff are generous with their time and will happily help with questions on their culture, and you can also chat with local artisans working in the gallery.

Play a Round on Montana's Oldest Golf Course

18-HOLE GREENS WITH MOUNTAIN VIEWS

Behind the Glacier Park Lodge, the **Glacier Park Lodge Golf Course** was built in 1928 by the Great Northern Railway for guests. Its 18 holes are a wonderful place to play a relaxing round for a couple of hours. The course is often empty and surrounded by dense forests and mountain views, plus there's a nine-hole pitch-n-putt course. Club rental is available at the hotel.

Sleep in the Park's First Historic Lodge

HOTEL BUILT WITH 900-YEAR-OLD TREES

Glacier Park Lodge (pictured) in East Glacier Park was built in 1913, loosely styled as a Swiss chalet and serving passengers in the halcyon days of the Great Northern Railway. It got its nickname as 'Big Tree Lodge' thanks to its lofty three-story lobby made from giant 900-year-old Douglas fir trees, although these timbers were actually sourced from Washington State. Guests can still stay in rustic rooms – with no TVs or air-conditioning – and lounge about in rocking chairs on a shaded porch with spellbinding views of the Glacier peaks.

There's a pool for cooling off in after park hikes and two on-site restaurants open to nonguests – the Great Northern Dining Room serves elegantly prepared dishes and the Empire Lounge, designed like a vintage dining train car, sells burgers, salads and sandwiches as sports play on TV.

BEST PLACES TO EAT AROUND TWO MEDICINE

Summit Mountain Lodge & Steakhouse
Cozy cabin dining, with great views. Locally sourced beef and organic produce. Deck dining for moose spotting. **$$$**

The Peak Restaurant
Reasonably priced steaks and enormous pizza in a bar setting with sport playing on multiple screens. **$$**

Two Medicine Grill
Basic diner set in wood-paneled walls, serving hearty breakfasts and good bison burgers. Open in winter. **$**

BEST PLACES TO DRINK IN EAST GLACIER PARK

Serrano's Mexican Restaurant
Serving excellent salty-rimmed spicy margaritas infused with huckleberry.

The Peak Restaurant
Go for the hard lemonade and angry orchard boozy cider or the twisted spiked tea.

Trailhead Saloon
A dive-bar vibe with pool tournaments and lots of fun, local indie beers to try.

VISITING AN INDIGENOUS RESERVATION

The 3000-sq-mile (7770-sq-km) Blackfeet Indian Reservation sits east of Glacier National Park and borders Canada, spanning an area twice the size of the park. It's home to 10,000 tribal members including those from the Northern Piegan (Blackfeet), Southern Piegan and Blood tribes, who lived in the Alberta area just north of the border in the 1700s.

The Blackfeet are known for their horse and gun skills and have a solid reputation for being some of the most formidable warriors in the West.

This warrior spirit continues today, especially through the Chief Mountain Hotshots, an elite firefighting crew based out of the Blackfeet headquarters of Browning. Known as the 'Warriors of the Forest,' this fierce crew works in large-scale wildland firefighting. Visitors to the east of the park will likely drive through the reservation to enter the park.

JUSTIN FOULKES/SHUTTERSTOCK ©

Blackfeet Indian Reservation

Tour with a Blackfeet Guide

INTERPRETIVE TOURS WITH INDIGENOUS INSIGHT

Sun Tours leave from various places around the park, including East Glacier Park, and visit Going-to-the-Sun Road in air-conditioned buses, while tribal member guides share invaluable insights on these Indigenous ancestral lands. Learn about cultural aspects of the Blackfeet people, their spiritual and philosophical perspectives, and how this area provided medicine through common plants and roots.

 BEST PLACES TO STAY BEYOND TWO MEDICINE

Brownies Hostel & Bakery
Rustic rooms and co-ed dorms inside a historic building. Shared bathrooms, communal lounge and kitchen. $

Circle R Motel
Tiny and slightly chintzy motel rooms with TVs and bathrooms. East of the station. Open year-round. $$

Lodgepole Gallery
Tipis and cabin dressed with Indigenous crafts near Browning run by a Blackfeet artist couple. $$

Skate on an Indigenous Reservation

SKATEPARK DONATED BY PEARL JAM

In the most unexpected location, off a quiet residential street among flat prairie lands, are some 12,500 sq ft (1161 sq meters) of concrete waves, plus a deep bowl, for skateboarding. The **Thunder Park Skatepark** in Browning was gifted by Jeff Ament, the bassist of the rock band Pearl Jam, to the Blackfeet people in 2018. During a moving opening ceremony of the skatepark, Chief Old Person honored Jeff with a Native American name, 'Holds Water.' If you've brought your board, it's a must-skate and a chance to meet some welcoming locals. Find it on Starr School Rd.

Sleep in a Vintage Locomotive

HISTORIC TRAIN HOTEL ON A HILL

Roughly 20 miles (32km) from East Glacier Park, off the scenic Hwy 2 southern route between each park entrance, is the mock-Tudor **Izaak Walton Inn,** built in 1939 as a refuge for Great Northern Railway winter workers tasked with clearing the snow from the rails between Essex and East Glacier Park. The place was dubbed the 'Inn Between' when plans to build a southern park entrance in the area never happened.

It's a short drive from East Glacier Park, and a stop on Amtrak's Empire Builder route in summer, where railway aficionados come from all over the world to experience sleeping in one of the painstakingly restored and refurbished locomotive rooms. Caboose cottages (the most luxurious of which has a king-sized bed and heated bathroom floor) overlook spectacular scenery and the nearby train tracks, and come with kitchenettes.

Meanwhile, the surprisingly spacious sky-blue GN441 diesel locomotive room, with the original operator's cab, was designed by a female locomotive mechanic. It has 400-year-old reclaimed oak hardwood floors, a switch that opens the engine access doors onto a view of the BNSF mainline, and a private deck complete with barbecue. Guests can also peruse the intact electrical control cabinet and eat locally sourced Flathead produce in a dining car restaurant. The inn, meanwhile, offers rental cabins and 'School House' rooms, with historic photos on the walls, plus country-style wood-paneled Empire Builder Rooms.

Activities in the area include snowshoeing, with access to 18 miles (29km) of Nordic trails (ski rentals available from the inn), and sauna bathing, plus (of course) train watching.

VISIT GLACIER'S QUIRKIEST STORE

The Spiral Spoon in East Glacier Park contains hundreds of beautiful hand-carved spoons made from local wood, plus black walnut, maple and rich cherry. Dozens of collector's items line the ceilings and display cabinets, including spoons from movies including *The Flintstones*, *Nacho Libre*, the Western TV show *Bonanza* and more.

Unusual spoons include a giant one carved with a chainsaw in Alaska and many baked maple serving implements with a caramelized tiger-striped wood appearance.

Harry Potter fans should check out the carved wand display, with a little box below reading: 'don't open me' – but do open it for a suitably Hogwarts-style prank.

The 14ft (4m) wooden spoon outside, made of papier-mâché sawdust recycled from spoon carving, ensures you can't miss it on the road into Two Medicine.

GETTING AROUND

Amtrak's *Empire Builder* train stops at East Glacier Park during the summer months. Shuttles run from the station to the Two Medicine park entrance. Tiny East Glacier Park is easily walkable.

POLEBRIDGE & THE NORTH FORK

● Polebridge & the North Fork

Forget about modern creature comforts, like cell signal and mains electricity. This area on the northwestern edge of Glacier National Park and the border of Flathead National Forest is the place to fully unplug and get away from the summer crowds, plus all the worries that come with our tech-heavy lives. Those who drive the bumpy, dusty road to get here can truly slow down, breathe in fresh mountain air, and wander with the wild things among grassy meadows and regenerated forests, plus hike some of the park's best backcountry trails. Recharge with freshly baked goods at the local Mercantile or sink a pint under propane lights in a historic rustic saloon in tiny Polebridge. Meanwhile, two dreamy lakes, Bowman and Kintla, plus the Flathead River, are ripe for water-based adventures, from boating and paddleboarding to rafting.

TOP TIP

Driving is the most common way to get to Polebridge – it's 27 miles (43km) from West Glacier, mostly on a dirt road known as North Fork Rd or Outside North Fork Rd. Camping is free just beyond Glacier's North Fork entrance along the Flathead River. There are toilets at the Polebridge Ranger Station at the entrance to the park.

LEFT: MELISSAMN/SHUTTERSTOCK © RIGHT: PATRICIA THOMAS/SHUTTERSTOCK ©

Polebridge Mercantile (p198)

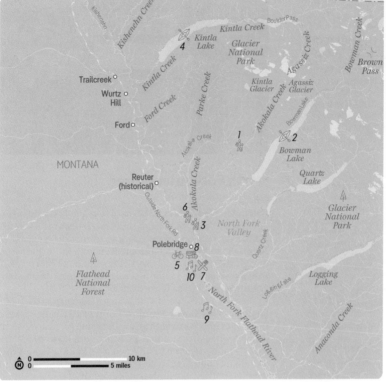

Deer, Bowman Lake (p198)

ACTIVITIES & TOURS
1 Akokala Lake Trail
2 Bowman Lake
3 Covey Meadow Loop Trail
4 Kintla Lake
5 Polebridge Outfitters
6 Polebridge Ranger Station

EATING
7 Polebridge Mercantile
8 Sasquatch Grill

ENTERTAINMENT
9 Home Ranch Bottoms
10 Northern Lights Saloon

 WHERE TO STAY IN POLEBRIDGE & THE NORTH FORK

Bowman Lake Campground
Spacious sites in forested grounds right next to Bowman Lake. It's rarely full, due to its remoteness. **$**

North Fork Hostel & Square Peg Ranch
A quirky hostel with a cabin, chalet, tipi, mixed dorm and camping. No wi-fi. **$**

Kintla Lake Campground
The park's most remote drive-in camping spot, at the top of Inside North Fork Rd. Pit toilet. **$**

KARIN HILDEBRAND LAU/SHUTTERSTOCK ©

Northern Lights Saloon

North Fork Adventures

RAFTING, BIKING AND HIKING

Polebridge Outfitters is the place to rent e-bikes, fat bikes,
rafts, paddleboards, kayaks and bear spray so you're fully kitted
out to explore the nearby creeks and rivers, plus the magical
(and uber quiet) **Kintla Lake** and **Bowman Lake** (the park's
third-largest lake after Lake McDonald and St Mary Lake).
Rent an e-bike early season and zoom the 6 miles (10km) from
Polebridge before roads are open for cars.

There are 10 hiking trails in the area, ranging from the short,
family-friendly **Covey Meadow Loop Trail** – starting near
the **Polebridge Ranger Station** and going 1.5-miles (2.4km)
through wildflower meadows in spring, with Rocky Mountain
views – to the medium 12-mile (19km) **Akokala Lake Trail**
– climbing 800ft (243m) for pristine views, alpine lakes and
wildlife spotting. For bird spotting and absolute solitude, hit
the 29-mile (46.6km) **Bowman Lake Trail**.

Pop into the Polebridge Mercantile

BAKERY, GIFT SHOP, COMMUNITY HUB

'The Merc,' as some locals call **Polebridge Mercantile**,
occupies an iconic wooden-fronted building that has served
as a general store since 1914. Visitors make the drive along
bumpy dirt tracks to try its legendary bear claws (sweet pastry
shaped into paws and filled with huckleberry jam) and hot,
gooey cinnamon buns. It's a meeting place at the center of
the community and also sells gifts, good coffee, craft beers,
wine and homemade sandwiches to go. For a more substantial
bite, try the seasonal **Sasquatch Grill** food truck next door,
serving everything from pulled pork to green curry.

 GETTING AROUND

Driving is the most common way to get
to Polebridge, 27 miles (43km) from
West Glacier mostly on a dirt road,
known as North Fork Road or Outside
North Fork Road.

There is a road running through the park
from just north of Apgar to Inside North Fork
Road, but it has been closed to vehicles from
Logging Creek to Camas Creek for some time.
Bikes, however, can use this road.

ST MARY & MANY GLACIER

St Mary & Many Glacier

St Mary in the east of the park is where prairies, mountains and forests converge. It's also the start or finish of any Going-to-the-Sun Rd drive. Centered around the second-largest lake in Glacier National Park – 9.9 miles (16km) from end to end – the area has multiple hikes darting off the road. Sadly, in 2015, parts of the forest (around 10 miles/16km from the visitor center) were decimated by the Reynolds Creek Fire, which also destroyed the historic Baring Creek Cabin, built in 1935. Hikers will see eerily apocalyptic scorched trees on routes, and the promising regeneration beneath them – stay on the trails.

Many visitors pair a visit to St Mary with a trip to Many Glacier to the north, often cited as Glacier's most beautiful valley. It's where hikers can reach the park's most accessible glacier, Grinnell, and is one of the best places in the whole park to spot bears.

TOP TIP

Shorten Many Glacier's legendary Grinnell Glacier hike with a boat shuttle across Swiftcurrent Lake from Many Glacier Hotel. Built by the Great Northern Railway in 1914–15, the hotel – with its old-world romantic Swiss-chalet facade – is a destination in itself.

ALMINTANG/GETTY IMAGES ©

Swiftcurrent Lake (p202)

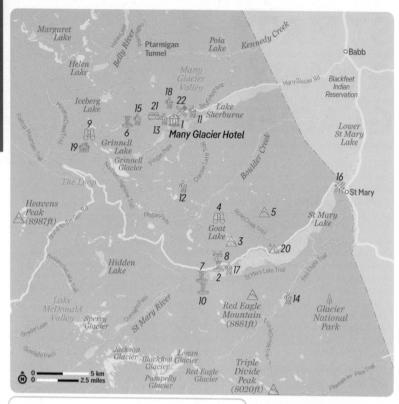

HIGHLIGHTS
1 Many Glacier Hotel

SIGHTS
2 Baring Falls
3 Goat Mountain
4 Otokomi Lake
5 Otokomi Mountain
6 Redrock Falls
7 St Mary Falls
8 Sunrift Gorge
9 Swiftcurrent Lookout
10 Virginial Falls

ACTIVITIES & TOURS
11 Apikuni Falls Trail
12 Cracker Lake

13 Grinnell Glacier Trail
14 Red Eagle Lake
15 Redrock Lake
16 St Mary Visitor Center
17 Sun Point
18 Swiftcurrent Pass

SLEEPING
19 Granite Park Chalet
20 Rising Sun Campground
21 Swiftcurrent Motor Inn

EATING
22 Ptarmigan Dining Room

Rockwell Falls (p190)

 BEST PLACES TO CAMP IN THE EAST SIDE

St Mary KOA Campground
Camping just outside the park, with impressive views, pet-sitting, pool and e-bike rentals. $

Cut Bank Campground
Peaceful campground off Hwy 89, with 14 first-come-first-served sites. No water. $

Many Glacier Campground
Primitive camping near amenities at Swiftcurrent Motor Inn – restaurant, laundry and camp store. $

Night sky above St Mary Lake

Attend a Star Party

LEARN ABOUT THE COSMOS

Glacier has **International Dark Sky Park** status, and throughout the park dark-sky-friendly lighting has been installed, which not only makes the dark sky above clearer, but reduces the impacts of artificial lighting on wildlife, especially nocturnal animals. Astronomy programs take place in various areas of the park – but the equipment is the most sophisticated outside **St Mary Visitor Center**, where an observatory with a 20-inch (51cm) telescope and astronomy camera helps visitors see projections of the cosmos on television monitors. Crowds gather and many people bring chairs during various summer star parties, usually in July and August, beginning at dusk and finishing around midnight – check at the visitor center for timings. Bring a headlamp and wrap up warm; the wind can be strong in St Mary.

WILD GOOSE ISLAND

Wild Goose Island Lookout sits 6 miles (10km west of St Mary Visitor Center on Going-to-the-Sun Road and offers a familiar view – one splashed on park promotional materials.

This is the place to stop for that quintessential Glacier park photo – with the tiny Wild Goose Island, rising just 14ft (4.3m) above the center of St Mary Lake, providing context to the enormity of the lake and soaring mountains of Red Eagle, Mahotopa, Little Chief and Dusty Star, Reynolds and Mount Logan.

The 2015 Reynolds Creek fire created a tree graveyard on the east side of St Mary Lake, but the thinned-out foliage has revealed new vistas and perspectives.

 BEST TOURS IN THE ST MARY AREA

Blackfeet Outfitters
Offers hiking and horseback-riding trips out of Babb, lead by local Blackfeet Native-certified guides.

Glacier Park Boats
Cruise St Mary Lake from the Rising Sun boat dock for an entirely different perspective.

St Mary Visitor Center
Rangers offer free guided walks of the St Mary Valley and evening talks.

Grinnell Glacier

One of the most accessible ways to view a glacier up close is via this terrific, and very popular, 10.6-mile (17km) day hike, passing epic lakes, traversing dense atmospheric forests and offering captivating mountain views, and plenty of bighorn sheep and mountain goat-spotting opportunities. Shorten the hike to 7.6 miles (12km) by taking the shuttle boat across Swiftcurrent Lake from Many Glacier Hotel and another shuttle across neighboring Lake Josephine.

1 Grinnell Glacier Trailhead

If you're not opting for the shuttle boat, full hikes start from here (just off Rte 3), where there's a large parking lot and restrooms, before heading into the dense forest.

The Hike: Continue through woodlands over a bridge on Swiftcurrent Creek and along the shore of the first astounding lake on the trail.

2 Swiftcurrent Lake

Soak in the astounding views across Swiftcurrent Lake, seeking out the distinctive conical 7600ft (2316m) Grinnell Point to the southwest of the lake, and the 7430ft (2264m) Angel Wing mountain.

The Hike: The lake views disappear and the trail continues on through the forest to the Morning Eagle boat dock (summer only).

Hiking the Grinnell Glacier Trail

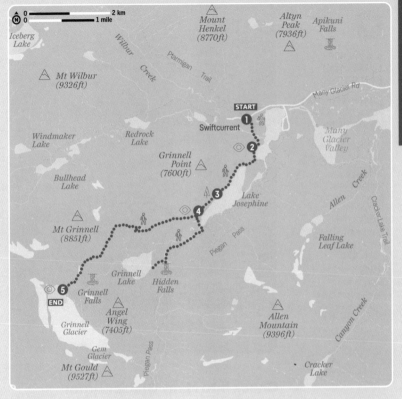

3 Lake Josephine

Hikers will approach this sublime body of water at its northern end, for views of still water, emerald green trees and snow-dappled peaks beyond. Due to its positioning, the lake will likely be iced over until May or even late June, making for a truly spectacular field of white ice, against big blue skies.

The Hike: The trail skirts the lake all the way to its southern end before coming to the Grinnell Glacier junction; bear left for Grinnell Lake and right for Upper Grinnell Lake.

4 Grinnell Lake

Those with time should pick up the short 0.6-mile (1km) round trip pathway from Grinnell Glacier junction to arguably the most impressive lake on this trail: the glacial Grinnell Lake. A peak-clasped turquoise blue bowl, its striking color was created by the silt from Grinnell Glacier.

The Hike: To get to Upper Grinnell Lake, it's a shaded walk back the way you came through ancient forests to Grinnell Glacier junction, with the sounds of the bubbling Grinnell Creek to the north.

5 Upper Grinnell Lake

Steep switchbacks up a rocky moraine lead to the piercing blue Upper Grinnell Lake and close-up views of Grinnell Glacier, where hikers can fully appreciate the 152-acre (61.5-hectare) hulk of ice, named after conservationist and explorer George Grinnell. Glaciologists have warned that it could disappear by the year 2030, due to rising temperatures.

Hikers should also look out for the smallest named glacier in the park, Gem Glacier, which sits on Garden Wall above Grinnell, and the Salamander Glacier (once connected to Grinnell Glacier) on a ledge above Grinnell.

GLACIER NATIONAL PARK ST MARY & MANY GLACIER

THE GUIDE

BEST PLACES TO EAT IN THE EAST SIDE

Johnson's of St Mary
Atmospheric Western log-cabin restaurant perched above St Mary serving steak, veal and fish dishes. $

Ptarmigan Dining Room
Fine dining inside historic Glacier Park Lodge, with lakeside views, craft cocktails and wagyu beef mains. $$$

Nell's
Diner fare at Swiftcurrent Motor Inn and open dusk till dawn in high season. Pizzas and burgers (including emu burger). $

Many Glacier Hotel

Check into Many Glacier Hotel

HISTORIC LODGE WITH OODLES OF CHARM

One of Glacier's three 'parkitecture' lodges (along with Lake McDonald Lodge in West Glacier and Glacier Park Lodge in East Glacier Park), **Many Glacier Hotel** was also built by the Great Northern Railway to serve travelers arriving at the park by trail.

Constructed in 1915, it has that similar old-world romantic Swiss-chalet facade and Western interiors to the other historic lodges, but instead is situated on the glistening southern shore of Swiftcurrent Lake. The more than 200 rooms have mostly rustic wood paneling and views of either the mountains or lake. Guests can play a tune on an almost 150-year-old piano in the grandiose lobby, where taxidermy

 BEST PLACES TO STAY IN THE EAST SIDE

St Mary Tiny Homes
Ten small pastel-colored cabins, sleeping up to four, with views of Glacier's eastern mountains. $$$

Duck Lake Lodge
Friendly fishing lodge in Babb. Cozy rooms, shared bathrooms and an on-site diner for breakfast and dinner. $$

Swiftcurrent Motor Inn
In Many Glacier, next to trailheads. Rustic cabins and motel-style rooms. Store, restaurant and laundry. $$

LEFT: TRAVELVOLO/SHUTTERSTOCK © ; RIGHT: PAULA COBLEIGH/SHUTTERSTOCK ©

adorns the walls and guests congregate around a large central fire, which is also a wi-fi hot spot. You may even spot members of staff wearing lederhosen. The **Ptarmigan Dining Room** serves a most satisfying breakfast buffet, and of an evening becomes the area's only fine dining restaurant, with dishes like rainbow trout and local wagyu top sirloin.

Set Off on Two Feet

TOP HIKES IN ST MARY

The best hikes St Mary has to offer begin from **Sun Point**, around 10 miles (16km) east of the visitor center, where the path to **Baring Falls** (1.2 miles/2km round trip), **St Mary Falls** (2.8 miles/4.5km round trip) and **Virginia Falls** (6.4 miles/10km round trip; pictured below) starts from the Three Falls trailhead and shuttle stop.

Along the easy trail (with only 200ft/61m elevation change), each waterfall is more impressive than the last, starting with Baring, which topples 25ft (7.6m) over a rock ledge. The path meanders through burned forest to the rushing 35ft (10.6m) **St Mary Falls**, charging down three separate tiers and through healthy green forests to the misty Virginia Falls, which plunge 50ft (15m) into an inviting pool below.

The **Red Eagle Lake** trail connects here, going a further 4.6 miles (7.4km) one way around the south side of St Mary Lake – much of the forest here was destroyed by a 2006 fire, which has dramatically changed the landscape. For spring wildflowers and mountain views, the 8.8-mile (14km) Otokomi Lake hike (around 5 miles west of the visitor center and climbing almost 2000ft) is convenient for those staying at the **Rising Sun Campground** off Going-to-the-Sun Road.

Keep your eyes peeled for purple coral root, red Indian paintbrush, pink wood's rose and lilac meadowrue on the trail before coming upon several waterfalls and climbing to vistas of **Goat Mountain**, **Otokomi Mountain** and the tranquil **Otokomi Lake**.

The shortest hike in the area can be done by the whole family – **Sunrift Gorge** is less than half a mile (800m) round trip and shouldn't be skipped. It sits around 7 miles (11km) east of Logan Pass and continues along a creek up stairs to a 131ft-deep (40m), 6.5ft-wide (2m) slot canyon.

WHERE TO GET A COFFEE IN THE EAST SIDE

Park Café
Family-owned retro diner with seriously good pies – try the Grizz-Bear-Y – and a strong cuppa joe.

Two Sisters Cafe
Quirky place for a brew, in Babb. It reads 'Aliens Welcome' on the roof and its walls are adorned with license plates.

Leaning Tree
Friendly Blackfeet family serving some of the best coffee for miles around.

Heidi's Snack Shop
Inside Many Glacier Hotel, serving espresso-based drinks of most varieties.

 BEST PLACES FOR SUPPLIES IN ST MARY

St Mary Grocery
Well-stocked seasonal store just outside the east park entrance, selling food and booze.

Park Cafe and Grocery
Open in the summer months with souvenirs, hats and T-shirts, plus limited groceries.

Trail & Creek Outfitters
The place for outdoor and camping gear before a St Mary adventure.

HIKE THE APIKUNI FALLS TRAIL

At only 2 miles long (3km) round trip, this is a fairly short hike, but it's a punchy, invigorating route, climbing 650ft (189m) in around a mile to a lean and graceful 100ft (30m) waterfall. Park at the small pull-out, off Rte 3 on the right, around 3 miles (4.8km) after the Many Glacier entrance station. There's room for around 10 cars, so get here early in summer.

The trail starts in a **1 dry meadow**. Look out for plants such as arrowroot, asters and lupine here before going into the **2 forest canopy** of aspen and Douglas fir trees and slowly gaining elevation. A **3 spur trail** to the right offers the option to walk through forest or continue on the more open path; both connect to the main trail ahead. The forest canopy opens on to a rocky surface and a clearing offers **4 soaring southern views** to Mt Allen, Siyeh and East Flattop Mountain, plus Sherbourne Reservoir to the east and Swiftcurrent and Josephine Lakes to the west.

Climb the **5 gradual switchbacks** to the finale, **6 Apikuni Falls**, which flows from Natahki Lake and dramatically tumbles through a narrow cleft over red-tinted limestone rock, formed in the Precambrian era. Apikuni Falls loosely translates to 'Spotted Robe,' a native name given to author James Willard Schultz in the 1880s when he was living with the Pikuni tribe.

Some adventurous hikers continue on to the summit of **7 Apikuni Mountain** (making it a 6.4-mile/10km round-trip hike), following the fork at the waterfall and climbing some 4000ft (1219m) overall. This turns the route into a very challenging hike, scrambling up loose, often treacherous, rocks. *Note: the trail becomes unmarked around half a mile (800m) after the waterfall, and is for experts only.*

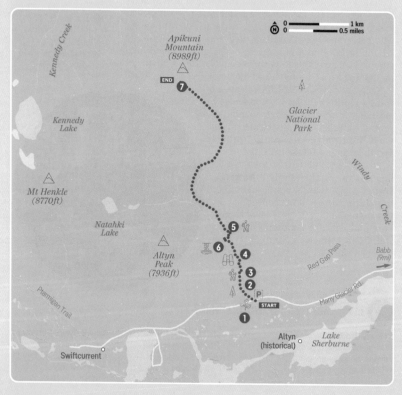

Apikuni Falls

Lace Up Your Walking Boots

TOP TRAILS IN MANY GLACIER

This mesmerizing part of the park is home to a handful of hiking corkers, from the short but very sweet 1.8-mile (2.9km) **Apikuni Falls Trail** (p206) to the phenomenal 10.6-mile (17km) **Grinnell Glacier Trail** (p202). The extraordinary turquoise 8.4-mile (13.5km) round trip trail to **Cracker Lake** gets its hyper-real color from glacial flour via Sayer Glacier, before the route continues (just under 1 mile (8.6km) round trip) to an abandoned cracker mine, built after copper ore was discovered near the lake in the late 19th century. Hikers can still spot abandoned machinery around the site. From **Swiftcurrent Motor Inn**, the challenging but memory-making 16-mile (25.7km) round trip hike to **Granite Park Chalet** passes **Redrock Lake** and **Redrock Falls** (3.6 miles/5.8km round trip), as it pours over bedrock, then goes onto **Swiftcurrent Pass** (via a series of heart-flutteringly steep switchbacks) en route. Don't miss the spur trail leading up to **Swiftcurrent Lookout** (gaining a total of 4300ft/1310m in elevation), and the highest point reachable on marked trails in Glacier National Park. From here, hikers can soak in humbling 360-degree views for miles and miles across Glacier and into Canada.

NATIVE AMERICA SPEAKS PROGRAM

Offered at the lodges and campgrounds around the St Mary area in peak season (and sometimes at Two Medicine Lake and Logan Pass), members of the Blackfeet, Salish, Kootenai and Pend d'Oreille tribes offer invaluable story-telling on their history and culture, plus traditional knowledge of plants and singing.

The timetable of speakers can usually be found at the visitor center and on the park website in June. Catch the Blackfeet Singers and Dancers for fancy, jingle, traditional and grass dance demonstrations.

For a deeper dive into local culture, it's also possible to book a certified Blackfeet guide with Blackfeet Tours on private and public lands.

GETTING AROUND

Private vehicles will need a reservation between July 1 and September 10 to enter Many Glacier and St Mary from 6am to 3pm.

A free shuttle operates in St Mary between July 1 and mid-September, and Red Bus tours operate in both areas of the park.

WATERTON LAKES NATIONAL PARK

FLAT PRAIRIES MEET ROCKY MOUNTAINS

Centered around a dramatic valley and two lakes, this mesmerizing park in Alberta's southwestern corner is a sanctuary for wildlife and a playground for hikers.

Paired with Glacier National Park, but over the border in Canada, Waterton is part of the first International Peace Park (separate entry fees).

Established in 1895, this 525-sq-km (203 sq-mile) wilderness gets less attention than its counterpart but is equally stunning, with one big advantage – fewer visitors, especially in the winter months. It's a day hikers' paradise, with almost instant access to stretches of rugged high alpine terrain, and an adorable tiny town on the edge of Upper Waterton Lake with dozens of restaurants, bars and accommodations options for its 250,000 visitors over the summer months.

The park's unique combination of flat prairies and mountains means 800 wildflower species, plus iconic animals including bighorn mountain sheep, chirping marmots and mighty moose (pictured), and the holy grail for wildlife spotters – grizzly bears and elusive mountain lions.

In 2017, the Kenow Wildfire tore through the park, causing devastating damage and destroying 80% of its trails. After a huge reconstruction project in the years following, all the trails have been rebuilt.

While the landscape has drastically changed, with graveyards of burned trees standing where dense green forests once were, there is regeneration everywhere. Forest floors are blanketed in new shoots and life. Hikers will notice that trails are now mostly without tree cover, but provide a new perspective – unobstructed views of the magnificent Rockies and an ever-evolving landscape.

THE MAIN AREA

WATERTON PARK
Adventure basecamp, with restaurants and hotels.
p212

Crypt Lake Trail (p224)

Find Your Way

One central road (Hwy 5) runs through the park, connecting to the scenic Red Rock Parkway and narrow Akamina Parkway. Another way into the park is by boat, via the Goat Haunt border, crossing Upper Waterton Lake.

BOAT

Shuttle boats run daily along Upper Waterton Lake from Waterton Park during summer, connecting hikers with trailheads including the popular Crypt Lake Trail and the Goat Haunt border.

CAR

Most visitors arrive by private vehicle from the USA in the southeast via Chief Mountain Hwy, then Hwy 6 and Hwy 5. Roads in the park are excellent, but they (and the parking lots) can get congested in peak season.

Waterton Park, p212

Epicenter of the park, located on Upper Waterton Lake with the historic Prince of Wales Hotel sitting on a bluff to the north.

MICHAEL_KENTUCKY/SHUTTERSTOCK©

Upper Waterton Lake (p218)

Plan Your Time

Only three roads go through the park, covering around 40km (25 miles), meaning it's easy to reach a lot of the main attractions quickly. Plan ahead if you need a boat crossing, as shuttles get booked up.

If You Only Have One Day

Soak in Waterton's beauty with a couple of short hikes – the terrific **Bear's Hump Trail** (p222) is a steep climb to iconic views over Waterton Valley, while the **Blakiston Falls** (p221) hike is an easy path from Red Rock Canyon to two rushing waterfalls. Recharge with scones and crustless mini-sandwiches during afternoon tea at the historic **Prince of Wales Hotel** (p213). Spend the rest of the afternoon kayaking on Waterton's sheltered **Cameron Lake** (p220).

If You Have Two Days

Get a boat shuttle to the thrilling **Crypt Lake Trail** (p224) for nail-biting pathways cut into the mountainside, steep drop-offs, and wire rails to cling onto, plus towering waterfalls and shimmering alpine lakes. Drive the scenic **Red Rock Parkway** (p227), through wildflower-scattered prairies and sweeping views of craggy mountains, and try a cycle-hike combo – **Snowshoe** (p223) to **Goat Lake** (p223) – for a glacial canyon and small emerald lake.

Seasonal Highlights

SPRING	SUMMER	AUTUMN	WINTER
Wildflowers are in bloom and wildlife emerges from hibernation. Seek out prairie trails for colorful blooms and nature spotting.	Park lakes come to life, and Waterton Park swells in population. Book ahead for camping, accommodations and shuttles.	Parts of the landscape turn from green to fiery orange and red. Visitor numbers are lower, but snowfall can close higher-altitude trails.	A blanket of snow covers the park. Some roads are closed, but winter adventures such as country skiing and snowshoeing abound.

WATERTON PARK

The tiny village of Waterton Park, inside the boundaries of the national park, consisting of just a dozen or so streets on the edge of Upper Waterton Lake, is an excellent base for park adventures. This low-profile place has a hardy local population of around 200, which goes down to just 40 in the winter months, and swells to around 250,000 visitors between July and August. Charming stone and wooden-fronted restaurants and shops line a pedestrianized street, while boutique and motel-style accommodations sit around the lake shores spanning a few blocks. It is easily walkable – 10 minutes maximum from one side of town to the other – with standout trails accessible via Tamarack Outdoors shuttle, private vehicle or Waterton Shoreline Cruises boats at the marina at Emerald bay. The new C$25 million visitor center on the edge of town has interactive exhibits and rangers to help with park planning.

Waterton Park

TOP TIP

Waterton Park has all the amenities visitors could need (book ahead for dining and overnight stays in peak months). Campers will find that laundry facilities are scarce – head to the Bayshore Inn for the area's only coin-operated laundromat. Open daily from 8am to 10pm, with vending machines for detergent.

BRIAN K HARRIS/SHUTTERSTOCK ©

Upper Waterton Lake

Prince of Wales Hotel

Drink Afternoon Tea in a Historic Hotel

WORLD HERITAGE RUSTIC ACCOMMODATIONS

The last of the historic 'parkitecture' hotels to be commissioned was the **Prince of Wales Hotel**, a looming green-roofed building that sits alone on a hill overlooking Upper Waterton Lake. It was built more than a dozen years after the park's other historic lodges, in 1927.

It was an attractive location in more ways than one: there was Prohibition in Montana, but over the border in Alberta, the ban on booze had ended in 1924. The building was designed by the Great Northern Railway's Louis Hill in the same rustic Swiss-chalet style as the other hotels in the collection, but marks the only Canadian property in the series. Listed as a World Heritage Site, it was close to being destroyed by the Kenow Wildfire in 2017, but thankfully it was saved by firefighters who doused it in water before flames dozens of meters high were knocking on the door.

Guests can experience a similar romantic old-world charm to that of the other accommodations in the Glacier Park Collection, including a huge lobby, with vintage details and furniture, plus original hand-carved woodwork. The Prince of Wales, however, distinguishes itself with an enormous wall of windows, offering that inside-outside feel, with panoramic views across the lake and mountains.

WHERE TO SEE LIVE MUSIC

One of few true drinking establishments in Waterton Park, the Thirsty Bear is decked out with wood, and is one of Southern Alberta's oldest bars. It's housed in the old Waterton Dance Pavilion – shared by the Lakeside Convention Center – which opened in 1926, and would lure dancers from 160km (100 miles) away. It's still where things get lively at the weekends, with craft beer on tap and a full calendar of live music – bands and acoustic musicians play every Friday and Saturday between mid-May to mid-September (and every night on holiday weekends). There are also pool tables, foosball tables and a big patio area for sunny evenings, plus nightly specials.

BEST PLACES FOR BREAKFAST IN WATERTON PARK

Pearls Café
Stacked pancakes, French toast and burrito wraps, plus the best coffee in town. **$**

Windflower Corner Coffee
Next to Waterton Lakes Opera House; the place to grab a pastry, smoothie and espresso-based coffee. **$**

Zum's Eatery & Mercantile
Breakfast classics from hot cakes and eggs to corned beef hash, served in a room filled with license plates. **$**

213

WATERTON PARK

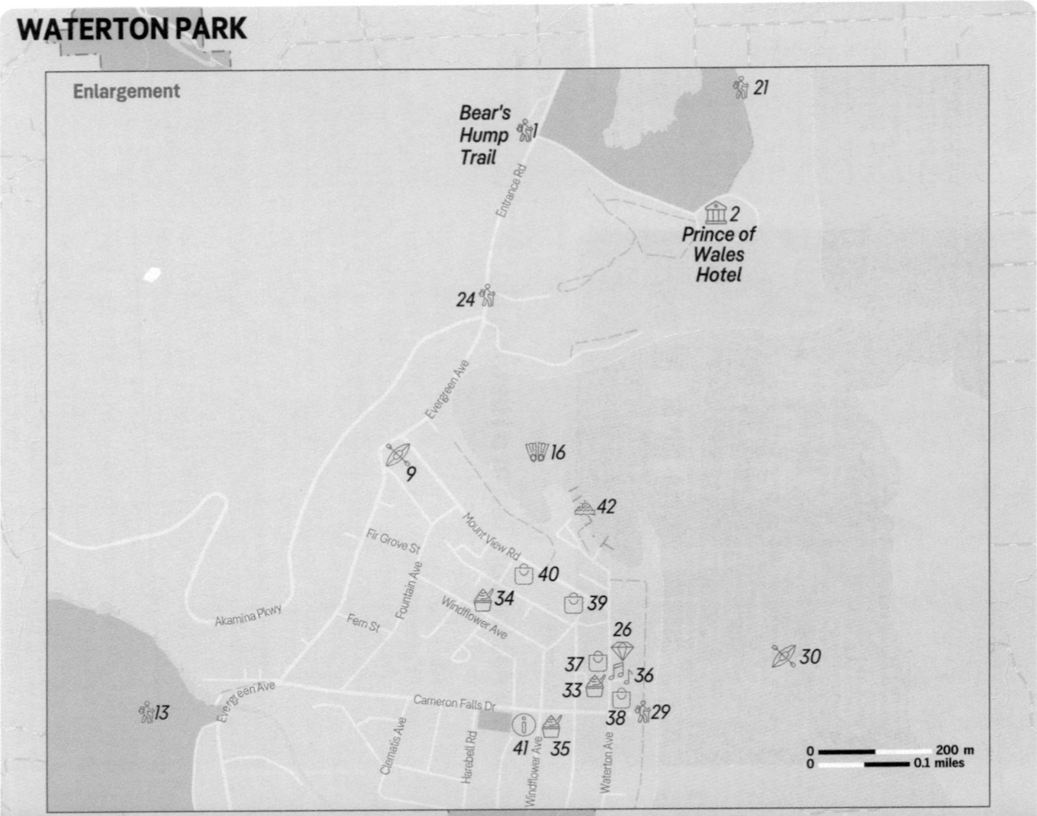

HIGHLIGHTS
1 Bear's Hump Trail
2 Prince of Wales Hotel

SIGHTS
3 Akamina Parkway
4 Goat Haunt Ranger Station
5 Red Rock Canyon
6 Red Rock Parkway

ACTIVITIES & TOURS
7 Alpine Stables
8 Bellevue Trail
9 Blakiston & Company
10 Blakiston Falls
11 Cameron Lake
12 Cameron Lake Boat Rentals
13 Carthew-Alderson Trail
14 Crypt Lake
15 Crypt Lake Trailhead
16 Emerald Bay
17 Goat Lake
18 Kootenai Brown Trail
19 Lakeshore, South Evergreen Avenue
20 Lineham Creek Trail
21 Linnet Lake Trail
22 Lonesome Lake
23 Maskinonge Lake
24 Prince of Wales Loop
25 Rowe Lakes Trail
26 Serenity Spa
27 Snowshoe Trail
28 Tamarack Trail

Enlargement

Prince of Wales Hotel

Bear's Hump Trail

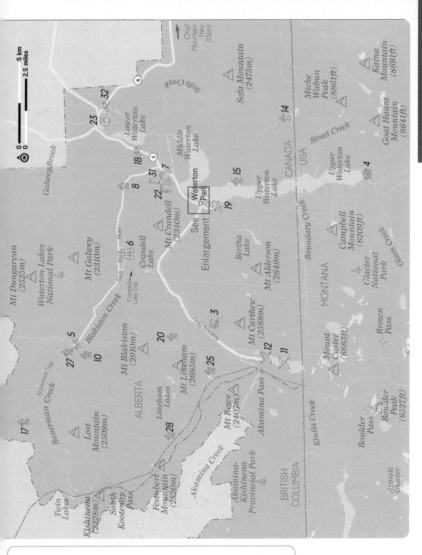

29 Townsite Hike
30 Upper Waterton Lake
31 Waterton Lakes Golf Course
32 Wishbone Trail

EATING
33 Big Scoop Ice Cream Parlor
34 Red Rock Trattoria
see 2 Royal Stewart Dining Room
35 Welch's Chocolates, Ice Cream & Desserts

ENTERTAINMENT
36 Thirsty Bear

SHOPPING
37 Akamina Gifts & Book Nook
38 Blackfoot Cultural Centre
39 Pat's
40 Tamarack Outdoor Outfitters

INFORMATION
41 Waterton Lakes National Park Visitor Center

TRANSPORT
42 Waterton Shoreline Cruises

The seasonal and stupendously scenic Chief Mountain Hwy – open between mid-May and late September – is the shortest driving route between Glacier National Park and Waterton Lakes.

It's a pretty 48km (30-mile) road trip that starts 7km (4 miles) north of **1 Babb**, beyond St Mary in East Glacier on the left, traveling through the prairie grasslands of the **2 Blackfeet Reservation**, along a winding and fragrant pine-tree-lined stretch of asphalt. Craggy peaks dominate the view to the west. Yellow Mountain and snippets of Apikuni Mountain appear to the south, and the commanding oblong-shaped Chief Mountain – it is known to the Blackfeet people as Nínaiistáko – comes into view. Its distinctive shape has been a beacon for travelers and tribes for centuries and is considered a sacred area.

Just beyond the reservation is the **3 border crossing** that marks the boundary between Canada and the US – passports are required here.

The road becomes Rte 6 as it winds its way to **4 Belly River Campground**. This terrific stargazing spot has 24 secluded, primitive first-come-first-serve pitches among aspen forest.

A 9.7km (6-mile) drive north leads to the **5 Waterton Lakes National Park Viewpoint**, with striking panoramic views from an elevation of 1600m (5250ft) of the peaks sculpted by glacial forces, including Vimy Peak, Mt Alderton, Bertha Peak, Mt Crandell and Mt Anderson. The rest area has benches and toilet facilities.

Continue on 7km (4 miles) to **6 Maskinonge Overlook and Lake**, Waterton's largest wetlands area, for picnic sites and an abundance of bird-spotting opportunities – look out for sandhill crane or osprey fishing. Continue less than 1.6km (1 mile) west, along Rte 5, to the entrance of **7 Waterton Lakes National Park**.

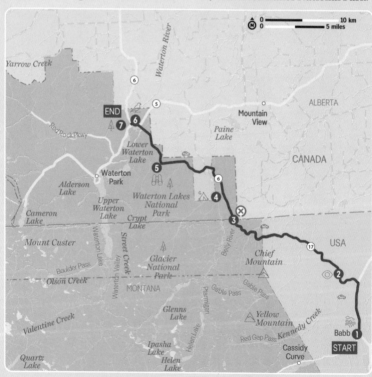

MELISSAMN/SHUTTERSTOCK ©

Prince of Wales Hotel

While it's certainly the most impressive accommodations in the area, the rooms (although renovated in recent years) are incredibly simple, with subtle vintage touches like iron headboards and Victorian-style sinks and bath fittings.

Non-guests are welcome at the hotel – visit for afternoon tea in the **Royal Stewart Dining Room**, where waitstaff in kilts serve plates of sandwiches and scones on traditional tiered tea stands every afternoon during peak season.

Venture into the Wilderness by Horseback

GUIDED TOURS ALONG SCENIC TRAILS

Family-run **Alpine Stables** has been in operation since 1969, when Dee and Lorna Barrus built their original barn in Waterton. Sadly it was destroyed by the Kenow Wildfire in 2017, but their new building opened in late 2019. Find it on the left before the Prince of Wales Hotel.

Horseback trail rides leave every hour except noon, and range from hour-long experiences for all the family into the hills around **Lonesome Lake** or through the flower-filled meadows of Blakiston Fan, to longer rides through water crossings and up to gorgeous viewpoints via switchbacks climbing up Vimy Peak. Overnight pack trips to the mountain meadows and crystal-clear lakes can be organized in advance, with all gear and campfire meals included.

BEST PLACES FOR A SWEET FIX

Welch's Chocolates, Ice Cream & Desserts
Family-run Waterton Park cubbyhole, with vintage pie counters and an adjacent store where kids can run wild along aisles of chocolates, fudge and candy. Scoff your loot on the deck. **$**

Red Rock Trattoria
This Italian restaurant knows its desserts – try the house-made cannoli shells with orange and white chocolate mousse or the melt-in-the-mouth tiramisu. **$$**

Big Scoop Ice Cream Parlor
Thirty-two different flavors are served in homemade chocolate-dipped waffle cones. Frozen yogurt and milkshakes too. **$**

 BEST PLACES TO CAMP IN WATERTON PARK

Belly River Campground
Primitive first-come-first-served site outside the park with 24 sites off Chief Mountain Hwy. **$**

Waterton Townsite Campground
Sprawling, near Waterton Park; 246 sites, over 100 suitable for RVs. Book ahead. **$**

Lone Lake
Super-isolated, pristine spot often dubbed one of Waterton's 'best-kept secrets.' Reserve ahead. **$**

THREE AMAZING PLACES TO STARGAZE

Keith B Robinson, *@dark_sky_guides*, president of Dark Sky Guides, runs night tours around the first International Dark Sky Park.

Lakeshore, South Evergreen Avenue
This nice, easily accessible spot to stargaze in Waterton Park has very limited streetlights for moon and planets, nebulae and star-clusters gazing.

Cameron Lake
About as far away from light pollution as you can get, while still remaining on the pavement. It has a significantly higher elevation than other spots so stargazers should dress warmly. The aurora borealis can be spotted here.

Chief Mountain Hwy
Locals call this great lookout Two Flags. It features a pull-out area with plenty of space and more than enough darkness to sit back, relax and take in the night sky constellations.

Emerald Bay (p220)

SHAWN.CCF/SHUTTERSTOCK ©

Cruise to the Loneliest Border Crossing

BOATING AND HIKING BETWEEN COUNTRIES

The southern end of Upper Waterton Lake serves as one of the quietest and most enjoyable border crossings on the continent.

The **Goat Haunt crossing** is reachable by a relaxing boat ride or a three-hour wild walk, around 11.2km (6.9 miles) from Waterton Park around the lake. **Waterton Shoreline Cruises** runs a summer hour-long Canada–USA Border Cruise to the cutline running through the forest up the sides of the mountains, indicating the boundary between the two countries.

The company also offers a longer Interpretive Sightseeing Cruise that stops at **Goat Haunt Ranger Station**. Passengers can check out the 'haunt's' boat dock and hiker shelter, fill up their drinking water, and see the Peace Pavilion interpretive

 BEST PLACES TO EAT IN WATERTON PARK

Pizza of Waterton
Solid thick-crust pizzas with lots of toppings. Pours huckleberry wheat ale or dry village cider. **$**

Vimy's Lounge and Grill
Inside Waterton Lakes Lodge Resort with Rocky views, nine types of burger and homey bowls of pasta. **$$$**

Kilmorey Lodge
Sophisticated plates in a lakeside dining room. Try maple whiskey prawns and elk meatballs. **$$$**

exhibit, chronicling the history of the park and exploring the meaning of the word 'peace' worldwide.

Unless you plan on staying more than 30 minutes – to hike the area or do a longer backpacking adventure – you will not need your passport. Those who wish to stay must clear US Customs ahead of time. Some people may be eligible to use the Reporting Offsite Arrival Mobile app for boaters.

The tiny ranger station, which doubles up as one of North America's smallest border posts, is often unmanned. Hikers can enjoy the unspoiled area on a series of wild hikes under the looming **Mt Cleveland**, the highest peak in the park, and book a later shuttle back to Waterton Park.

Play a Super-Scenic Round

STANLEY THOMPSON–DESIGNED GOLF COURSE

Play an 18-hole round where the mountains meet the prairies, at the **Waterton Lakes Golf Course**, dreamed up by Stanley Thompson – who designed and remodeled 145 golf courses in Canada between 1920 and 1953 including the Banff Springs and Jasper Park Lodge. Golfers can play a wild game through 97 hectares (240 acres) of parkland among 1400 types of flora, and witness the occasional deer, moose and bear in the Rocky Mountain setting. There's also a putting green and clubhouse with club rentals and golfing gear for sale.

Bird-Watch on Waterton's Largest Wetlands Area

EXPLORE A NATURE-RICH WETLAND

Often overlooked in favor of the shimmering lakes and craggy peak hikes beyond, **Maskinonge Lake**, near the park gates, is one of Waterton's most nature-rich habitats. Its wetlands are home to swans and geese, ducks, waterfowl and dragonflies, and an eruption of wildflowers in spring. This is a sacred place for the Blackfoot community – wetland creatures are believed to have shared their power with the Blackfoot here. Gifts are preserved each year in a sacred collection called the Beaver Bundle. Each spring's rebirth of the wetlands is celebrated with ritual and song and a beaver bundle containing preserved animal hides and waterfowl skins.

Come here at dawn or dusk for big-game spotting, and search out deer and elk. Or find sandhill crane and osprey fishing, with a pair of binoculars or aboard a canoe or kayak. There are picnic facilities by the parking lot.

GO FISHING

Waterton offers excellent fishing, with 24 species of fish, including Arctic grayling, rainbow trout, brown trout, brook trout, lake trout, northern pike and mountain whitefish (catch limits apply).

The fish can be big here. One angler famously hauled in a record-sized lake trout, weighing more than 23kg (50lb), in Waterton.

The hike in Bertha Lake is a pristine spot for anglers, as the easily accessible Cameron Lake and the bird-watching haven of Maskinonge Lake.

Permits (available at the visitor center or Pat's, which also sells tackle) are required for fishing inside the park.

Outside the park, the Waterton River has excellent fly-fishing opportunities for large brown and rainbow trout. Dave Brown Outfitters offers guided trips, including transport and gear.

Lakeside Chophouse & Wine Bar
Upmarket lakeside dining room serving international cuisine using local ingredients. **$$$**

Zum's Eatery & Mercantile
Casual hiker joint decorated with license plates serving North American fare – burgers, chili and veggie options. **$$**

The Taco Bar
Awesome burritos and tacos with all the trimmings served in a colorful space. **$**

Scuba Dive in Rocky Mountain Lakes

EXPLORE CAMERON BAY OR EMERALD BAY

Around 20m (60ft) deep, on the bottom of **Emerald Bay**, sits a sunken paddle wheeler called the *Gertrude,* which was built in 1907. It was used as a workboat for a sawmill before becoming a floating tearoom and then being deliberately sunk near the Prince of Wales in 1918. Much of the wreck is decayed, and the bow is buried in silt, but machinery, pistons, shafts and a big boiler can be viewed by divers. It's also possible to explore the rocky walls and underwater meadows at **Cameron Bay**. No one rents scuba gear in Waterton Park, but a full kit can be hired in Lethbridge (around an hour away) at Awesome Adventures.

Paddleboard or Kayak on Waterton's Lakes

EXPLORE HARD-TO-REACH CORNERS

One of the best ways to explore the area, and get into the wilderness away from the crowds, is to climb aboard a kayak or canoe. **Cameron Lake** is a sheltered and popular spot for water adventures, only a stone's throw from the parking lot (for easy gear transportation). **Cameron Lake Boat Rentals** is the place to get stand-up paddleboards, kayaks and row boats in the summer months. **Blakiston & Company** rents crafts on Emerald Bay for explorations of **Upper Waterton Lake**. If you have enough paddle power, you can skip the boat shuttle and power over to the **Crypt Lake trailhead**, but check the wind forecasts before you set off; the return journey can be difficult in high winds. Those staying overnight at a backcountry campsite accessible by water (Bertha Bay and Boundary Bay) should get a backcountry use permit from the **Waterton Lakes National Park Visitor Center** before they set off.

Take a Short Ramble into the Wilderness

EASY HIKES WITH QUICK ACCESS TO NATURE

Waterton has 200km (120 miles) of trails to hike, ranging from easy to strenuous through rugged high-alpine terrain, offering soaring plateaus, tranquil glacial lakes and cascading waterfalls – all within easy access of the main town. Around 80% of the trails were damaged by wildfire in 2017, but,

---

 BEST HOTELS IN WATERTON PARK

Aspen Village Inn
Slightly dated but very comfortable motel-style rooms, walkable to all that Waterton Park offers. $

Bayshore Inn Resort & Spa
Lakefront rooms, some with mountain views. Adjacent spa, restaurant and laundry. $$

Bear Mountain Motel
Nostalgic 1950s-style motel, with pristine rooms and a warm welcome. Some have kitchenettes. $$

CHRISTOPHER BABCOCK/SHUTTERSTOCK ©

Waterton Lake

ICONIC MULTIDAY BACKCOUNTRY HIKING

Waterton has epic wilderness trails including the standout two- to three-day 36km (23-mile) Tamarack Trail, starting from either the Rowe Lake trailhead or Red Rock Canyon.

It's probably the park's most notorious and demanding trail, skirting the Continental Divide along high ridges with awesome views, through larch forests and stream crossings, and to a stunning canyon and alpine lakes, including camping at the spectacular Lone Lake.

Shuttle pickups are available with Tamarack Outdoor Outfitters. Permits are required for all overnight stays in the backcountry; get them at the visitor center up to three months in advance by calling +1 (403) 859-5133 to reserve.

incredibly, all of them have been rebuilt in the years following. While trails are regularly maintained, hikers should still be cautious of fallen debris displaced in storms and high winds; dead trees are more likely to be unstable.

Those looking for easy, family-friendly hikes should try the 8km (5-mile) **Rowe Lakes Trail** for quick access to a shimmering alpine lake, while the terrific 2.8km (1.8-mile) **Bear's Hump Trail** (p000) has a steep climb up to sublime views over Waterton Valley. The 2km (1.2-mile) round-trip **Blakiston Falls** hike starting at **Red Rock Canyon** is an easy, almost flat, newly rebuilt path going to two waterfall viewpoints. Other easy hikes include the 3.2km (2-mile) accessible paved **Townsite Hike** beside Upper Waterton Lake, and the gentle 2km (1.2-mile) **Prince of Wales Loop** going along Middle Waterton Lake's shore and up to the bluff where the iconic hotel sits, via Emerald Bay. The 3.8km (2.4-mile) **Bellevue Trail** is the one for flower fans, with pretty wild blooms in spring and early summer through prairies, and a mosaic of aspen groves and fescue grasslands, bordered by Rocky Mountain views. In winter it offers favorable conditions for cross-country skiers.

Crandell Mountain Lodge
Tudor-style beams meet country rustic at this 1940s lodge, with homey rooms, some with kitchenettes. **$$**

Northland Lodge
A characterful historic house once owned by Louis Hill, with rustic rooms and period furniture. **$$**

Prince of Wales Hotel
Grand hotel exuding romantic old-world charm. Rooms are simple with vintage touches. **$$$**

BEAR'S HUMP TRAIL

This terrific 2.4km (1.6-mile) out-and-back moderate hike sits right outside Waterton Park and climbs almost 300m (1000ft). Blackfoot Indigenous Peoples know this lump of rock as Bear Mountain – see if you can make out the shape of a **1 grizzly bear** from a distance.

The family-friendly hike begins on Hwy 5, just north of the town, near Linnet Lake, where there's a small parking lot that fills up fast in peak season. Bring a hat and some water as there's no shade. Take the gravel path through the remains of burned trees, casualties of the 2017 Kenow Wildfire, and past **2 green meadows** of regrowth, where you can spot wildflowers in spring and the shoots of new trees emerging.

The trail becomes steep almost immediately with a calf-pounding **3 series of switchbacks**, but has plenty of benches along the way where hikers can sip water

and take in the views of the legendary **4 Prince of Wales Hotel** below, with its distinctive green roof.

The trail turns into steps at particularly steep points around halfway up. The lack of trees means the views just get better the higher you climb. At the **5 hump** are 180-degree mountain panoramas and the vast 11km (7-mile) **6 Waterton Lake**, the deepest lake in the Canadian Rockies, appears in its entirety.

Some climb further up the hump on grippy limestone for an even better vantage point of Mt Boswell and Cleveland to the southeast, Cathedral Peak to the south, and Campbell Mountain and Mt Richards to the southwest of Upper Waterton Lake. Keep your eyes peeled along the rebuilt Akamina Parkway to Cameron Lake below for mountain goats and bighorn sheep – both enjoy this rocky terrain.

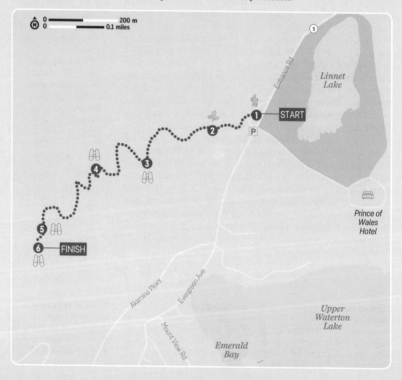

CAVAN IMAGES/ALAMY STOCK PHOTO ©

Bear's Hump Trail

Embark on a Long Hike

DAY HIKES TO REMOTER PARTS OF THE PARK

Hikes ranging from three to nine hours can be done over a day and will get visitors much further into the wilderness for better nature-spotting possibilities, plus bags of solitude. The **Lineham Creek Trail** is a wonderful hike to start with. It has a round-trip distance of 8.4km (5.2 miles) going uphill through fire-ravaged hills, and on to dense forest and a 125m (410ft) waterfall, with soaring views of Mt Lineham and Mt Blakiston (the park's highest mountain). **Crypt Lake** (p224) has become notorious among daredevils, and is busy as a result. The trail includes a metal stepladder on the side of a steep cliff, and small pathways with big drops and a rock tunnel to navigate, and is peppered with lakes and waterfalls.

For those who are not sure how much stamina they have, the **Rowe Lakes Trail** offers the chance to do a shorter or longer version. It's an 8km (5-mile) round-trip hike to Lower Rowe Lake, which can be extended to 10.4km (6.4 miles) to Rowe Meadow, and 12.6km (7.8 miles) to Upper Rowe Lake, for forests, meadows, and awesome valley and mountain views.

The hike to **Goat Lake** can be combined with a 9.2km (5.7-mile) round-trip cycle along the **Snowshoe Trail**, picked up at Red Rock Canyon, before following the 5km (3.2-mile) round-trip pathway to Goat Lake along steep switchbacks. You'll climb around 425m (1400ft), and enter a glacial canyon with a small emerald lake, surrounded with pretty wildflowers like purple phacelia, blue lupines, and red Indian paintbrushes in spring and early summer.

Last but not least, the 20km (12-mile), one-way with shuttle **Carthew-Alderson Trail** is an iconic climb up gradual switchbacks from Cameron Lake through meadows and subalpine forests to beautiful sweeping views from Carthew Ridge – it finishes in Waterton Park.

BEST PLACES TO STAY IN WATERTON PARK

Waterton Glacier Suites
Rustic yet modern suites with whirlpool baths, satellite TV, gas fireplaces and air-con. **$$$**

Waterton Lakes Lodge Resort
With a gym, indoor pool, hot tub and restaurant. Deluxes have Jacuzzis. **$$$**

Kilmorey Lodge
Smart 1926 lodge with spacious rooms, some with balconies/patios. On-site pub and restaurant. **$$$**

Hike Crypt Lake

Often labeled one of the best hikes in Canada, the seasonal six- to eight-hour Crypt Lake Trail is certainly the most hyped adventure in the park due to its thrill factor and variety. The 10.8-mile (17.2 km) round-trip advanced trail climbs 2214ft (675m), has steep drop-offs, a skinny tunnel and a cliffside stepladder. Hikers are rewarded with towering waterfalls, a dreamy alpine lake and jaw-on-the-floor views.

1 Emerald Bay

The adventure starts with a 15-minute Shoreline Cruise boat shuttle across Upper Waterton Lake (June to September only; advanced booking is required) to the trailhead. Strong paddlers can kayak across.

The Hike: Those wanting to add another 23km (14 miles) to their day can trek or bike around the lake, along the Wishbone Trail, to the trailhead.

2 Crypt Landing

Boats alight here, where the start of the trail travels through dense forests of Engelmann spruce pine and fir, and begins to ascend moderate switchbacks.

The Hike: In just over 1.6km (1 mile), hikers will reach the Hell Roaring Falls junction.

3 Hell Roaring Falls

With a unique turquoise pool before its cascade, this makes for a lovely mini spur (adding 20 minutes), but many save their legs for the main trail, tacking this on to the return trip if they have time before their shuttle back to Waterton Park.

The Hike: A 1.9km (1.2-mile) side trip along a narrow trail.

CHRISTOPHER BABCOCK/SHUTTERSTOCK ©

Crypt Lake Trail

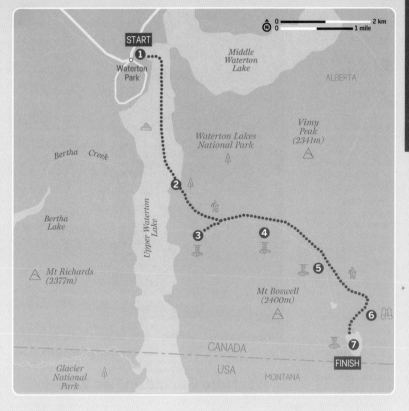

4 Twin Falls

The junction to Twin Falls appears around 3.7km (2.3 miles) along the main trail. This provides a much shorter detour to a scenic resting spot and a picturesque cascade – rushing hardest in spring and early summer – in two sections.

The Hike: On the main trail, continue another 1.6km (1 mile) along the path, crossing little creeks. A clearing in the trees offers impressive views.

5 Burnt Rock Falls

This slender waterfall comes into view, with the rare vantage point of it rolling through a green valley above before tumbling off an iron-stained rocky ledge.

The Hike: The trail gains elevation rapidly as it ascends to the end of the valley for the next 1.9km (1.2 miles).

6 Crypt Tunnel

The 18m-long (60ft) Crypt Tunnel is plenty wide, but only 1.5m (5ft) high – it requires crouching or scrambling to get through. Those who do are rewarded with dramatic valley views.

The Hike: Continue on a perilous trail with a steel cable running along a rocky ledge, which climbers use to steady their nerves over a 213m (700ft) drop-off.

7 Crypt Lake

The trail levels out on the final push to Crypt Lake. An unmarked trail offers a short detour to view Crypt Falls as it plunges into the lake below.

The Hike: The main trail descends to meet the lake. Those who still have steam in the tank can cross an unmarked border into Montana by taking the path around the lake to its southern end.

BEST WINTER ACTIVITIES

Fat Biking
Pedal along the Townsite Loop or Wishbone Trail and rent a fat bike at Pat's – the RAD Rover e-bikes are perfect for cruising along in the snow.

Nordic Skiing
Popular cross-country skiing trails include the 3.1-mile (5km) round trip Cameron Ski Trail through a coniferous forest and the single-width 3.4-mile (5.5km) Dipper Ski Trail through wooded slopes. Tamarack Outdoors runs guided cross-country skiing trips in January, February and March.

Snowshoeing
Many of the flatter trails in the park are ideal for snowshoeing, including Linnet Lake Trail and the Prince of Wales Hill to the Kootenai Brown Trail or book a tour with Uplift Adventures.

Cyclists, Upper Waterton Lake

Cover More Ground on Two Wheels

BIKE INTO THE WILDERNESS

Several of Waterton's trails are open to bikers, including the 13km (8.1-mile) **Wishbone Trail**, which was originally a wagon route and starts just off Alberta Hwy 6 before the park entrance. The trail goes past low wetlands, where songbirds serenade your ride, past Middle Waterton Lake and all the way to the Crypt Lake trailhead. Set off early and combine the bike path with the thrilling Crypt Lake Trail (p224).

The **Kootenai Brown Trail** runs parallel to the road leading into the park with gorgeous views of Waterton Lakes and the mountain ranges. It's also the place to learn about Waterton's early resident George 'Kootenai' Brown, who helped Frederick Godsal mark Waterton as a future national park. He lived on the shore of this lake in a cabin, and was

 BEST PLACES TO STAY AROUND WATERTON PARK

Thistle Ridge Villa
Clean and spacious three-bedroom house near Payne Lake, ideal for families that like seclusion and nature. **$$**

Waterton Country Villas
Immaculately finished villas outside the park entrance, with gyms, lounge areas and wraparound porches. **$$$**

Bear Country Inn and Suites
In Mountain View, run by the owners of the Barn Store. Small, comfy, great-value motel-style rooms. **$**

appointed a forest ranger in 1910, patrolling an area of more than 320km (200 miles) on horseback or in snowshoes. His grave can be found here, between those of his two wives, one of whom died before him and the other who lived in the area for 19 years after his death.

Snowshoe Trail is accessible from Red Rock Canyon, and offers another great 16.4km (10.2-mile) ride along a former fire road, with minimal elevation change and the possibility of backcountry camping, plus many hiking options to Lost Lake, Twin Lakes, Blakiston Valley and the **Tamarack Trail** beyond. Bike rentals are available at **Pat's** and **Blakiston & Company** in Waterton Park.

Drive Waterton's Scenic Parkways

ROCKY MOUNTAIN ROAD TRIPS

Non-hikers and bikers can still enjoy the epic vistas the park has to offer on its repaved and reopened – after extensive repairs following the Kenow Wildfire of 2017 – roads. The narrow **Akamina Parkway** leaves from Waterton Valley and winds 16km (10 miles) along the Cameron Valley. Trailheads and picnic areas line the route, and stop-offs include the first oil well in Canada. Oil was struck in the Akamina Valley in 1902 and the Western Oil and Coal Company collected one barrel a day in 1905. But, luckily for us, the oil soon dried up and locals focused on tourism instead. Look out for a family of bighorn sheep that hangs out on the rocky terrain near Bear's Hump on route to Waterton Park.

Another must-drive inside the park is the 14km (8.7-mile) **Red Rock Parkway** (pictured), which goes northwest from Rte 5 (just beyond the park entrance) through Blakiston Valley. The road snakes past wildflower-scattered prairies and sweeping views of Mt Crandell, Bellevue Hill and Mt Galwey, finishing at the iron-rich beetroot-hued **Red Rock Canyon**. On the outskirts of the park, the scenic **Chief Mountain Hwy** (p216) is a standout drive.

BEST SHOPPING IN WATERTON PARK

Akamina Gifts & Book Nook
With the largest selection of books in town, pick up some lakeshore reading or trail maps here.

Tamarack Outdoor Outfitters
For camping gear, backpacks, hats and anything else you might need for exploring the great outdoors.

Pat's
Part gas station, part adventure rentals, part gear shop – Pat's has everything from fishing tackle to firewood.

Blackfoot Cultural Centre
For great local maps, affordable artwork and Indigenous gifts.

GETTING AROUND

Inside the park, those without their own vehicle can book shuttles to trailheads with Tamarack Outdoor Outfitters. Boat shuttles can be organized at Emerald Bay with Waterton Shoreline Cruises.

Cycling is another great way to get around the park, which has many bike-friendly trails. Rentals are readily available in Waterton Park at Pat's gas station and Blakiston & Company.

TOOLKIT

The chapters in this section cover the most important topics you'll need to know about when you're visiting Banff, Glacier & Jasper national parks. They're full of nuts-and-bolts information and valuable insights to help you understand and navigate the parks and get the most out of your trip.

Arriving
p230

Getting Around
p231

Money
p232

Accommodations
p233

Family Travel
p234

Health & Safe Travel
p235

Food, Drink & Nightlife
p236

Responsible Travel
p238

LGBTIQ+ Travelers
p240

Accessible Travel
p241

Parkitecture Lodges
p242

Traveling with Dogs
p243

Safe Bear Encounters
p244

Nuts & Bolts
p246

Bow Lake (p119)

Arriving

International visitors to Banff, Glacier and Jasper usually arrive at Calgary International Airport, just over an hour, three hours and four hours, respectively, from each of the parks. Domestic flyers land at Glacier Park International Airport (Kalispell) and Edmonton International Airport. The most evocative way to visit Glacier is by train, alighting at the West Glacier and East Glacier train stations.

Visas

At the time of writing, international visitors did not need an eTA to visit Canada by land (required by air). Land and air visitors to the US must complete an ESTA before they reach the border.

Trains

The super-scenic Amtrak *Empire Builder* travels from Seattle to Chicago, stopping at two Glacier National Park entrances in the summer months, plus the towns of Whitefish in the west and Browning in the east.

Driving in Winter

Many park roads are closed in winter due to snowfall and ice. Plan ahead for road closures. It's advisable – and legally required in areas of Banff and Jasper – to carry snow chains in winter.

Wi-Fi & Cell Signal

Download offline maps before you enter the parks, as wi-fi and cell signal are virtually non-existent in many areas, besides access points at visitor centers and hotels.

Public transportation between national park hubs

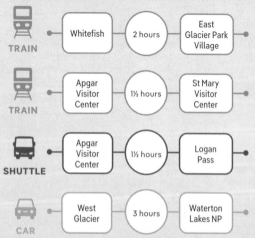

TRAIN — Whitefish — 2 hours — East Glacier Park Village

TRAIN — Apgar Visitor Center — 1½ hours — St Mary Visitor Center

SHUTTLE — Apgar Visitor Center — 1½ hours — Logan Pass

CAR — West Glacier — 3 hours — Waterton Lakes NP

BORDER CROSSINGS

Those exploring Glacier and Waterton will need their passports when traveling between the land borders dividing Alberta in Canada and Montana in the United States. The border at Eureka, closest to the west side of Glacier National Park, is open 24/7, while the Piegan port of entry opens at 8am and closes at 6pm daily. The most scenic border is by far the Chief Mountain Summer Station crossing, only open in peak months, with a gorgeous winding drive through Rocky Mountain views on either side of the border.

Getting Around

Driving is often the most convenient way to navigate the stunning scenery inside the parks, but personal vehicles can encounter queues and congestion. Many choose to use the excellent free shuttle systems instead.

RENTAL COSTS

Snowshoes
$10/day

Cross-country skis
$20/day

Snow chain
$8/day

Fat bike
$60/day

Renting a Car

Major rental companies can be found in the feeder towns near the national parks, plus at nearby airport terminals. Prebook before your arrival and check if car insurance covers border crossing between the US and Canada if traveling between Glacier and Waterton national parks.

Shuttle Hopping

Banff, Jasper and Glacier offer free buses, which ferry park-goers to the most popular trails and attractions. Use them to avoid parking queues and help reduce traffic and pollution in the parks. Be aware that some park buses only run in peak season.

VEHICLE REGISTRATION

In 2023, a car-reservation system was implemented in Glacier (May 26 to September 10) to reduce congestion at the North Fork, Camas and West Entrance. In Many Glacier and Two Medicine, the system kicks in later (July 1 to September 10). Reservations can be made between four months and 24 hours before your visit (nps. gov) – numbers are limited per day. Reservations are usually included with prebooked lodging stays within the park. Visitors arriving on foot or bicycle do not require a day-use reservation.

TIP

Avoid Glacier National Park's summer vehicle reservation system by driving into the park before 6am or after 3pm.

DRIVING ESSENTIALS

Drive on the right

10

Speed limits can be as low as 10mph (16kph) in national parks

.08

Blood alcohol levels must be lower than 0.08% in Montana and Alberta

Tours

One of the best ways to see the park is aboard a distinctive vintage Red Bus (like an elongated Rolls Royce). These striking vehicles have been touring visitors around the valleys for almost 100 years. Alternatively, Sun Tours offers a fascinating insight into Indigenous culture, told by Blackfleet guides.

Shuttle Boats

Shuttle boats whisk hikers to various trailheads in the summer months, shortening trail lengths and offering wilderness without the legwork. Passengers on the historic MV *International* boat can opt for a Canada–US Border Cruise across Waterton Lake to the loneliest border crossing in North America.

Two Wheels

Bikes can be rented at all the parks and offer an easy way to avoid crowds, traffic and being tied to a shuttle timetable. All park roads are open to bikes, and are well maintained and signposted, but check which trails bikes are allowed before you set off.

 # Money

CURRENCY: **US DOLLAR ($)** AND **CANADIAN DOLLAR (C$)**

Credit Cards

Credit cards are widely accepted in all areas of the parks, apart from walk-in campgrounds (which will require cash). Book your pitch online to avoid using cash.

Digital Payments

Contactless payments are used in most businesses in the parks. Some local places outside the park may not be set up for touch payments or may prefer cash.

Money & the Border

If traveling from Glacier to Waterton, bring your US dollars. Most businesses accept US currency, but you may lose out on exchange rates. Canadian dollars are not usually accepted in Glacier. There's no sales tax in Montana; sales tax is 5% in Alberta.

Tipping

Restaurants, cafes & bars A tip of 18% to 20% for good service is standard.

Hotels $1 or $2 per bag for porters, and a tip for the cleaners at your discretion.

Taxis 10% of the fare, or more for good service.

Tour guides 10% to 20% of the tour price is standard.

HOW MUCH FOR A...

burger
$15–20

coffee
$3–6

guided minibus tour
$100

three-course meal with wine
$80–100

HOW TO... Change Money

Changing international currency is not as easy as it once was. While banks do this in towns like Whitefish, they're only open at certain times. Coinstar automated machines are a good option (with hefty exchange rates) for all-hour money exchanges. Before a trip, look into getting a bank card that doesn't charge to withdraw cash in local currency when abroad, and a credit card that doesn't charge for international transactions.

LOCAL TIP

If traveling between Canadian national parks, the Discovery Pass (adults: C$72.25; group of seven in a car: C$145.25; 17s and under: free) covers admission to over 80 destinations for 12 months.

CASH VERSUS CARD

Although most places in and around Glacier National Park and Waterton Lakes National Park now take cards, wi-fi connections for payments have been known to go down in these remote areas. It's advisable to make sure you have some cash on you before leaving the nearby towns (where ATMs are available).

Keep some change – quarters and smaller notes – as this will come in handy for walk-in campgrounds (you may need to deposit cash into an honesty box – overnight fees range from $10 to $30), doing laundry or buying food inside the park.

Accommodations

Guesthouses & Motels

There are numerous ranch and B&B-style stays around the park for that homey feel and personal touch, with hosts offering plenty of tips about the local area; breakfast is usually included. These are usually midrange in price. For a more anonymous stay, without the frills, many opt for an inexpensive motel. There are a handful of motels inside the park boundaries.

Quirky Stays & Hostels

Less-conventional places to stay are situated around the parks, including tipis on an Indigenous reservation, yurts in more secluded areas and rooms inside train carriages. These will be on the mid- to high end of the scale. The few hostels in the area are excellent; affordable places for solo travelers to meet new friends and hiking buddies.

Historic Lodges

The parks have a range of luxurious lakeside retreats to rustic backcountry lodges. Glacier's grand romantic properties were built by the Great Northern Railway – their legendary 'parkitecture' offers the most iconic stays in the area, with atmospheric details like huge lobbies, open fires and taxidermy trimmings. Book months ahead, as these are highly sought-after.

In-Town Resorts

More luxurious accommodations can be found in the larger towns. These will likely have in-room amenities and sizable rooms with plush furnishing, plus communal facilities like a pool, restaurant, spa and great service – but they're the most expensive of all the accommodations options and are likely to be a longer drive to the park.

HOW MUCH FOR A NIGHT IN A...

historic lodge
$200–400

motel
$100–200

campground
$10–25

Camping

The most economical and immersive way to sleep in the parks: cook s'mores on the fire, sleep under the stars and wake up in nature to the sound of birdsong. Book ahead for popular campsites, but walk-in sites and free camping are available in certain areas. Most backcountry camping spots will require a permit from the wilderness office. Camping gear is easy to rent in and around the parks.

HIGH SEASON

If you haven't booked well in advance of high season, you may be sorely disappointed. All accommodations options (including campgrounds) fill up very quickly between mid-June to early September. However, there are a number of walk-in sites available at the park, plus backcountry camping, and free camping in certain areas just beyond park boundaries (such as along the Flathead River in Polebridge, near Glacier). It's hit or miss as to whether these will be full. The best bet is to book well in advance before your visit.

Family Travel

Many families make some of their best memories in the Rocky Mountain parks. Camping out in the wild for the first time is one big adventure for kids, as is spotting wildlife in its natural habitat. On arrival, pop into the visitor center to see what activities are on offer. Children qualify for discounted or free entry to all the parks.

Hiking & Camping

Wildlife walks don't have to be strenuous, although plenty of families tackle longer hikes with babies in slings or baby pack carriers, which can be rented from gear shops for a daily fee. And families don't have to fork out for new camping gear either – with a little bit of pre-planning, camping equipment can be rented in or around all the parks.

Facilities

Choose the bigger campgrounds for restrooms with flushing water and washing facilities. Backcountry trails have drop toilets or no toilets. Private campgrounds outside the parks are often more convenient for families, due to their shower facilities. Most park campgrounds don't have showers. There are a few public showers in the parks that require an admission fee.

Eating

Most restaurants inside and outside the park have child-friendly menus or separate children's menus. Bring your favorite snacks (or anything for special dietary needs); groceries stores in and around the parks only stock the basics.

Supplies

Bring diapers, wipes, baby formula, kids' sunscreen and other essential supplies with you to the park. Park stores will have a limited stock of these and it may be a long drive out of the park to source them.

CHILD-FRIENDLY PICKS

St Mary Visitor Center, Glacier (p201)
Join a star party here, where there's an observatory with a 20-inch telescope.

Flathead River, Glacier (p175)
Ideal for a family white-water rafting trip. Teenagers will enjoy a thrilling rapid ride on faster-flowing river sections.

Trail of the Cedars, Glacier (p172)
Boardwalk and flat trail, perfect for young families.

Banff Legacy Trail, Banff (p79)
Explore the wilderness on two wheels during a biking adventure.

JUNIOR RANGERS & EXPLORERS

One of the best ways to get children engaged with the wilderness is to set them a challenge. Those who complete the self-guided Glacier Junior Ranger Activity Booklet, which teaches young people about plants, wildlife and how to protect the park – including rules for visitors like 'leave no trace' – will be sworn in as a Junior Ranger at any visitor center or ranger station. In Banff, Waterton and Jasper, kids can complete the Xplorers program, with activities on tracking animals and identifying different kinds of poop. On completing it, kids get a collectible souvenir.

Health & Safe Travel

ICE & SNOW

Ice and snow are guaranteed in winter, and often remain at the highest altitudes in summer. Do not walk on frozen lakes, and turn back if snow is too deep on the trail, unless you're an expert mountaineer with the correct equipment. When driving (with snow chains) through snowy conditions, carry a charged phone, and supplies (blankets, food, water, matches) in your car.

Heat & Wildfires

Alberta and Montana have suffered severe wildfires in recent years, caused by lightning and improperly maintained campfires. Check the weather before a hike, especially on overnight hikes; there will be wildfire warnings at the visitor centers. If the risk is high or extreme – don't risk it. Bring a high-factor sunscreen on warmer days to prevent harmful UV rays and sunburn.

Ticks

Check for ticks regularly when in the park. These tiny creatures – most active in spring and early summer – bury themselves into skin and can transmit serious diseases including Rocky Mountain spotted fever and Lyme disease. If you find a tick, completely remove it and disinfect the bite site. Antibiotics may be required after a bite, especially if rashes or lesions form. Consult a doctor.

WATER

Fill bottles at bigger campgrounds and visitor centers. If you fill up from rivers or lakes, boil (at least 10 minutes), treat or filter the water.

TRAIL SIGNS

Avalanche
Pinpointing risk areas on the trail

Bear sighting
Indicating a recent encounter

Wildfire warnings
Usually color-coded from 'extreme' to 'low risk'

Stay on trail signs
Signaling loose rocks, uneven terrain and regeneration

Wildlife Encounters

When encountering animals, including moose, bighorn sheep, mountain goats, deer and coyotes, keep your distance – it's recommended that visitors stay at least 23m (75ft) away. While attacks on people are very rare, an animal will do so if it feels threatened. If you stumble upon an animal, make your presence known and slowly back away in the direction you came.

BEAR ENCOUNTERS

Hike in groups to avoid bear encounters; talk or sing along the trail to avoid surprising a bear. Bear attacks are rare, but always carry bear spray and learn how to use it before you set off. Only use it if you are attacked. Never turn your back to the bear or run.

Food, Drink & Nightlife

When to Eat

Opening hours Restaurants in and around the national parks are not open as late as you would find in international cities. Many places close at 9pm or 10pm.

Low season Many restaurants close altogether between October and May, taking down their signs outside and boarding up their windows to prevent weather damage. Bring food supplies when visiting smaller towns in low season.

Where to Eat

Lakeside Chophouse & Wine Bar (p219) Fresh salads and inter-national mains with Waterton lake views. **$$**

Whitefish Lake Restaurant (www.whitefishlakerestaurant. com/ Top steakhouse set on a golf course. **$$$**

Brownie's Bakery (www. brownieshostel.com) East Glacier institution serving huckleberry bear claws, hot cinnamon rolls and brownies. **$**

Sweet Peaks (www.sweetpeaksice cream.com/whitefish) Whitefish ice cream made with Montana dairy and local mountain flavors. **$**

Polebridge Mercantile (p198) In an iconic wooden-fronted building with excellent baked goods, coffee and handmade sandwiches to go. **$**

Zyka Elevated Indian Restaurant (p66) Indo-Chinese and tandoori favorites in Banff. **$$**

MENU DECODER

Entrée Derived from the French verb 'to enter' and meaning the opening act; appetizer or starter in Europe, but the main dish in North America.

House-made Made from scratch, rather than out of a bottle or packet.

Vegan Food made without meat or dairy produce.

Farm-to-table Fresh produce from local farms, rather than from hundreds of miles away.

Organic Meat, dairy and veggies produced without using chemicals.

Service charge A 10% to 20% added fee on the bill. If it is labeled 'discretionary' ask for this to be removed if you're unhappy with the service.

To go Taking food 'to go' is common-place in the US and Canada. If you have leftovers on your meal, wait-staff will gladly box it up for you.

Eat in the Rockies

HOW TO... Try these specialty foods while visiting Montana and Alberta.

Rocky Mountain oysters Known as 'prairie oysters' in Canada, these breaded and fried bull testicles are often served as an appetizer or bar snack. They have the consistency of calamari, with a mild gamey flavor.

Elk Lower in fat content and higher in protein than beef, this tender, dark-red meat makes a great burger or steak (pictured above).

Huckleberries The sweet round maroon or blue-colored berries are a delight in pastries, pancakes, ice creams and jams, and thrive in this high-elevation terrain.

Trout Nearly all upmarket restaurants in the area will have this lake and river fish, rich in protein, vitamin B12 and omega, on their menu.

Bison This enormous land animal is used to restore landscapes, while offering a low-maintenance livestock species. Find bison burgers, stews and jerky throughout Alberta and Montana, for a lighter and sweeter alternative to beef.

HOW MUCH FOR...

a steak
$20–40

an ice cream
$2–5

a sandwich
$10–15

an upscale main
$20–50

a burger
$15–20

a coffee
$3–6

a beer
$5–8

a cocktail
$13–17

HOW TO...

Get a Good Cuppa Joe

Good coffee is hard to come by in remote areas around the US and Canada, with diners often serving weak brown water. Luckily independent producers serving freshly made espresso-based drinks can be found if you know where to look. Try these great coffee shops.

Leaning Tree Blackfeet family-owned joint serving some of the best coffee in East Glacier.

The Cedar Tree Serving Montana Coffee Traders roasts inside Glacier National Park next to Lake McDonald.

Heidi's Espresso Stand Freshly made brews inside Many Glacier Hotel.

Montana Coffee Traders Get a cup fresh from the roastery in Whitefish.

Swift Creek Cafe Whitefish hole in-the wall with perfectly prepared caffeinated drinks.

Wild Coffee Company A designer's dream setting: a minimalist modern airy space with natural woods and great coffee.

SnowDome Coffee Bar Jasper favorite sourcing coffee from local Alberta roasters; down it with a side of banana bread.

Good Earth Coffee House The place in Banff to get a cup of caffeine with a clear conscience. It sources beans from farms with sustainability practices, and Fair Trade and Organic certifications.

Folklore Coffee Whitefish micro-roastery making artisan brews from beans sourced in Mexico, Kenya, Tanzania and Ethiopia.

Mountain Coffee

Mountainous regions produce great coffee due to well-drained soils on angled growing slopes and cooler temperatures, which mean a slower growth cycle for the coffee tree. Conditions in the Rocky Mountains produce small yet flavorful beans with complex flavors.

GOING OUT

The drinking age in Montana is 21 years old and above, while just across the border in Alberta it's 18 and over. There's a fast-evolving craft beer scene in each state above and below the border, plus a scattering of craft distilleries popping up in recent years. But don't expect an all-night party – distilleries and breweries close early, around 8pm or 9pm, with the latest bars closing at 2am.

Try Spotted Bear Spirits for Whitefish-distilled whisky, vodka and gin-based cocktails. Latitude 48 Bistro serves cocktails in a chic basement lounge. Bonsai Brewing Project is the place for creative craft brews; its microbrewery has a cozy bar and outdoor garden area near City Beach, Whitefish. The hippest spot near Glacier, however, is the Great Northern Bar & Grille, with a younger crowd and bar games. Freda's West Glacier Bar is right outside the park entrance and gets packed with a post-rafting crowd, but closes at 10pm.

The off-grid community of Polebridge is a surprisingly good option for live music in summer months, with the Northern Lights Saloon and Home Ranch Bottoms hosting bands all season. Jasper Brewing Co Brewpub was a first in a Canadian national park – it uses glacial water to make its fine ales. Bear Street Tavern in Banff serves ridiculously good hiker-themed craft beer on tap and thin-crust pizzas. Thirsty Bear in Waterton is housed in a former dance hall, and still gets hikers up on their feet with live music every weekend during the summer months.

Responsible Travel

Climate Change & Travel

It's impossible to ignore the impact we have when traveling, and the importance of making changes where we can. Lonely Planet urges all travelers to engage with their travel carbon footprint. There are many carbon calculators online that enable travelers to estimate the carbon emissions generated by their journey; try https://calculator.carbonsavvy.uk. Many airlines and booking sites offer travelers the option of offsetting the impact of greenhouse gas emissions by contributing to climate-friendly initiatives around the world. We continue to offset the carbon footprint of all Lonely Planet staff travel, while recognizing this is a mitigation more than a solution.

Pack In, Pack Out

When hiking around the parks, remember to leave no trace. Take all trash with you – even biodegradable items like fruit peel can impact nature, as they take time to decompose.

Doing a Number Two

Backpackers on multiday trips will have to go at some point. If no toilets are available, go at least 30m (100ft) from a trail or water source, dig a small hole and take any paper away.

Don't Feed the Wildlife

Never feed animals; this makes them associate humans with food and lose their fear of people. It's dangerous for both the wildlife and for humans.

Storing Food Properly

Never store food or scented products (soaps and shower gels etc) in your tent. Use bear lockers or a canister if available, or store food on a cable or bear pole away from your campground.

Trail Etiquette
Bikers should generally yield to hikers on the trail. Horses have right of way over hikers and bikers.

Campsites
Use campsites previously used by other campers to avoid unnecessary impact to the landscape.

A fed bear is a **DEAD BEAR**

DO NOT FEED WILDLIFE

FOOD PREPARATION

Many backcountry campsites have food-preparation areas away from camping sites. Use these to avoid attracting wildlife and keep your campground clean.

STAY ON TRAIL

Established pathways help hikers find the way, but also stop walkers from trampling on regrowth and regeneration on the forest floor. Popular trails may see hundreds of people walk them a day. Stay on trail to allow biodiversity to thrive.

Avoid Chemicals

Take biodegradable soap to wash camping dishes, and do it well away from rivers and streams.

Learn about Indigenous Culture

Broaden your understanding of these protected places, used by the Blackfeet, Salish, Kootenai and other tribes for thousands of years. Book a cultural tour at the visitor center or explore the park with an Indigenous guide.

Alleviating Human Impact

Many North American parks have adopted reservation systems in recent years to reduce congestion in the parks. Visiting responsibly can help pressure points and prevent further restrictive policies.

Fire Restrictions

Check fire restrictions before you set off on a trail. Use a stove instead of a fire where possible to reduce impact, scorching the ground and using firewood.

Leave What You Find

The saying 'leave only footprints, take only memories' rings true. Don't take rocks, plants or anything else in the wild.

Low-Impact Vehicles

To reduce carbon emissions and traffic, avoid driving in the parks where possible. There are shuttle buses to the major trailheads in peak season, plus e-bikes for rent in and around the parks.

RESOURCES

leavenotrace.ca
The principles of Leave No Trace.

nps.gov/glac/blogs/ poop-out-side.htm
How to poop outside.

nps.gov/subjects/watching wildlife/7ways.htm
How to safely encounter wildlife.

CLOCKWISE FROM TOP: WESTEND61/GETTY IMAGES ©, ZACK FRANK/SHUTTERSTOCK ©, AMELIA MARTIN/SHUTTERSTOCK ©

LGBTIQ+ Travelers

Acceptance and tolerance toward LGBTIQ+ travelers is generally high in the national parks and among outdoor enthusiasts in general who may be traveling to the area. Banff and Jasper have crosswalks painted in rainbow colors and many businesses display rainbow flags. Canada legalized same-sex marriage in 2005, and Montana in 2014. Pride events take place in Alberta and Montana.

Banff Pride

Held in October, Banff National Park (banffpride.ca) hosts a 10-day celebration of diversity in the great outdoors, in one of the most picturesque settings. Activities and events range from guided hikes, rock climbing and mountain-top drag to open-mic nights, drag bingo, art markets, comedy shows and even free haircuts for the LBGTIQ+ community. The event also typically has more than a dozen musicians performing, and celebrated its 10th anniversary in 2023.

JASPER PRIDE

Jasper holds a four-day annual Pride festival (jasperpride.ca) in April. Hit the slopes and indulge in safe-space après-ski, plus outdoor events, film screenings, a drag show and a mini food festival where you can try special Pride tipples, attend themed brunches and tuck into heart-shaped pizzas.

Discounted Hotels

LGBTIQ+ visitors will benefit from visiting during Pride events. The world-famous Fairmont Banff Springs, plus Mount Royal Hotel, Moose Hotel and Suites, and the Rimrock Resort Hotel are LGBTIQ-friendly spaces, offering discounts on rooms for the rainbow community. Enquire during booking (or check banffpride.ca/visit-banff for discount codes).

GLACIER PRIDE

This embryonic Pride event is the smallest in the areas surrounding the national parks, with a tiny but passionate LGBTIQ+ community running events and activities in the fall. Bonsai Brewing and Montana Raft both host community Pride events, run by the Glacier Queer Alliance (glacierqueeralliance.org). Other LGBTIQ-friendly businesses include Home Ranch Bottoms, Stumptown Snowboards, Glacier Lanes and Backslap Brewing.

AD-HOC LGBTIQ+ EVENTS

Keep an eye out for queer events throughout the year, run by local Pride centers and local associations. Roller Disco, organized by the team at Banff Pride, is a groovy event where participants dress up in fabulous disco attire for an evening of skating at the Fenlands Banff Recreation Centre (banffpride.ca/events).

The Scene

There's no gay or LGBTIQ+ scene to speak of in or around the parks, but some venues host regular LGBTIQ+ drinks, including the tap room at Banff Ave Brewing Co, which does 'Beers for Queers' on the first Wednesday of every month from 8pm.

Accessible Travel

There's work to be done in Banff, Jasper and Glacier to make visits for those with auditory, visual or physical disabilities seamless, but the parks have made progress in their facilities, including accessible campgrounds, shuttles and ranger programs. Check at visitor centers before setting off to make sure facilities are running.

Trails for Wheelchairs

Banff National Park Bow River Loop, Fenland Trail, Banff Legacy Trail, sections of the Johnston Canyon and Lake Minnewanka shoreline trails, the Lake Louise shoreline trail and the Sundance Canyon Trail.

Jasper National Park Lake Annette shoreline trail and Pyramid Lake's Pyramid Island. Part of the Mary Schäffer Loop is paved.

Glacier National Park Trail of the Cedars, Running Eagle Falls Trail and the cycle path from Apgar Village.

Waterton Lakes National Park Linnet Lake Trail and Waterton Townsite Trail.

Airport

Calgary International Airport (yyc.com) is the best airport near the parks for wheelchair and mobility assistance, plus services for other disabilities. These must be booked well in advance of travel.

Accommodations

Most park hotels have at least some wheelchair-accessible rooms. Campgrounds with wheelchair-friendly campsites and washrooms include Fish Creek and Apgar in Glacier; Lake Louise in Banff; Whistlers, Wilcox and Icefield in Jasper; and the Waterton Townsite campground.

SIGHTS

Banff's Lake Louise, Upper Hot Springs Pool and Peyto Lake along the Icefields Parkwsy are wheelchair-accessible, as is the main visitor center.

Park Shuttles

Glacier's shuttles are ADA accessible, making exploration of Going-to-the-Sun Road areas possible. Parks Canada shuttles have limited accessibility. Roam Public Transit is wheelchair-accessible with routes between the town of Banff and Lake Louise.

ACCESSIBLE PROGRAMS

Accessible ranger-led programs are available in Glacier for those with mobility issues, and for people requiring audio assistance. Several of the amphitheaters are accessible. Check in advance what programs are running.

RESOURCES

Park and tourism board websites have information on accessible travel to each of the parks.

Glacier National Park

Banff National Park

Jasper National Park

The **Disabled Traveler's Companion** is a great resource for travelers with additional needs.

RESTAURANTS

Many restaurants in Banff, Jasper, Glacier and Waterton are on the ground floor, and should have provisions for wheelchair users. Check about accessible bathrooms before you dine.

Parkitecture Lodges

Parkitecture is architecture that's specially designed to blend with its surroundings, bring the outside in and not distract from the staggering beauty of the scenery.

Glacier & Waterton Lakes

The first International Peace Park has several classic examples of this romantic style, starting with Glacier Park Hotel (now Glacier Park Lodge), built in 1913, with Swiss-chalet features combined with Wild West elements – taxidermy trimmings, Indigenous crafts. Located just outside the Two Medicine park entrance, and commissioned by the Great Northern Railway for passengers alighting at Glacier Park Station (now East Glacier Park), it had music and writing rooms, a sun parlor and an emergency hospital. It was given the moniker 'Big Tree Lodge' thanks to its enormous log frame, constructed with 900-year-old Douglas fir timbers, up to 1.2m (4ft) in diameter. The four-story hotel could sleep up to 400 visitors, and the giant 'forest' lobby was like bringing the nature outside indoors.

RUSTIC STYLE

When the first national parks were established in the US at the end of the 19th century, lodges, ranger stations and other public buildings were thoughtfully constructed in a rustic style to blend in with their surroundings and not distract from the beauty of the landscape. This arts-and-crafts-style construction used materials commonly found in the area, such as stone or wood. As the national park system grew, so did the phrase 'parkitecture' to describe their distinctive structures.

Multiple Lodges

Other grand lodges around the park soon followed, including the hunting-style Lake McDonald Lodge (originally known as the Lewis Glacier Hotel), built on Glacier's largest lake in 1913, on its northeastern edge; it was originally reached by steamboat from the south, where the West Glacier station was located. Many Glacier Hotel joined the series on Swiftcurrent Lake in 1914–15, plus a number of backcountry chalets – including Sperry Chalet and Granite Park Chalet, both constructed with stone to blend into their surroundings, with huge fireplaces and situated in the most scenic areas of the park.

PRINCE OF WALES HOTEL

Waterton's historic castle-like lodge, up on a bluff overlooking Upper Waterton Lake, was commissioned much later, in 1927, in the same rustic Swiss chalet style as Glacier's lodges. It was also built by the US company Great Northern Railway, despite being over the border in Canada. It's arguably grander than the others, standing at 37m (121ft) tall, with seven floors and a wall of windows out onto Waterton Lakes. Plus, it was an early adopter of nifty features like power outlets in guest rooms plus irons and curling tongs. A big draw for early US guests was that Prohibition had ended in Alberta when it opened, whereas across the border in Montana Prohibition would continue until 1933.

Traveling with Dogs

Taking pets to the national parks in this book is a mixed bag. Those in Canada will find it noticeably more pet-friendly, whereas Montana's Glacier National Park is far more strict. If you intend to bring your pooch, plan ahead…

Dog Rules

While pooches may be taken camping, pets are not permitted on trails, lakeshores or in any buildings in Glacier. In Waterton pets on a leash are allowed on trails, and in picnic areas, parking areas and boats on lakes where motorized watercraft are permitted. They can also go on certain Waterton Shoreline Cruises while leashed. Dogs on leashes can be taken on most hiking trails in Jasper, aside from trails considered caribou country, such as Bald Hills, Opal Hills and Cavell Meadows (check with rangers which trails you can walk with your dog). Leashed dogs are allowed on almost all of Banff's 1500km (932 miles) of hiking trails, and there are lots of dog-friendly spots in Banff Town, including off-leash dog parks.

Pet-Friendly Hikes

For a gentle and incredibly scenic walk, try the 3.7km (2.3-mile) Maligne Canyon Loop in Jasper, for mountain views and a gorgeous gorge. Get out of the sun on Banff's shaded 3.4km (2.1-mile) Marsh Loop for Bow River and Valley views, or do some climbing on the 4.3km (2.6-mile) Tunnel Mountain Trail to a soaring panorama over Banff Town. For epic valley views over Waterton Lakes, try the short, steep and very rewarding 2.4km (1.5-mile) Bear's Hump Trail. Keep a good grip on leashes on high-altitude trails – there are big drops.

SLEEPING

Pet-friendly hotels and campgrounds can be found in or around all the parks. West Glacier KOA allows guests to bring up to two pets.

Inside the park, Apgar House allows dogs for no extra fee, and all front-country campsites within the park's boundaries allow dogs on leashes.

Waterton, Jasper and Banff have the same leash rules when it comes to camping in the parks.

For a comfier lakeside location try the Bayshore Inn in the center of Waterton Park. For a plusher stay, try the mountain-chic Elk + Avenue Hotel in Banff, with modern design features.

TIPS FOR TRAVELING WITH DOGS

Pack everything your pet might need for a holiday – food, leash, towel for dogs, poop bags, and a crate if your dog needs it in the hotel room.

Book accommodations well in advance, especially in peak season when pet-friendly hotels book up fast.

Keep dogs on leashes on all trails, at a maximum of 1.8m (6ft) long. Pick them up if you encounter wild animals, especially moose or bears.

Consider booking a pet-sitter for your hotel or local dog kennel so you can go on longer trails and explore worry-free.

Safe Bear Encounters

The parks featured in this book are natural habitats for both black and grizzly bears. Visitors are usually excited, apprehensive and often downright terrified of running into a bear, but the truth is bear attacks are very uncommon. According to the National Park Service, the chance of being injured by a bear is one in 2.1 million. While encounters are rare, visitors should understand more about these mammals and what to do if they do run into one.

LIFESPAN
An average grizzly bear lives 20 to 25 years; for black bears it's 10 years. But both species can live upward of 30 years in the wild.

Population

There are an estimated 55,000 grizzly bears in North America, living in only five or six states – Alaska, Wyoming, Montana, Idaho, Washington and occasionally southern Colorado. Around 30,000 grizzly bears reside in Alaska followed by 25,000 in Canada. There are around 1000 grizzly and black bears in Glacier National Park, some 170 bears in Waterton, just over 100 bears in Banff and approximately 200 in Jasper.

Camping in Bear Country

Use the communal food-preparation areas, which are available at most campgrounds, including backcountry sites. Store food and anything with a scent, like toiletries, in bear lockers where possible, or canisters at least 30m (100ft) away from tents and hung at least 3m (10ft) off the ground. These are issued free of charge with backcountry permits in Glacier. Canisters fit into a backpack or the hatch of a kayak, but only have space for a certain amount of supplies – campers can borrow as many as they need for their hike.

Don't run on trails as this could surprise a bear – a surefire way to agitate it.

Bear Identification

Black bears tend to be shy toward humans; grizzlies are not. Black bears have a prominent rump, pointed ears, dark claws, no hump and a straight, dog-like muzzle. Grizzlies have a hump, rounded ears and long, light-colored claws. A male grizzly can be more than 2.1m (7ft) tall when standing, and can weigh more than 227kg (500lb).

IF YOU DO ENCOUNTER A BEAR

Bears may stand on their hind legs if they are curious to get a better look at you or your group. They are irritated when they huff, clack their teeth and sway their heads. A lowered head and laid-back ears could also be a sign of aggression.

Keep your distance. You want to be at least 91m (300ft) away. If a bear is on your trail, get out of the way and let it pass if you can. If moving agitates the bear, stand your ground.

Talk calmly and quietly in a low voice to the bear. Don't look the bear directly in the eye. Use your judgment to move away when the situation allows.

PREVENTING AN ENCOUNTER

- Hiking in a group significantly reduces your chance of having a negative encounter with a bear. Solo hikers should team up with other hikers on trails, or try a ranger-led activity, which are conducted in groups.

- Make noise as you walk. Bear bells are pretty ineffective, but calling out when going around blind bends is effective, as is singing, clapping and generally chatting. Be aware near rivers and streams, which create white noise, or in winds and dense mossy vegetation, as bears may not hear you approach.

- Be on high alert in feeding areas like fields of glacier lilies and berry patches.

If a Bear Attacks

Prepare to deploy your bear spray. If you are unable to use bear spray, get on the ground and protect your chest and abdomen by lying face down on the ground. Hold the back of your neck with your hands for protection. Leave your pack on to protect your back. Stay lying down; the bear may leave if it knows you're not a threat. If the attack continues, fight back as hard as you can, but do not run.

Diet & Habitat

Bears are omnivores with varied diets. They eat mammals, including badgers, rabbits, foxes and rodents, plus insects, roots, fish, pine nuts, grass and fruit. They like large forests, alpine meadows and prairies with a variety of fruits and nuts, plus rivers and streams with healthy fish populations. If you're hiking with small children and spot a bear, immediately pick up your child. An adult may be too big to eat but a child could be an attractive prospect.

BEAR SCAT

Look for bear scat on trails. Bear poop is tubular with a blunt end and in a sizable pile around 30cm (12in) long; likely larger than a man's hand. The fresher it is, the more recently a bear has been on the trail. If it's dried out, it's probably been there for a while and the bear has likely moved on from the area.

DEPLOYING BEAR SPRAY

Use two hands to hold the can out in front of you. Put one hand on the trigger, and pull the safety clip off (usually a glow-in-the-dark piece of plastic). When the bear is within 10m (30ft), aim slightly down, pull the trigger and spray in a zigzag motion – discharge the whole contents. Don't forget to check the expiry date on the bear spray before you set off and store it somewhere easily reachable, on your belt or in a water-bottle holder rather than inside a backpack. Bear spray can be bought and rented around the parks, from outdoor stores to gas stations.

Nuts & Bolts

Electricity
120V/60Hz

GOOD TO KNOW

Time Zone
GMT -6

Country Code
1

Emergency Number
911

Populations
Banff 7840, Jasper 4590,
Glacier 142, Waterton 200

PUBLIC HOLIDAYS

Canada
New Year's Day January 1
Good Friday March/April
Easter Monday First Monday after Good Friday
Victoria Day Monday preceding May 25
Canada Day July 1
Labor Day First Monday in September
Thanksgiving Day Second Monday in October
Remembrance Day November 11
Christmas Day December 25
Boxing Day December 26

USA
New Year's Day January 1
Martin Luther King Day Third Monday in January
President's Day Third Monday in February
Memorial Day Last Monday in May
Independence Day July 4
Labor Day First Monday in September
Columbus Day Second Monday in October
Veterans' Day November 11
Thanksgiving Day Fourth Thursday in November
Christmas Day December 25

OPENING HOURS

Low-season hours may be reduced or businesses may close altogether.
The following are for peak season.

Shops 9am–5:30pm (grocery and convenience stores may open later)

Restaurants 7–10:30am (breakfast), 11am–3pm (lunch), 5–9pm (dinner)

Bars 4pm–midnight or slightly later; breweries and distilleries can close as early as 8pm

Banks 9am–5:30pm Monday to Friday

Wi-Fi

Cell signal is virtually non-existent in most areas of Glacier

Weights & Measures

Kilometers are used in Canada with elevations in meters. It's miles and feet in the US. Both use imperial pounds for weights.

Smoking

Smoking is banned in enclosed public spaces in both Montana and Canada.

Moraine Lake (p108)

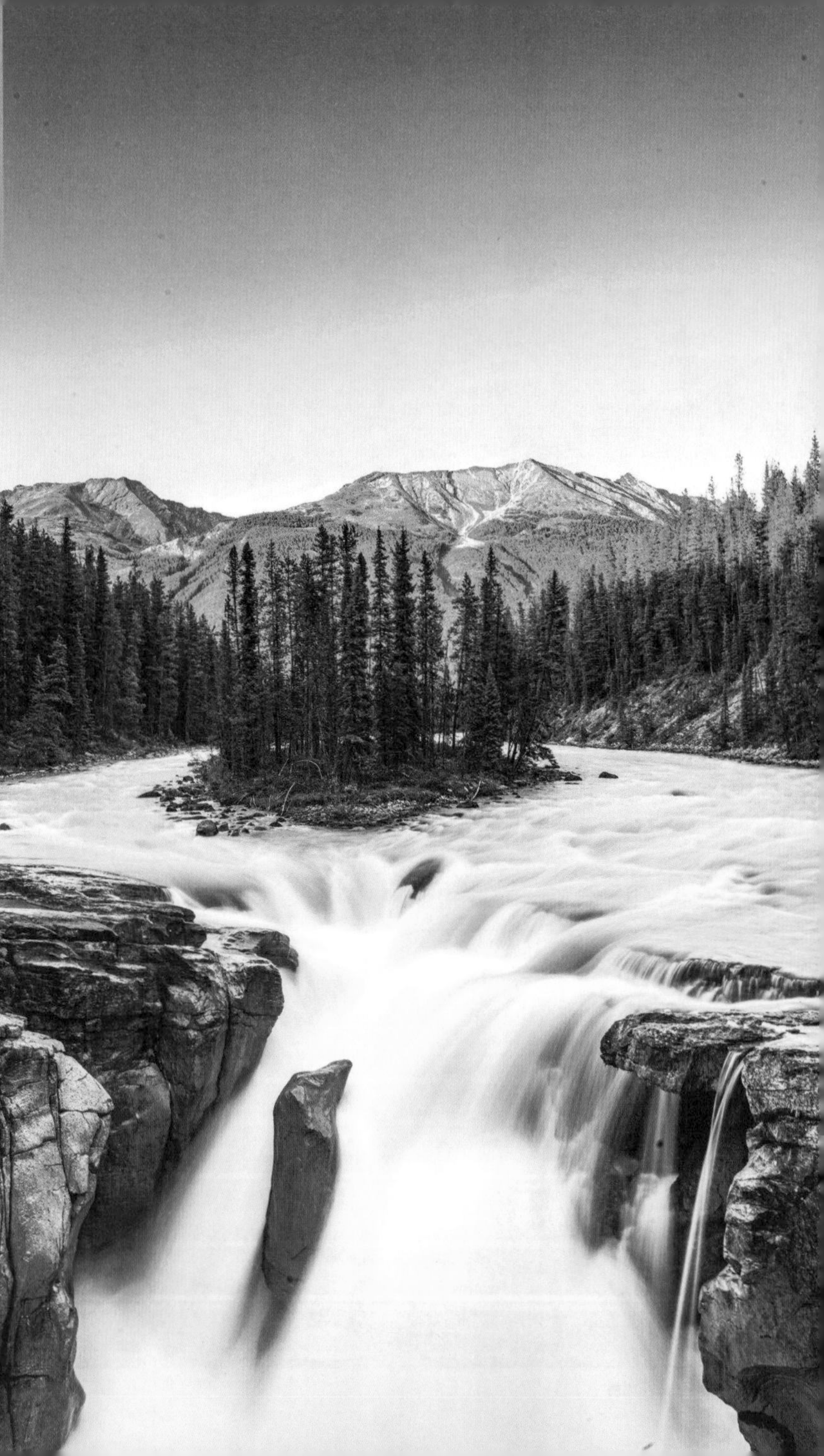

STORYBOOK

Our writers delve deep into different aspects of park life

Sunwapta Falls (p162)
FRANCESCO RICCARDO IACOMINO/GETTY IMAGES ©

A HISTORY OF BANFF, JASPER & GLACIER NATIONAL PARKS IN

15 PLACES

Some 550 million years ago, the area we now know as the Rocky Mountains was an inland sea. Marine sediments turned into soaring and humbling sandstone and limestone peaks, and their rugged shapes formed over millions of years as a result of erosion. By Jade Bremner

VARIOUS INDIGENOUS GROUPS lived for millennia in the areas that eventually turned into Jasper, Banff, Glacier and Waterton Lakes. European expeditions edged west in the late 18th century and these pristine lands were ravaged for their natural resources before conservationists campaigned for their protection.

Banff, Jasper, Glacier and Waterton were opened between 1885 and 1910 thanks to an unlikely partnership forged between environmental activists and profit-hungry railway entrepreneurs (looking to lure wealthy visitors to America's version of the Swiss Alps).

Banff, created in 1885, is the third-oldest national park in the world, and just as Europe protected its medieval castles and ancient ruins, this park became a benchmark for the preservation of wild spaces in Canada. Waterton Lakes National Park came 10 years later, followed by Jasper and Glacier 25 years after that. Glacier and Waterton share an international border between Canada and the US, and became the first-ever International Peace Park in 1932. The latter offers an incredibly scenic border crossing (Chief Mountain; passport required), which passes breathtaking snowcapped mountains, high-altitude lakes, and ancient cedar-hemlock forests.

1. Sulphur Mountain

NATURAL SPRINGS AND HEALING WATERS

The Stoney Indigenous people were aware of the supposed healing powers of the springs at Sulphur Mountain for hundreds of years. In 1882, three railroad laborers, William and Tom McCardell and Frank McCabe, stumbled upon these geothermal waters, and without them Banff National Park may not exist at all. The craze for spa bathing was crucial in attracting early visitors to the park in the late 19th century, and the trio brought the waters to the attention of the masses. In 1958, the construction of the Sulphur Mountain gondola began and now whisks half a million tourists per year to the peak's sweeping scenes of six mountain ranges.

For more on Sulphur Mountain, see page 66.

2. Banff Springs Hotel

ICONIC HOTEL ARCHITECTURE

Canadian Pacific Railway entrepreneurs seized the opportunity to make the area a tourist hot spot, building a train line and grand hotels along the network to lure wealthy tourists to the area's recuperative springs and Swiss-esque scenery. In 1888, the chateau-style Banff Springs Hotel opened and became one of the grandest properties in Canada. The fairytale-like, five-story wooden building sleeps hundreds of guests, notably King George VI and Queen Elizabeth in the 1930s, and plenty of movie stars over the years, including Marilyn Monroe in the 1950s, when she was filming *River of No Return*. Rising above Banff's Bow Falls, the landmark, now known as the Fairmont Banff Springs hotel, is a Canadian icon.

For more on Banff Springs hotel, see page 63.

3. Lake Louise

HAMLET BECOMES PART OF BANFF PARK

More than 5000 tourists had visited the embryonic park, and its rejuvenating spring water, by 1888. The demand was so great that in 1892 the nearby turquoise, glacier-fed Lake Louise was incorporated into the park, and with it came another castle-like hotel: Chateau Lake Louise. A coach road, opening in 1911, made the area more accessible to the general public, rather than just the wealthy. Hiking trails were forged around the lake, including an enjoyable ramble up to the Lake Agnes Teahouse, believed to be the oldest teahouse in Canada, offering bird's-eye views of the water beneath.

For more on Lake Louise, see page 102.

4. Icefields Parkway

MAKING THE PARK ACCESSIBLE TO ALL

During WWI, immigrants were forced to work in prisoner-of-war camps in Banff National Park – they built much of the established infrastructure we enjoy today, including many of the roads, which were once horse tracks. In the 1930s came the Icefields Parkway, an iconic 230km (143-mile) highway that connects Lake Louise with Jasper along scenes of virgin wilderness, mind-blowing waterfalls, epic mountain vistas, peacock-colored lakes, and the mighty Columbia Icefield, home to the Athabasca Glacier, which can be visited on foot or in an Ice Explorer all-terrain vehicle.

For more on Icefields Parkway, see page 116.

5. Banff Town

HIGH TOWN INCORPORATED WITHIN A PARK

Named Banff in 1884 by Canadian Pacific Railway boss George Stephen, after his birthplace near Banff in Scotland, this was the first municipality to be incorporated within a Canadian national park. Banff Town's economy further boomed around a century later, in 1988, during the Winter Olympics in Calgary. This added attention and further strengthened the

Banff Springs hotel (p63)

JEFF WHYTE/SHUTTERSTOCK ©

tourism infrastructure. It's still the highest town in Canada (at an elevation of 1383m (4537ft) and is a lively mini-metropolis of 7500 permanent residents, with numerous historic monuments and a cosmopolitan mix of shops, bistros, pubs and museums. Around 4 million people visit per year.

For more on Banff Town, see page 60.

6. Athabasca Valley
ANCIENT U-SHAPED SETTLEMENT

The land that is now Jasper National Park was a hunting, fishing and gathering ground for Indigenous Peoples before the 1800s, when fur traders came to the area and caused a number of Indigenous groups to relocate after claiming their territory in the Athabasca Valley. A dispute with the Piegan group over access to Howse Pass prompted British-Canadian explorer David Thompson to find a new trade route across the Rockies. He ventured over Athabasca Pass in the winter of 1811 to establish a fur route over the Continental Divide. The superb 45.6km (23-mile) backcountry Skyline Trail offers seemingly endless skyline views stretching from the Colin Range to the Athabasca Valley.

For more on Athabasca Valley, see page 163.

7. Maligne Lake
DISCOVERED BY AN EARLY OUTDOORSWOMAN

Mary Schäffer was the first non-Indigenous person to explore Jasper's Maligne Lake, trailblazing in a time when most women couldn't even vote. Schäffer, a Philadelphia widow, was a true park pioneer who, in 1908, went in search of the hidden mountain lake named Chaba Imne by the Stoney people. The only knowledge she had was a map sketched from memory by a Stoney man named Samson Beaver, 14 years earlier. Her successful exploration led the Geological Survey of Canada to commission her to survey Maligne Lake in the Canadian Rocky Mountains in 1911. She later published the book *Old Indian Trails of the Canadian Rockies*, recounting her daring adventure.

For more on Maligne Lake, see page 144.

8. Jasper Park Lodge
HISTORIC RAILWAY RESORT

The idea for a lodge started with a 10-tent site on the shore of Lac Beauvert. A resort suitable for contemporary travelers was built in 1921 by the Canadian National Railway, after the railway reached the tiny settlement of Fitzhugh and brought with it a host of adventurous tourists. The town swelled in size and was renamed Jasper after fur-trading manager Jasper Hawse. It originally had eight log cabins, followed by dozens of other distinctive structures, including a huge dance hall, restaurants and an 18-hole golf course. The main building was overhauled following a 1952 fire, and renovations continued over time, with fresh cedar replacing the original cabin wood.

For more on Jasper Park Lodge, see page 136.

9. Peyto Lake
STORY OF JASPER'S PIERCING BLUE LAKE

Peyto Lake was named after English-Canadian mountain guide and early Jasper park warden Ebenezer William 'Bill' Peyto, who originally came to the area as a railway worker. He decided to stay and built himself a small log cabin before becoming a mountain guide leading climbs up to Mt Assiniboine. Bill discovered the famous glacially fed lake in 1894 after crossing Bow Summit and exploring the Misty Valley – the piercing blue Peyto Lake, bordered by Caldron Peak, Peyto Peak and Mt Jimmy Simpson, is splashed over many park marketing brochures. Its waters get their striking color from the glacial rock flour that pours from Peyto Glacier, also named after Bill.

For more on Peyto Lake, see page 115.

10. Jasper SkyTram

ACCESSIBLE VIEWS FOR EVERYONE

Albertan adventurer William McGregor summited Whistlers Mountain in 1960, and made it his mission for everyone to be able to experience these epic views and alpine tundra, no matter their ability. Jasper Park authorities were convinced to build a high-speed cable car to the lofty height of 2466m (8088ft) and the summit of Whistlers Mountain. Some six million people have been transported on the Jasper SkyTram up the mountain since the 1960s. From the gondola's highest point, hikers can climb a steep 1.25km (1-mile) trail to the mountain's real pinnacle, where on a clear day it's possible to spy the highest peak in the Canadian Rockies, Mt Robson.

For more on Jasper SkyTram, see page 138.

11. Great Northern Railway

THE TRAIN LINE THAT STARTED IT

The Blackfeet lived in and controlled most of the areas now known as Glacier National Park. The notoriously fierce tribe held off European invaders until smallpox ravaged the Indigenous community of 30,000 in 1837 and killed 6000 people. Local tribes were forced into reservations.

Conservationist Dr George Bird Grinnell lobbied for a decade for the bill that created Glacier National Park. The Great Northern Railway was constructed by Canadian entrepreneur James J Hill in the 1890s, transporting visitors to some of America's most captivating wild spaces. Trains still run daily between West Glacier and East Glacier Park train stations in peak season on Amtrak's *Empire Builder* line.

For more on Amtrak's Empire Builder *train, see page 175.*

12. Glacier Park Lodge

RUSTIC ACCOMMODATIONS IN THE PARK

Pre-1930s, Two Medicine Valley was one of East Glacier's most accessible hubs. The grand Glacier Park Hotel (now Glacier Park Lodge) was built for passengers alighting at East Glacier on the Great Northern Railway. It was the first of several atmospheric lodges to be built for visitors and was dubbed 'Big Tree Lodge' thanks to the stacks of 900-year-old Douglas fir timbers that made up the four-story high lobby, adorned with taxidermy trimmings and Native American artwork. Visitors would venture into the wild park interiors by horse, but the halcyon days of rail and mule rides would soon to come to an end, with the popularity of motor cars.

For more on Glacier Park Lodge, see page 193.

13. Going-to-the-Sun Road

NEW TARMAC CROSSES THE PARK

In 1921, to link the east and west sides of Glacier National Park, a new road through the interior of the park was proposed. The 80km (50-mile) Going-to-the-Sun Rd, traveling from the south of Lake McDonald to St Mary, was opened in 1932. It crosses the Continental Divide at 2026m (6646ft) Logan Pass and makes the wilderness accessible to visitors in their millions. This incredible feat of engineering was designated a National Historic Landmark, and remains one of the most scenic drives in the US, passing waterfalls, jaw-dropping Rocky Mountain views, and stop-offs at astounding hikes. Today, hybrid shuttle buses ferry tourists along the route to reduce congestion.

For more on Going-to-the-Sun Road, see page 178.

14. Chief Mountain Highway

INTERNATIONAL PEACE PARK BORDER CROSSING

The union of Waterton and Glacier national parks in 1932 is thanks to individuals including George 'Kootenay' Brown – the first ranger of Waterton Lakes National Park – and Rotary International members in Alberta and Montana. Although the two parks are administered separately and have two separate entry fees, they share a long and wild border – plus a truly spectacular road crossing (the Chief Mountain Hwy). The winding ride through Chief Mountain Border Crossing is an experience in itself, with viewpoints onto Rocky Mountain panoramas and winding tarmac through cedar-hemlock forests. In 2007, the International Dark Sky Association named Waterton-Glacier an International Dark Sky Park.

For more on Chief Mountain Hwy, see page 216.

Going-to-the-Sun Road (p178)

15. Waterton Park

HOME TO A LEGENDARY HOTEL

This tiny settlement established on the shore of Waterton Lakes, named after British naturalist Charles Waterton, has around 200 residents, only 40 of whom stay all year-round. In 1902 oil was discovered in the Cameron Valley nearby, and Canada's first oil well was established. The place would have a very different feel if the oil had not dried up soon after. Those who moved and worked here pivoted into tourism. Louis W Hill, son of James J Hill (the Great Northern Railway boss), built the Swiss-style Prince of Wales Hotel over Upper Waterton Lake in 1927. The arrival of the hotel marked a new era for the sleepy town.

For more on Waterton Park, see page 212.

MEET THE RANGER

Glacier National Park Interpretive Ranger NATALIE SWAIM guides us through her everyday duties in the park, and offers invaluable tips on visiting the area.

THE WHOLE PARK is basically my office – it's pretty sweet. My day-to-day duties vary. I might be prepping new staff or working a shift at the visitor center, where I'm helping people plan their trips, answering questions and swearing in Junior Rangers – it's really fun seeing young children get excited about learning about national parks and resources. I might go on what we call a 'roam,' which is where we get out in the park, and be a presence and answer questions. In peak season, I'll run a program or two, such as the wildlife encounters program, which educates people about some of the animals in the park and what to do if they encounter them out on a trail.

The best part of my job is that I get paid to talk to people and meet people from all over the country and the world, and connect with them. The park is over 1000 million acres, so it can be kind of intimidating. Chatting with me at the visitor center helps people feel a little more confident.

I fell in love with Glacier National Park later in life. I grew up in western North Carolina – the Great Smoky Mountains were kind of in my backyard. In my sophomore year of college, I applied for a term of service with AmeriCorps and got stationed in Fort Benton, Montana. I did a lot of hiking in the area and figured out that I loved it. Even if I have signal, I'll put my phone on airplane mode, and just really try and enjoy nature. One weekend, I drove up to Glacier and camped and hiked and I formed this connection with the park. It's so beautiful, such a special place. It made me realize that I wanted to work for the Park Service and help educate people on why we need to protect these beautiful parks and ecosystems. I was able to work here for the first time last summer and 2023 was my second season.

Glacier stands out from other places due to its sheer diversity. We've got waterfalls, alpine lakes, hikes with sweeping mountain views. We also have amazing wildlife diversity, from things as big as grizzly bears to things as small as pikas. In spring, there are the wildflowers like paintbrush, shooting stars and pasqueflowers.

My favorite memory so far was last summer, after a kind of east-side grand tour, we stopped in Many Glacier where we saw five moose – they're just so, so majestic. I also remember driving on Going-to-the-Sun Road, coming home from hiking Swiftcurrent Pass, and a grizzly just walked right across the road in front of me, not a care in the world. It's so humbling. I feel like you could spend forever here and still want to see more.

Be Prepared

If you're someone who really enjoys hiking 16km to 24km (10–15 miles), bring a water bladder so that you can do the trails safely. If you're going overnight in the backcountry, store your food correctly, carry bear spray on all hikes, and learn how to use it properly.

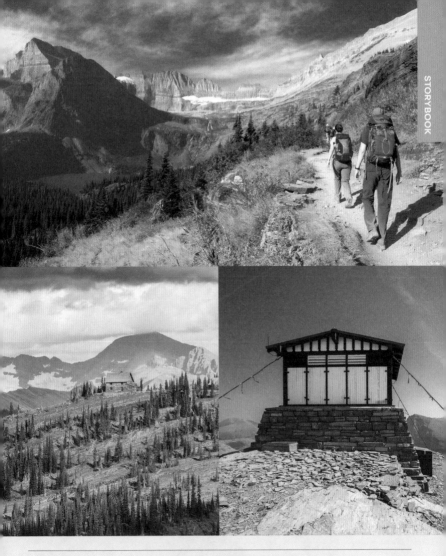

MY THREE FAVORITE HIKES

Grinnell Glacier
Length: 16.5km (10.3 miles)
Area: Many Glacier

On this trail, you will see the Grinnell Glacier as well as the Salamander Glacier. There's also Grinnell Lake, which is glacially fed and a really stunning turquoise color.

Highline Trail
Length: 18.9km (11.8 miles)
Area: West Glacier

Starting at Logan Pass, this hike gives you some beautiful views of the mountains. There's the Granite Park Chalet and Logan Pass for wildlife spotting – you might encounter mountain goats or bighorn sheep, even a bear – and wildflowers bloom in spring.

Swiftcurrent Pass to Swiftcurrent Lookout
Length: 27.3km (17 miles)
Area: Many Glacier

There is a phenomenal view from the Swiftcurrent Fire Lookout. It's a challenging hike, especially the last mile from Swiftcurrent Pass up to the Fire Lookout. I just take it one step at a time, and it is absolutely stunning.

257

MEET THE
BEETLES

A small insect with a ravenous appetite, the mountain pine beetle
has greedily bored its way through huge tracts of Canadian forest.
By Brendan Sainsbury

BEARS ARE UNNERVING, and moose are huge, but arguably the most destructive creature in the Rocky Mountain ecosystem is a tiny 5mm (0.2in) insect with club-shaped antennae called the mountain pine beetle.

Starting in the late 1990s, mountain pine beetles tunneled their way into the bark of millions of healthy pines in British Columbia, killing the trees and annihilating 160,000 sq km (61,776 sq miles) of forest in the process; an area the size of Tunisia.

Some scientists have called it the largest forest-disturbance event in recorded history; the work of a vast army of diminutive beetles each measuring no bigger than a small ant.

So, what caused this epidemic and why is it potentially dangerous?

Bionic Beetles

Mountain pine beetles are wood-boring insects native to western North America that burrow their way into various species of pine tree, including lodgepoles and ponderosas, to lay their eggs. Excavating deep into the bark, they cut off the tree's water movement and deprive it of the nutrients necessary for survival.

At first, attacked trees will display few ill effects of a beetle infestation but, within a year, their needles will turn from green to rust-red as they fall into an irreversible decline. Two years down the line, the infected pines appear ashen and gray and undisputedly dead.

Anyone who has visited the Rocky Mountains in the last 20 years, particularly British Columbia, will have seen the devastating effects the infestations can wreak – vast swathes of formerly lush forest rendered gray and lifeless by pine beetles.

The recent epidemic began in the mid-1990s in central British Columbia, peaking in 2005, before migrating north and east to areas well beyond the pine beetle's normal range. By 2014, it had jumped over the Continental Divide and begun to appear in parts of Banff and Jasper.

A Vicious Cycle

Pine-beetle infestations aren't a new phenomenon. There were outbreaks in Kootenay and Banff national parks in the 1940s. In the 1970s an epidemic in the US spread north to Waterton and Kootenay, and was followed by another small outbreak in Banff in the 1980s.

The problem with more recent pine-beetle infestations is their unprecedented scale. The worry for many environmentalists is that a mixture of climate change and 20th-century forestry interventions might be pushing the forests to a tipping point; a watershed moment where natural forces become unnatural, and the pine beetles get the upper hand. This, in turn, creates a vicious cycle. Fewer living trees means less of a carbon sink to absorb the increasing amounts of CO_2 humans are pumping into the atmosphere. Added to this, the presence of more dead trees in the canopy creates more inflammable material to burn in the event of a fire.

Natural & Necessary

In a healthy forest, there is nothing unnatural about mountain pine beetles. They are a necessary part of the ecosystem. Rather like fires, they help clear out old trees and aid in the forest's long-term regeneration.

Normally, they attack old or weak trees, but natural checks and balances are usually sufficient to repel a full-scale epidemic. Flourishing pine trees release a defensive toxin in their sap that wards off some of the beetles' deadly potential. Furthermore, several days of freezing temperatures below -35°C (-31°F) – not uncommon in the Rockies – is enough to kill them off en masse.

The problem is when humans intervene, inadvertently or otherwise, in the ecosystem.

The Human Factor

A succession of warm winters and dry summers in the early 21st century played a part in exacerbating the recent epidemic. Temperatures weren't cold enough to kill the beetles. The infestation survived to fight another year with increased vigor. At the same time, drought put more stress on the surviving trees, reducing their defenses and dampening their ability to produce beetle-deterring toxins. With more vulnerable trees in the forest, there was more wood for the insects to work on.

Climate change isn't the only way human actions have indirectly affected the pine-beetle epidemic. Fire suppression has been another contributing factor. Beginning in the early 1930s, land management strategies aggressively attempted to control and extinguish large natural fires. These policies, which had been mostly discredited by the 1970s, left large tracts of unnaturally dense forests in the Rockies full of old, weakened trees that were susceptible to pine-beetle infestation.

The result? More infected trees, more dry dead wood, and a tinder box of highly combustible material waiting for the next thunderstorm or recklessly discarded cigarette butt to go up in flames. When the fires inevitably started, they were far more intense than usual, burning for longer and threatening people and property.

Fire suppression was compounded by a third factor: monocultural replanting – the introduction of similar tree species (often lodgepole pine) of the same age to a logged or rehabilitated forest. This lack of arboreal diversity sent the beetles into an egg-laying frenzy, jumping from tree to tree like gatecrashers at a drunken party with nothing to stop them.

The Pine Beetle Reaches Jasper

Pine beetles have been a feature in Alberta since the early 2000s but became particularly meddlesome around 2017 when the current BC-imported epidemic gained traction. After several unusually warm winters, Jasper, which had long resisted the blight thanks to its high mountains and cold winters, was particularly badly hit. By 2019, an astounding 30% of the national park's lodgepole pines had been colonized by pine beetles, with the affected area increasing exponentially between 2017 and 2018 from 930 sq km (359 sq miles) to nearly 1630 sq km (629 sq miles). Today, it's impossible to travel along the Icefields Parkway or look down on the forest canopy from the Jasper SkyTram without being treated to an eyeful of reddish-brown trees, sometimes covering whole mountain slopes.

Intervention

Following the failure of erstwhile fire and replanting policies, debate has raged in recent years about when (or, indeed, if) to curtail pine-beetle infestations.

Arguments for intervention are strong. As well as damaging huge tracts of forest, the epidemic has had big ramifications for the timber industry. Lumber prices rose between 200% and 300% in the three years following 2019 thanks to a shortage of wood in British Columbia. It is estimated that the province lost a decade's worth of lumber supplies between 2000 and 2015 as production fell by 40%.

Aside from raising the fire risk, ravaged forests also indirectly affect tourism and sow worry and uncertainty. The beetle's work has a similar knock-on effect on certain species of wildlife. Pine trees provide food, shelter and a home for numerous birds and animals. Pine martens use their foliage to make dens. The seeds of the whitebark pine are eaten by grizzly bears.

Responses

In Jasper, Parks Canada has responded to the outbreak with a policy of controlled burns and selective mechanical thinning to manually remove dead trees and help restore a healthier forest. Banff, though less badly hit than Jasper, has also been proactive, pruning approximately 34 hectares (84 acres) of forest around its townsite in early 2023 in an effort to impair future beetle and fire activity.

But the biggest game changer in the battle to date has been Mother Earth.

A succession of cold winters beginning in 2018–19 killed off the bulk of Jasper's mountain pine beetle population and sent the local epidemic into retreat. By December 2022, it was reported that the oblivious little pests had seen their numbers fall by 94% in four years thanks primarily to consecutive cold snaps. Indeed, in January 2020, the temperature in Jasper dropped to a near record -44.8°C (-48.6°F). As far as the near term is concerned, the worst seems to be over – at least, for now.

The Future

The future is less certain. While frigid winters may have pushed the epidemic into remission and given the forest a welcome bit of breathing space, the war is far from over. The fire-suppression and mono-planting policies of yore have been adapted for the better since the 1970s, but the blight's other root cause, climate change, hasn't disappeared.

Furthermore, with thousands of hectares of forest rendered dead or dying in the medium term, much of the damage has already been done. Authorities can't and won't remove all dead trees. They remain in situ, a looming fire risk for the future. Regrettably, we must live with the consequences.

It'll be a tricky tightrope walk. For millennia, the Rocky Mountain forests have existed as changing and evolving organisms. The question is, are they losing their resilience?

Meanwhile life goes on for mountain pine beetles. The endemic if universally loathed insects that measure no larger than a grain of rice continue to play an important role in forest life in North America. They haven't gone away, nor should they. We have to learn to live with them, adhere to a few ecological ground rules and hope they don't go on another bender.

For millennia, the Rocky Mountain forests have existed as changing and evolving organisms. The question is, are they losing their resilience?

Dead pine trees after a pine-beetle infestation

NATURE'S CHARM/SHUTTERSTOCK ©

A LAST CHANCE TO SEE GLACIER'S GLACIERS?

Our generation could be the last to witness a glacier in person in the park. By Jade Bremner

THE NATIONAL PARK Service has stated that Glacier National Park is warming at nearly two times the US global average, and according to a study conducted by NASA – based on the decline of the Sperry, Agassiz, Jackson and Grinnell Glaciers – the park's fast-shrinking glaciers could be gone by as early as 2030. In 1850, at the end of the Little Ice Age, there were about 150 glaciers in the area; more than a century later in 1968 the US Geological Survey (USGS) recorded 83 ice-and-snow bodies larger than 0.1 sq meter (1 sq ft). The number of named glaciers today stands at 25, and those that do still exist have lost more than 35% of their volume since the 1960s.

Recent Studies

At the time of writing in 2023, Alberta was in a state of emergency due to wildfires ravaging the province. 'The onset of melt has been really, really rapid,' explained USGS Glaciologist Caitlyn Florentine on her recent research, which showed more melt than ever recorded before – national parks in general have seen relatively more warmth than the global average. This is partially because many national parks are covered in snow and ice. 'You start to get these feedbacks where if the snow is coming off earlier, then there's actually more heat kept within the system,' said Florentine. On a glacier in particular, if the snow melts off earlier in the spring, it means that the bare ice is exposed earlier in the melt season: 'the reflectivity of the surface, known as the albedo, is such that more of the radiative energy or the sun's warmth is kept on the glacier surface. Rather than a nice, clean, snowy blanket, there's more reflection, so the reflectivity is higher,' explained Florentine. The spring of 2023 was uncharacteristically warm, compared to the previous spring, which was very wet. 'It's sort of this concept of climate weirding. You know, things just getting a little weird,' said Florentine.

Effect on Park Biodiversity

The easily accessible Grinnell Glacier presents some of the most obvious changes firsthand – around 10 years ago it had a 7.6m (25ft) wall of ice, now the glacier slopes into the water. Changes to the glaciers not only have an effect on tourism, and change the physicality of the landscape, but also on the park's ecosystems, including its animal populations, which depend on glacier flow. Glaciers are frozen reservoirs of slowly released water, held back for decades, but now this water is more quickly released thanks to rising temperatures, adding to streams that might have low

flows or no flows. Surrounding plant life and alpine gardens will likely disappear when the water eventually dries up. The 2019 study 'Seeking snow and breathing hard – Behavioral tactics in high elevation mammals to combat warming temperatures', conducted by researchers Wesley Sarmento, Mark Biel and Joel Berger, found the decline in glaciers could have an impact on mountain goats. 'I found that on hot summer days, during the hottest part of the day, the goats tend to gravitate towards snow passes,' explained Sarmento, who used their respiration as a metric of how hot their bodies were, and found that being near glaciers reduced their metabolic output. 'On hot summer days, you frequently see these mountain goats panting really hard. They're visibly heat-stressed. So having that snow and that persistent ice is really important for them.' Sarmento would observe goats going into snow, and lying down and splaying out trying to maximize their body contact with the snow to try to cool down. He predicts that goats could die out in these areas if the glaciers disappear. 'Just like the Harrington mountain goats that lived in Grand Canyon National Park about 10,000 years ago during the last glacial maximum extent…as the climate became hotter and drier, the goats died out of those southern areas,' he said. 'Hotter weather has so many different impacts.'

When the Glaciers Are Gone

If Glacier's glaciers disappear, what does it mean for a park named after them, which attracts 3 million visitors per year? As Al Gore previously quipped, it will have to be retitled 'The Park Formerly Known as Glacier.' But others predict that most

Changes to the glaciers not only have an effect on tourism, and change the physicality of the landscape, but also on the park's ecosystems, including its animal populations, which depend on glacier flow.

Melt water, Grinnell Glacier (p202)

DESTINI44/SHUTTERSTOCK ©

visitors won't notice a difference, as many don't come for the glaciers themselves, but the staggeringly scenic glacially carved, ice-sculpted landscape, formed over millions of years. These epic valleys and craggy mountains are not going anywhere in our children's children's children's lifetimes.

Where to See a Glacier

For most of the year, glaciers are cloaked in snow and hard to identify. Snow will be a lot whiter than a glacier, which will likely look a bit grimy and be covered in or have patches of dirt and rocks on it. Most of Glacier's glaciers are hidden in shadowy pockets high along the Continental Divide. But a number can be seen from viewpoints on prominent roads, and others can be seen close up after an exhilarating hike. Late summer and early fall, when snowy blankets have melted, are the best seasons to witness the ice sheets.

The easiest glacier to see in the park is Jackson Glacier, which is visible from Going-to-the-Sun Road at the overlook 8km (5 miles) east of Logan Pass. Salamander Glacier is easy to spot when driving into the Many Glacier area, just beyond the entrance station. Grinnell Glacier, which sits below Salamander, can be viewed on an excellent 16.4km (10.2-mile) return hike from Rte 3 (the main road through the area), passing mystifying lakes and forests and climbing 488m (1600 ft). Sperry Glacier can be reached by a challenging 27km (17-mile) hike, climbing 1524m (5000ft) from Lake McDonald Lodge. Pack a park map and a pair of binoculars when going in search of glaciers, and explorers heed this warning – travel soon to see these bodies of ice before it's too late.

RISING FROM
THE ASHES

Life beyond the wildfires that decimated the flora and fauna of
Waterton Lakes National Park.
By Brendan Sainsbury

SHAWN.CCF/SHUTTERSTOCK ©

**Prince of Wales Hotel, visible from Bear's
Hump Trail (p213) after the Kenow Wildfire.**

WATERTON NATIONAL PARK'S scenery
dramatically changed in the summer of
2017, after lightning sparked a wildfire
during a severe storm 10km (6.2 miles)
from the park boundary, on Kenow
Mountain in British Columbia. Dry lands,
hot weather and strong winds fueled the
blaze, directing it into Waterton where
it would burn for more than a week,
destroying more than 190 sq km (73 sq
miles) of the park.

Spreading Like Wildfire

Sadly 80% of Waterton's trails were ravaged
by the fire, which moved like a freight train
at speed during the night, changing the
landscape for an entire generation, and
killing many animals and their habitats
in the process.

Much to residents' surprise, however,
many animals survived; smaller creatures
had burrowed into the ground and larger
ones fled to safer areas. Elk, bears, deer,
moose, and sheep were spotted in the ashes
soon after, although many would seek out
new areas with feeding opportunities in
the days following the fire.

265

Impact on Residents

The psychological impact of the fire was felt throughout the town, with scorched, almost post-apocalyptic scenes replacing the verdant valleys and dense green forests that carpeted the mountains only days before. Locals mourned their landscape in the years following the fire, but many speak of a bright future – millions of dollars of federal funding has been invested in rebuilding projects in the park, including brand-new Akamina and Red Rock parkways, shiny new day-use and picnic facilities, new restrooms and state-of-the-art viewing platforms, plus a fancy C\$25 million dollar visitor center in Waterton Town, which is now open for visitors.

Wildfire Causes

In 2023, at the time of writing, a state of emergency was declared in Alberta, as 100 fires burned across the province. In the same year, the number of fires had doubled compared to the same time the previous year. Wildfires are becoming more dangerous. Firefighters across North America are seeing more frequent and larger fires, which cause more damage. One theory is that global warming is creating more intense weather patterns, and drying out vegetation and soil, therefore creating a more flammable landscape.

Regeneration

While visitors cannot avoid the stark difference between the green forest on one side of Waterton Lakes and the seemingly endless charred landscape made up of branchless trunk graveyards on the other side, they will also notice positive signs everywhere – including artificial and natural regeneration. Hikers will witness wildflowers and tree shoots sprouting up, and new life emerging from forest floors.

Wildfires do occur naturally and it's important to remember that fires can fulfil critical ecosystem functions. The endangered Karner blue butterfly caterpillar, for example, feeds on wild lupine, which needs overhanging plants to be reduced so it can have access to sunlight. Fires can also clear decaying plants that build up on the forest floor, preventing organisms in the soil from gaining nutrients. Fire increases soil fertility and creates regeneration – certain trees, plants and flowers require fire for seed germination. Suppression is not the answer when it comes to fire; nature needs it – controlled fires are key. Waterton now offers something truly unique for visitors – the opportunity to see Mother Nature rebound from destruction.

How to Be Fire Safe

Before you set off on a trail in the parks, always check the weather and the fire warnings. Thunderstorms can cause all sorts of problems on a trail – from avalanches and fallen trees to wildfires.

If you see a fire in the wild, do not hike toward the flow of smoke. Keep an eye on the column of smoke, as wind can make it change direction in an instant. Get away from the fire as quickly as possible. Carry a physical map with alternate trails in case you need an escape route. Call 911 in an emergency, or to report a fire.

Backpackers should check for campfire bans before they set off. If you have a campfire, make sure it's lit away from tree cover and foliage – don't leave it unattended and make sure it is fully out when you leave.

INDEX

Map Pages **000**

Take on the challenge of climbing the Athabasca Glacier (p161) in Jasper National Park.

'A wave of emotion hit when I first clapped eyes on a real-life grizzly bear in Many Glacier. It was nonchalantly wandering through a flat prairie near the entrance station. Nothing can prepare you for that rush of adrenaline when you see one of these majestic beasts in the wild – followed by total relief and amazement when you're at a safe distance.'

JADE BREMNER

Mapping data sources:
© Lonely Planet
© OpenStreetMap http://openstreetmap.org/copyright

THIS BOOK

Destination Editor
Sarah Stocking

Production Editor
Claire Rourke

Book Designer
Dermot Hegarty

Cartographer
Mark Griffiths

Assisting Cartographer
Eve Kelly

Assisting Editors
Janet Austin, Sarah Farrell, Kate James, Mani Ramaswamy

Cover Researcher
Kat Marsh

Thanks
Sofie Andersen, Charlotte Orr, Katerina Pavkova

MIX
Paper from responsible sources
FSC™ C021741
www.fsc.org

Paper in this book is certified against the Forest Stewardship Council™ standards. FSC™ promotes environmentally responsible, socially beneficial and economically viable management of the world's forests.

Published by Lonely Planet Global Limited
CRN 554153
7th edition – Feb 2024
ISBN 978 1 83869 675 7
© Lonely Planet 2024 Photographs © as indicated 2024
10 9 8 7 6 5 4 3 2 1
Printed in China